SUPER SIMPLE
MATH

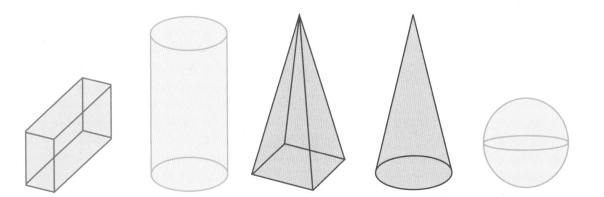

Penguin
Random
House

DK LONDON
Senior editor Sarah MacLeod
Senior art editor Samantha Richiardi
Project editors Edward Aves, Ben Morgan
Editor Alexandra Di Falco
US editor Kayla Dugger
US executive editor Lori Cates Hand
Illustrators Adam Brackenbury, Gus Scott
Managing editors Rachel Fox, Lisa Gillespie
Managing art editor Owen Peyton Jones
Production editor George Nimmo
Production controller Laura Andrews
Jacket designer Akiko Kato
Jackets design development manager Sophia MTT
Publisher Andrew Macintyre
Art director Karen Self
Associate publishing director Liz Wheeler
Publishing director Jonathan Metcalf

Authors Belle Cottingham, John Farndon, Tom Jackson,
Ben Morgan, Michael Olagunju, Jenny Skene, Karl Warsi
Consultants Amber Kuang, Allen Ma, Karl Warsi

DK DELHI
Senior editor Anita Kakar
Project art editor Sanjay Chauhan
Editors Aashirwad Jain, Sonali Jindal
Art editor Sonakshi Singh
Assistant art editor Aparajita Sen
Senior picture researcher Surya Sankash Sarangi
Picture research manager Taiyaba Khatoon
Senior managing editor Rohan Sinha
Managing art editor Sudakshina Basu
Senior DTP designer Vishal Bhatia
DTP designer Nityanand Kumar
Pre-production manager Balwant Singh
Production manager Pankaj Sharma
Jacket designer Juhi Sheth
Senior jackets designer Suhita Dharamjit
Jackets DTP designer Rakesh Kumar
Design head Malavika Talukder
Editorial head Glenda R. Fernandes

First American Edition, 2021
Published in the United States by DK Publishing
1450 Broadway, Suite 801, New York, NY 10018

Copyright © 2021 Dorling Kindersley Limited
DK, a Division of Penguin Random House LLC
21 22 23 24 25 10 9 8 7 6 5 4 3 2 1
001–322042–June/2021

All rights reserved.
Without limiting the rights under the copyright reserved above, no part of this publication may be reproduced,
stored in or introduced into a retrieval system, or transmitted, in any form, or by any means (electronic, mechanical,
photocopying, recording, or otherwise), without the prior written permission of the copyright owner.
Published in Great Britain by Dorling Kindersley Limited

A catalog record for this book is available from the Library of Congress.
ISBN: 978-0-7440-2889-8

DK books are available at special discounts when purchased in bulk for sales promotions, premiums,
fund-raising, or educational use. For details, contact: DK Publishing Special Markets,
1450 Broadway, Suite 801, New York, NY 10018
SpecialSales@dk.com

Printed and bound in China

For the curious
www.dk.com

Smithsonian

Established in 1846, the Smithsonian is the world's largest
museum and research complex, dedicated to public education,
national service, and scholarship in the arts, sciences, and history.
It includes 19 museums and galleries and the National Zoological
Park. The total number of artifacts, works of art, and specimens in
the Smithsonian's collection is estimated at 156 million.

MIX
Paper from
responsible sources
FSC™ C018179

This book was made with Forest Stewardship
Council™ certified paper—one small step in
DK's commitment to a sustainable future.
For more information go to
www.dk.com/our-green-pledge

SUPER SIMPLE
MATH

THE ULTIMATE BITE-SIZE STUDY GUIDE

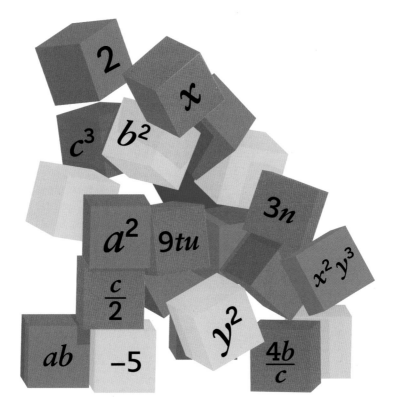

Contents

Angles and shapes

Fractions, decimals, and percentages

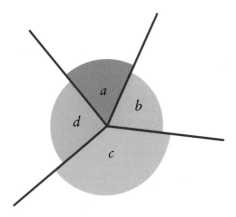

Measure

Introducing algebra

Powers and calculations

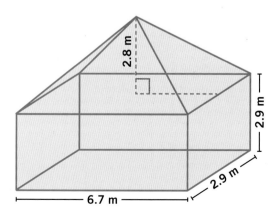

Equations and graphs

Ratio and proportion

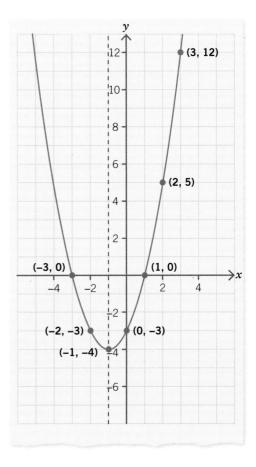

Geometry

Trigonometry

Probability

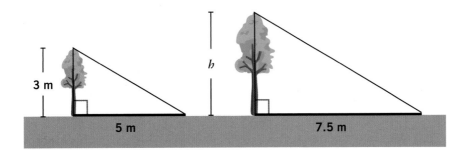

Statistics

Further graphs

Sequences

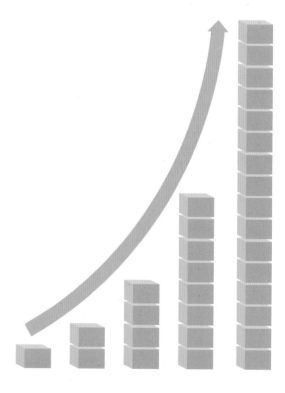

Number and arithmetic

Introducing numbers

Numbers form the foundation of math. The number system we use today is called the decimal system and is based on thinking and counting in groups of 10.

Types of numbers

In the decimal system, all numbers are represented by just 10 "digits": 0, 1, 2, 3, 4, 5, 6, 7, 8, and 9. These digits are put together in different combinations to show any number from zero to infinity. They are also used to represent different kinds of quantities, such as negative numbers, fractions, and decimals.

📌 Key facts

✓ All numbers in our decimal system are comprised of the digits 0 to 9, put together in different combinations.

✓ Numbers can be positive or negative.

✓ Part numbers are represented either as fractions, such as ¾, or as decimals, such as 0.75.

✓ Integers include all positive and negative numbers, including zero, but exclude part numbers such as fractions.

Whole numbers
Whole numbers are the simplest type of number. They comprise all the complete positive numbers, as well as zero.

Negative numbers
If a positive number is every number greater than zero, such as 2, a negative number is every number less than zero, such as −2.

Fractions
Fractions represent numbers in between whole numbers. If 1 represents a whole, the fraction ¼ represents one part of a whole that has been divided into four parts.

Decimals
A decimal is another way to express numbers in between whole numbers. The digits to the right of the decimal point represent a value less than 1.

Zero
Zero is itself a number, and the zero symbol is added to other digits as a "placeholder." So, for example, we use zero to distinguish between 4, 40, and 400.

🔍 Natural numbers, whole numbers, and integers

In this book, we refer to natural numbers, whole numbers, and integers. There is a subtle but important distinction between these terms, but none of them are used to describe part numbers (fractions or decimals).

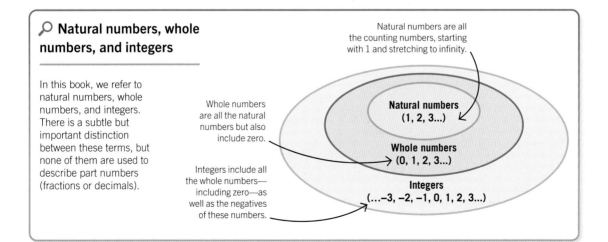

Natural numbers are all the counting numbers, starting with 1 and stretching to infinity.

Whole numbers are all the natural numbers but also include zero.

Integers include all the whole numbers—including zero—as well as the negatives of these numbers.

Natural numbers
(1, 2, 3...)

Whole numbers
(0, 1, 2, 3...)

Integers
(...−3, −2, −1, 0, 1, 2, 3...)

Decimals

Like fractions, decimals are a way of expressing numbers that are not whole. A decimal is a number that includes parts that are less than 1. The parts of the number that are more than 1 are separated from the parts that are less than 1 by a dot called the decimal point.

Key facts

✓ Decimals are a way of expressing numbers that include parts that are less than 1.

✓ Whole numbers go to the left of the decimal point, and the parts of the number less than 1 go to the right.

✓ When putting decimals in order of size, work through the digits from left to right.

Decimals and place value

To understand decimals, it helps to lay the digits out in a place value table, in which each digit is placed into a column that represents its value.

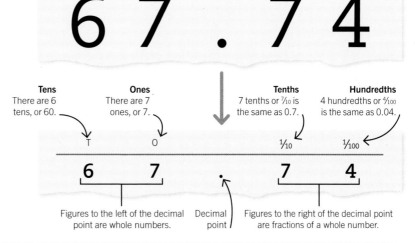

Tens
There are 6 tens, or 60.

Ones
There are 7 ones, or 7.

Tenths
7 tenths or $\frac{7}{10}$ is the same as 0.7.

Hundredths
4 hundredths or $\frac{4}{100}$ is the same as 0.04.

T	O		$\frac{1}{10}$	$\frac{1}{100}$
6	7	.	7	4

Figures to the left of the decimal point are whole numbers.

Decimal point

Figures to the right of the decimal point are fractions of a whole number.

Ordering decimals

When putting numbers with decimals in order of size, work through each number from left to right.

Question
Three runners run a very tight race.

Runner A	9.4 seconds
Runner B	9.37 seconds
Runner C	9.42 seconds

Place the runners in order from first to last place.

Answer

1. All the runners ran the race in 9 ones, or 9 seconds, so move on to the first decimal column.

3. 9.4 is the same as 9.40. As 0 hundredths is smaller than 2 hundredths, runner A came in second.
2nd = Runner A 9.4 seconds
3rd = Runner C 9.42 seconds

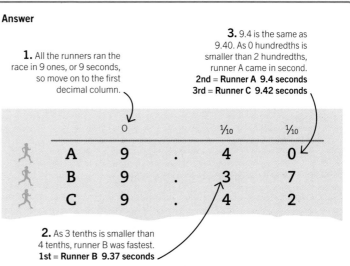

	O		$\frac{1}{10}$	$\frac{1}{10}$
A	9	.	4	0
B	9	.	3	7
C	9	.	4	2

2. As 3 tenths is smaller than 4 tenths, runner B was fastest.
1st = Runner B 9.37 seconds

Written addition and subtraction

When you need to work out larger sums using a pen and paper, it helps to arrange the numbers to be added or subtracted into place value columns (see page 11). It's always a good idea to make an estimate of the answer first that you can check against once you've completed the calculation.

Key facts

✓ In written addition and subtraction, the numbers are arranged one on top of the other in columns.

✓ You find the solution by adding or subtracting the numbers column by column.

✓ Always work through the calculation from the right-hand column to the left-hand column.

Adding large numbers

Find the sum of the numbers 342 and 297. Round the numbers to make an estimate: 340 + 300 = 640.

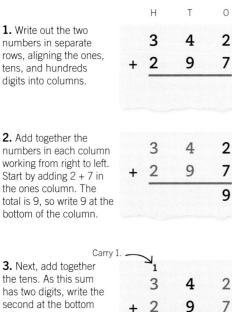

1. Write out the two numbers in separate rows, aligning the ones, tens, and hundreds digits into columns.

	H	T	O
	3	4	2
+	2	9	7

2. Add together the numbers in each column working from right to left. Start by adding 2 + 7 in the ones column. The total is 9, so write 9 at the bottom of the column.

	3	4	2
+	2	9	7
			9

3. Next, add together the tens. As this sum has two digits, write the second at the bottom of the tens column and "carry" the first to the hundreds column.

Carry 1.

		¹		
		3	4	2
+		2	9	7
			3	9

4. Add together the hundreds, then add the carried digit. The answer is 639, which is close to your estimate, so it is likely to be correct.

Add the carried over 1.

		¹		
		3	4	2
+		2	9	7
		6	3	9

Subtracting large numbers

Subtract 195 from 927. Again, make a quick estimate first: 930 − 200 = 730.

1. Write the numbers out in columns. Place the amount to be subtracted below the number it is to be subtracted from.

	H	T	O
	9	2	7
−	1	9	5

2. In the ones column, start by subtracting the bottom number from the top number. The answer is 2, so write that at the bottom.

	9	2	7
−	1	9	5
			2

3. In the tens column, you cannot subtract 9 from 2, so you need to "borrow" 1 from the hundreds column and carry it to the tens, turning 2 into 12. Now subtract.

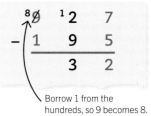

	⁸9̷	¹2	7
−	1	9	5
		3	2

Borrow 1 from the hundreds, so 9 becomes 8.

4. Subtract 1 from 8 (which is the new number in the hundreds column) to find the total. The answer is 732, which is close to your estimate.

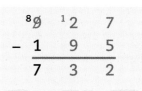

	⁸9̷	¹2	7
−	1	9	5
	7	3	2

Adding and subtracting decimals

Adding and subtracting decimals works in the same way as adding and subtracting whole numbers (see opposite). You just need to line up the decimal points.

Adding with decimals
Work out 26.97 + 14.8. Write out the sum in columns, aligning the decimal points. It's a good idea to make a quick estimate of the answer first by rounding each part of the sum to the nearest whole number: 27 + 15 = 42, so the answer will be around 42.

Subtracting with decimals
You have $5 in cash and you want to buy a bar of chocolate that costs $1.34. How much change will you get? Make sure the numbers in each column have the same number of decimal places. Five can be written as 5.00, so work out $5.00 − $1.34.

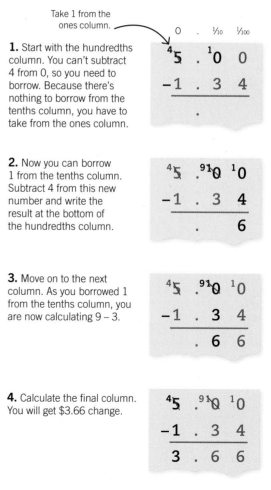

1. Add a zero to 14.8 to give the numbers the same number of decimal places. Add together the digits in each column, working from right to left. Write 7 at the bottom of the hundredths column.

1. Start with the hundredths column. You can't subtract 4 from 0, so you need to borrow. Because there's nothing to borrow from the tenths column, you have to take from the ones column.

2. Add together the digits in the tenths column. As 9 + 8 = 17, you need to carry 1 to the ones column.

2. Now you can borrow 1 from the tenths column. Subtract 4 from this new number and write the result at the bottom of the hundredths column.

3. Add the digits in the ones column, including the carried over 1. Because 6 + 4 + 1 = 11, you need to carry over another 1.

3. Move on to the next column. As you borrowed 1 from the tenths column, you are now calculating 9 − 3.

4. Calculate the final column, taking in the second carried over 1. The answer is 41.77, which is close to your estimate, so it is probably right.

4. Calculate the final column. You will get $3.66 change.

Negative numbers

Negative numbers are numbers less than zero. We use them all the time in real life, such as to record temperatures below 0°F. Negative numbers are indicated with a minus sign, such as −7.

Adding and subtracting

A number line, such as the one below, can be used to help understand adding and subtracting with negative numbers. Move right along the line for addition and left for subtraction.

Adding a positive number to any negative number makes it shift right along the number line. If the positive number is greater than the negative number, the result is positive.

Adding a negative number to any number is the same as subtracting the equivalent positive number from that number.

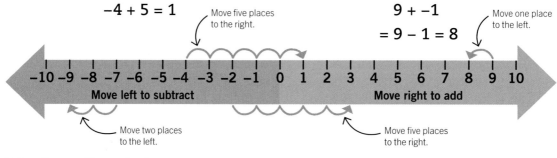

$$-4 + 5 = 1$$
Move five places to the right.

$$9 + -1$$
$$= 9 - 1 = 8$$
Move one place to the left.

−10 −9 −8 −7 −6 −5 −4 −3 −2 −1 0 1 2 3 4 5 6 7 8 9 10

Move left to subtract **Move right to add**

Move two places to the left.

Move five places to the right.

Subtracting a positive number from a negative number makes it shift left along the number line.

$$-7 - 2 = -9$$

Subtracting a negative number from any number creates a "double negative." The two minus signs cancel each other out, making a positive.

$$-2 - -5$$
$$= -2 + 5 = 3$$

Multiplying and dividing

The rules for multiplying and dividing negative numbers are easy to remember. When the two signs in the numbers being multiplied or divided are alike, the result is positive. When the signs are different, the result is negative.

Multiplying or dividing a positive by a negative gives a negative.	+ − makes −	$2 \times -3 = -6$ $6 \div -3 = -2$
Multiplying or dividing a negative by a positive gives a negative.	− + makes −	$-2 \times 3 = -6$ $-6 \div 3 = -2$
Multiplying or dividing a negative by a negative gives a positive.	− − makes +	$-2 \times -3 = 6$ $-6 \div -3 = 2$

Multiplying and dividing by 10, 100, and 1,000

Multiplying a whole number by 10, 100, or 1,000 is easy—you just add one, two, or three zeros on to the end of the start number, so for example, $5 \times 10 = 50$ or $62 \times 100 = 6{,}200$. Multiplying or dividing numbers containing decimals is only a little trickier and just requires remembering a few rules.

Key facts

✓ To multiply by 10, 100, or 1,000, move the digits one, two, or three places to the left on a place value table.

✓ To divide by 10, 100, or 1,000, move the digits one, two, or three places to the right on a place value table.

✓ The decimal point in the number being calculated moves one place for 10, two places for 100, and so on.

Multiplying by 10, 100, or 1,000

When a number is multiplied by 10, all the digits move one place left on a place value table. This is the equivalent of the decimal point in the number shifting one place to the right. Multiplying by 100 and 1,000 works the same way: the number of places the digits shift to the left on a place value table (and that the decimal point in the number shifts to the right) equals the number of zeros in the number you are multiplying by. You add zeros to the end of the result as necessary.

Multiplying by 10

$$2.82 \times 10 = 28.2$$

The decimal point moves one place to the right.

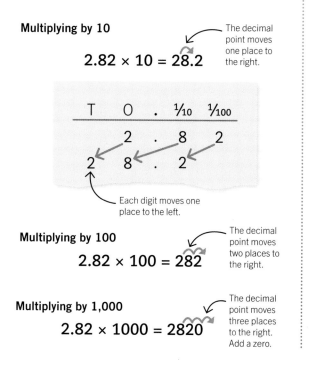

Each digit moves one place to the left.

Multiplying by 100

$$2.82 \times 100 = 282$$

The decimal point moves two places to the right.

Multiplying by 1,000

$$2.82 \times 1000 = 2820$$

The decimal point moves three places to the right. Add a zero.

Dividing by 10, 100, or 1,000

When a number is divided by 10, all the digits move one place to the right on a place value table. This is the equivalent of the decimal point shifting one place to the left. Dividing by 100 and 1,000 works the same way: you shift the number to the right on a place value table (two places for ÷ 100, three places for ÷ 1,000), the decimal point the same number of places to the left, and remove zeros as necessary.

Dividing by 10

$$762 \div 10 = 76.2$$

The decimal point moves one place to the left.

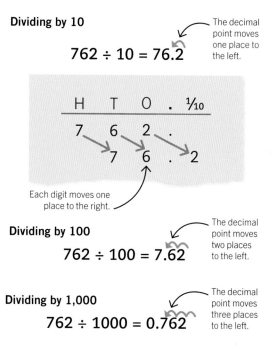

Each digit moves one place to the right.

Dividing by 100

$$762 \div 100 = 7.62$$

The decimal point moves two places to the left.

Dividing by 1,000

$$762 \div 1000 = 0.762$$

The decimal point moves three places to the left.

Methods of multiplication

Multiplication is very easy using a calculator but can also be done in your head or on paper. When the numbers in a multiplication contain two or more digits, it is more appropriate to use a written rather than a mental method. The result of a multiplication is called the product.

Long multiplication

Long multiplication is a standard way of multiplying two numbers that contain two or more digits. Place the numbers, one above the other, in columns of ones (O), tens (T), hundreds (H), thousands (Th), ten thousands (T Th), and so on. Here, we are calculating 162 × 143. First, make an estimate of your calculation (see box below).

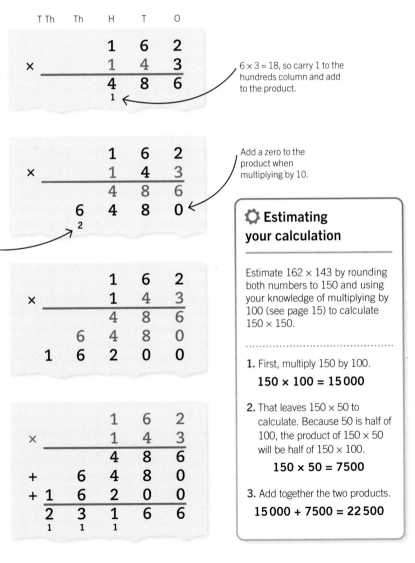

1. Multiply 162 by 3 in the ones column and place the result beneath the bar. Work through the digits from right to left, starting with 2 × 3, then 6 × 3 (carrying 1 to the hundreds column), then 1 × 3 (adding in the carried over 1).

6 × 3 = 18, so carry 1 to the hundreds column and add to the product.

```
        T Th   Th    H    T    O
                     1    6    2
    ×                1    4    3
                     4    8    6
                     1
```

2. Next, add a row and add a zero to the product, because you are moving on to multiplying 162 by 4 in the tens column. Work through the digits from right to left.

4 × 6 = 24, so carry 2 to the thousands column and add to the product.

Add a zero to the product when multiplying by 10.

```
                     1    6    2
    ×                1    4    3
                     4    8    6
                6    4    8    0
                2
```

3. Then add another new row and add zeros to the product in the ones and tens columns, because you are multiplying by 100. Multiply 162 by 1 in the hundreds column and add to the product.

```
                     1    6    2
    ×                1    4    3
                     4    8    6
                6    4    8    0
           1    6    2    0    0
```

4. Now, add together the products of the three multiplications, carrying over numbers and adding to the result as necessary. The answer is 23,166, which is close to your estimate of 22,500, so it is probably right.

```
                     1    6    2
    ×                1    4    3
                     4    8    6
    +           6    4    8    0
    +      1    6    2    0    0
           2    3    1    6    6
           1    1    1
```

> ### ⚙ Estimating your calculation
>
> Estimate 162 × 143 by rounding both numbers to 150 and using your knowledge of multiplying by 100 (see page 15) to calculate 150 × 150.
>
> **1.** First, multiply 150 by 100.
>
> **150 × 100 = 15 000**
>
> **2.** That leaves 150 × 50 to calculate. Because 50 is half of 100, the product of 150 × 50 will be half of 150 × 100.
>
> **150 × 50 = 7500**
>
> **3.** Add together the two products.
>
> **15 000 + 7500 = 22 500**

Long multiplication involving decimals

Long multiplication can be used to multiply decimals, too. You first need to take out the decimal points, then work through the long multiplication, and finally put the decimal points back in at the end. Here, we are calculating 2.91 × 3.2.

Key facts

✓ **Long multiplication is a useful method of calculating the product of larger numbers.**

✓ **Long multiplication can also be used for multiplying with decimals.**

✓ **When calculating with decimals, you take out the decimal points at the beginning of the calculation and put them back in at the end.**

1. First, make a quick estimate of the answer by rounding each number to 3. Because 3 × 3 = 9, you expect the answer to be around this figure. To take out the decimal points, multiply each number by 10, 100, and so on as needed in order to convert each to a whole number.

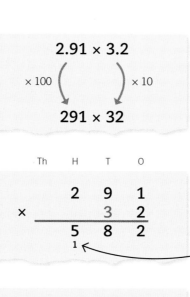

2.91 × 3.2

× 100 ( ) × 10

291 × 32

2. Then multiply each of the digits in 291 by 2, starting with the ones column and working from right to left. Carry over numbers to the next column as necessary.

	Th	H	T	O
		2	9	1
×			3	2
		5	8	2
		1		

Add the carried over 1 to the product.

3. Then add a zero to the ones column and move on to calculating 291 × 3 in the tens column. Work through the digits one by one and carry over numbers as necessary.

	2	9	1
×		3	2
	5	8	2
8	7	3	0
₂			

Add the carried over 2 to the product.

Add a zero to the product when multiplying by 10.

4. Add together the products of the two multiplications, carrying over digits as necessary. The sum is 9,312, but you still need to put the decimal points back in.

	2	9	1
×		3	2
	5	8	2
+ 8	7	3	0
9	3	1	2
1	1		

5. To convert the sum back into decimals, you multiply together the 100 and the 10, which you used to convert the decimals to whole numbers, then divide 9,312 by this number. The answer is 9.312.

100 × 10 = 1000

9312 ÷ 1000 = 9.312

Because this is close to your estimate of 9, the answer is probably correct.

Methods of division

Division is about finding out how many times one number can be divided by another. It is slightly more complex than multiplication.

Short division

Short division is commonly used when the number being divided (the dividend) is divided by a number (the divisor) less than 10. If the dividend doesn't divide exactly by the divisor, the amount left over (the remainder) is carried over to the next digit. The result of a division is called the quotient.

1. To divide 753 by 6, start by dividing the first digit in the dividend (7) by 6. The result is 1 with a remainder of 1. Put 1 directly above the 7 and carry over the remainder.

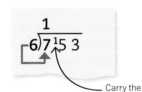

Carry the remainder to the next digit.

2. Move on to the next digit. Because of the remainder being carried over, you are dividing 15 by 6. The result is 2 with a remainder of 3. Add this to the next digit.

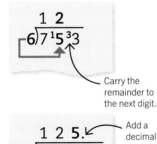

Carry the remainder to the next digit.

3. Divide 33 by 6. The result is 5 with a remainder of 3. As it doesn't divide exactly, you add decimal points above and below the line and add a zero to the dividend. Carry the remainder.

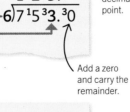

Add a decimal point.

Add a zero and carry the remainder.

4. Divide 30 by 6. It divides exactly, so add 5 above the zero of the dividend after the decimal point. You now have your answer.

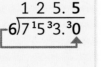

Short division: dividing a decimal by a whole number

You can use the same method when dividing a decimal number. Start by adding a decimal point in the quotient just above the decimal point in the dividend. Here, you are working out 42.6 ÷ 3.

1. Add a decimal in the quotient to line up with the one in the dividend. Divide the first digit by the divisor and carry the remainder.

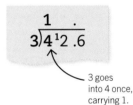

3 goes into 4 once, carrying 1.

2. Move on to the next digit and place the result above the line.

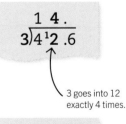

3 goes into 12 exactly 4 times.

3. Then move on to the digit after the decimal point. Because 3 divides into 6 exactly, you have your answer.

Long division

Long division is a method of division that is particularly helpful when working with larger numbers. As with long multiplication, it involves working step-by-step, carrying over remainders as you go.

1. To divide 450 by 36, begin by dividing 45 by 36.

Align 1 with the last digit of the number being divided.

2. Calculate the remainder by subtracting the 36 from the first two numbers of the dividend, so 45 − 36. The remainder is 9.

Amount left over from the first division

3. Bring the last digit of the dividend down next to the remainder and divide this by the divisor, so 90 ÷ 36.

Because 36 goes into 90 twice, add 2 above the line.

4. Work out the amount left over by calculating 90 − 72 = 18.

5. There are no more digits in the dividend you can bring down, so add a decimal point and a zero to the dividend. Bring down the zero to make 180.

6. Add a decimal point after the 12 and divide 180 by the divisor, so 180 ÷ 36. Because 36 goes into 180 exactly 5 times, you now have the answer.

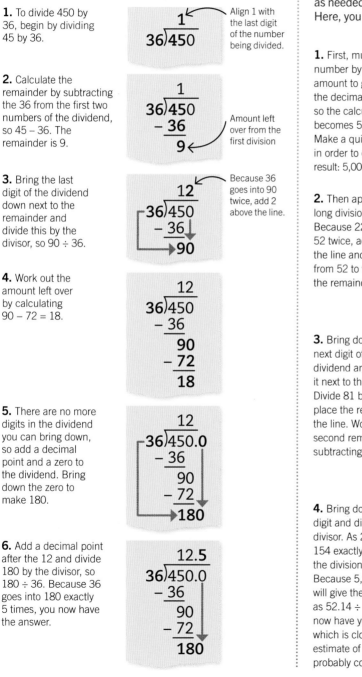

Long division involving decimals

A useful way to divide by a number that contains a decimal is to convert both numbers to whole numbers first. You get rid of the decimals by multiplying both numbers by 10, 100 (and so on) as needed to convert them to whole numbers. Here, you are calculating $52.14 \div 0.22$.

1. First, multiply each number by the same amount to get rid of the decimal places, so the calculation becomes $5{,}214 \div 22$. Make a quick estimate in order to check to result: $5{,}000 \div 20 = 250$.

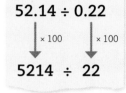

2. Then apply the long division method. Because 22 goes into 52 twice, add 2 above the line and subtract 44 from 52 to work out the remainder.

3. Bring down the next digit of the dividend and place it next to the remainder. Divide 81 by 22 and place the result above the line. Work out the second remainder by subtracting 66 from 81.

4. Bring down the final digit and divide by the divisor. As 22 goes into 154 exactly 7 times, the division is complete. Because $5{,}214 \div 22$ will give the same result as $52.14 \div 0.22$, you now have your answer, which is close to your estimate of 250, so it is probably correct.

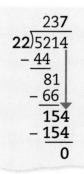

Mental addition and subtraction

Many everyday calculations can be simplified so that you can find the answer in your head or by using a scrap of paper without needing a calculator or a formal written method.

Key facts

✓ The partition method simplifies calculations by breaking them down into easier steps.

✓ In the compensation method, you adjust the numbers you're working with to make the calculation easier.

Partition method

One way of making an awkward calculation simpler is to break it down into a series of easier calculations. You then combine the results of each easier calculation to get the answer. This is called partitioning. Here, you are calculating 352 + 414.

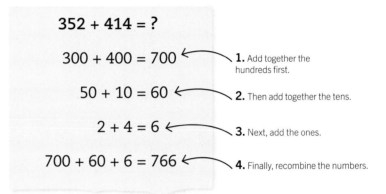

352 + 414 = ?

300 + 400 = 700   **1.** Add together the hundreds first.

50 + 10 = 60   **2.** Then add together the tens.

2 + 4 = 6   **3.** Next, add the ones.

700 + 60 + 6 = 766   **4.** Finally, recombine the numbers.

Compensation method for addition

The compensation method is another way of simplifying calculations. When adding, you add to one number to make it an easier number to work with and subtract the same amount from the other number in order to compensate. Calculate 196 + 234.

1. Make the calculation easier by adding 4 to 196 to make 200.

2. To balance it out, you need to subtract 4 from 234.

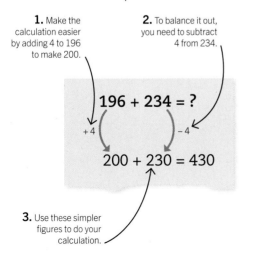

196 + 234 = ?

+ 4   – 4

200 + 230 = 430

3. Use these simpler figures to do your calculation.

Compensation method for subtracting

The compensation method for subtraction is slightly different from the method for addition. Instead of adding to one side and subtracting from the other, we apply the same operation to both numbers. Calculate 27.6 – 18.8.

1. Add 1.2 to 18.8 to make 20.

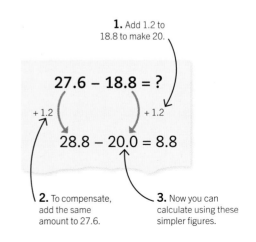

27.6 – 18.8 = ?

+ 1.2   + 1.2

28.8 – 20.0 = 8.8

2. To compensate, add the same amount to 27.6.

3. Now you can calculate using these simpler figures.

Mental multiplication and division

Some numbers are easier to work with than others. Harder calculations using multiplication and division can be done in your head if you break the numbers down into easier calculations.

Partition method

The partition method can be used to break tricky multiplication and division calculations down into more manageable chunks. Here, you are calculating 43×52.

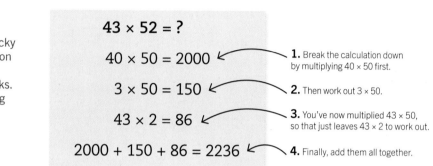

$43 \times 52 = ?$

$40 \times 50 = 2000$ — **1.** Break the calculation down by multiplying 40×50 first.

$3 \times 50 = 150$ — **2.** Then work out 3×50.

$43 \times 2 = 86$ — **3.** You've now multiplied 43×50, so that just leaves 43×2 to work out.

$2000 + 150 + 86 = 2236$ — **4.** Finally, add them all together.

Compensation method for multiplication

If you know your times tables, another handy method is to keep multiplying the first number by something and dividing the other by the same number until you have a simpler calculation. This is most useful when calculating even numbers. Here, you are working out 24×36.

1. As both 24 and 36 are divisible by 3, multiply the first number by 3 and divide the other by 3.

2. Keep multiplying and dividing by 3 until the calculation becomes simpler.

3. Now switch to multiplying and dividing by 2 to get the answer.

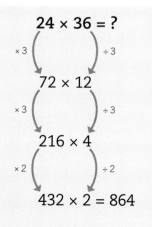

$24 \times 36 = ?$

$\times 3 \qquad \div 3$

72×12

$\times 3 \qquad \div 3$

216×4

$\times 2 \qquad \div 2$

$432 \times 2 = 864$

Compensation method for division

The compensation method can also be used for division. Simplify a division calculation by dividing both parts of the calculation by the same number until you have numbers that are easier to work with. Calculate $224 \div 28$.

1. Divide both sides by 2 to simplify.

2. Continue dividing by 2.

3. You can now recognize you're working in the 8 times table.

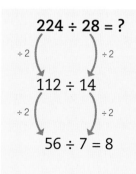

$224 \div 28 = ?$

$\div 2 \qquad \div 2$

$112 \div 14$

$\div 2 \qquad \div 2$

$56 \div 7 = 8$

Powers of numbers

When a number is multiplied by itself a number of times, this is expressed using powers. The power of the number is indicated with a smaller-sized number, called an exponent (or index), written to the right of the main (or "base") number. So, for example, 2×2 is written as 2^2.

Key facts

✓ Powers provide a shorthand for multiplying a number lots of times.

✓ A square number is multiplied by itself once.

✓ A cube number is multiplied by itself twice.

✓ Powers are written using a small exponent, also known as an index.

Square numbers
When you multiply a number by itself, it is said to be squared. It's a square, because it works like the area of a square. We've shown one example below, but any number can be squared. It's a good idea to learn the first few.

3 rows, each with 3 units, make up this square, so $3 \times 3 = 3^2 = 9$.

$3^2 = 9$

This is the power symbol for squared.

1^2	2^2	3^2	4^2	5^2	10^2
1×1	2×2	3×3	4×4	5×5	10×10
1	4	9	16	25	100

Cube numbers
When you multiply a number by itself twice, it is said to be cubed. It's a cube, because it works like the volume of a cube. We've shown one example here, but any number can be cubed.

There are 3 horizontal rows and 3 vertical rows, each with 3 units, so $3 \times 3 \times 3 = 3^3 = 27$.

$3^3 = 27$

This is the power symbol for cubed.

1^3	2^3	3^3	4^3	5^3	10^3
$1 \times 1 \times 1$	$2 \times 2 \times 2$	$3 \times 3 \times 3$	$4 \times 4 \times 4$	$5 \times 5 \times 5$	$10 \times 10 \times 10$
1	8	27	64	125	1000

🔍 Using a calculator

Scientific calculators have buttons you can use to find squares, cubes, and higher powers, such as 2^4 $(2 \times 2 \times 2 \times 2)$, 2^5, and so on.

Squares and cubes
Enter the number to be squared or cubed, then press the dedicated button.

$2^2 =$ [2] [x^2] $= 4$

$2^3 =$ [2] [x^3] $= 8$

Higher powers
For higher powers, you use the exponent button. Enter the number, tap the exponent button, and then enter the power.

$2^5 =$ [2] [x^y] [5] $= 32$

Factors and multiples

The factors of a number are all the whole numbers that it can be divided by exactly. The multiples of a number are the result of multiplying it by another whole number.

Visualizing factors
A simple way to understand the factors of 10 is to imagine a chocolate bar with 10 square chunks. The factors are the different ways in which the bar can be divided into equal sections of whole squares. There are four ways, which give four factors of 10: 1, 2, 5, and 10.

10 ÷ 1 = 10

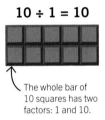

The whole bar of 10 squares has two factors: 1 and 10.

10 ÷ 2 = 5

Splitting the bar in half gives you two more factors, 2 and 5.

10 ÷ 5 = 2

Dividing into five sections of two squares each repeats the factors 2 and 5.

10 ÷ 10 = 1

Dividing into individual squares repeats the factors 1 and 10.

Factor pairs
Factors always come in pairs, which multiplied together make up the original number exactly. To work out the factor pairs of 20, you list the numbers that can be multiplied by another number to give 20.

1. Start with the factor pair of 1 and 20 and list them together.

$1 \times 20 \longrightarrow$ **1, 20**

2. As $2 \times 10 = 20$, add 2 and 10 to the list.

$2 \times 10 \longrightarrow$ **2, 10**

3. 3 is not a factor of 20, as $3 \times 6 = 18$ (too low) and $3 \times 7 = 21$ (too high).

~~3~~

4. Because $4 \times 5 = 20$, add these two numbers in.

$4 \times 5 \longrightarrow$ **4, 5**

5. Stop when the numbers start repeating.

5×4

6. List the factors in order. These are all the factors of 20.

1, 2, 4, 5, 10, 20

Multiples
Multiples are the result of multiplying a number by another whole number. In other words, they are simply that number's times table.

First five multiples of 7
$7 \times 1 = 7$
$7 \times 2 = 14$
$7 \times 3 = 21$
$7 \times 4 = 28$
$7 \times 5 = 35$

First five multiples of 11
$11 \times 1 = 11$
$11 \times 2 = 22$
$11 \times 3 = 33$
$11 \times 4 = 44$
$11 \times 5 = 55$

Prime numbers

A prime number is a number (apart from 1) that can only be divided exactly by 1 and itself. Therefore, prime numbers only have two factors. Every other number has more than two factors and is called a composite number.

Prime numbers up to 100
There are 25 prime numbers between 2 and 100. Apart from 2 and 5 (see below), all prime numbers end in 1, 3, 7, or 9, though not all numbers ending in these digits are prime numbers.

Since 1 does not have two different factors, it is not a prime number.

The only even prime is 2. All other even numbers can be divided by 2, so they are not prime.

Prime numbers are shaded in pink.

1	2	3	4	5	6	7	8	9	10
11	12	13	14	15	16	17	18	19	20
21	22	23	24	25	26	27	28	29	30
31	32	33	34	35	36	37	38	39	40
41	42	43	44	45	46	47	48	49	50
51	52	53	54	55	56	57	58	59	60
61	62	63	64	65	66	67	68	69	70
71	72	73	74	75	76	77	78	79	80
81	82	83	84	85	86	87	88	89	90
91	92	93	94	95	96	97	98	99	100

Is a number prime?

There is a simple way of finding out if a number up to 100 is a prime number or not—if it cannot be divided exactly by 2, 3, 5, or 7, it is a prime.

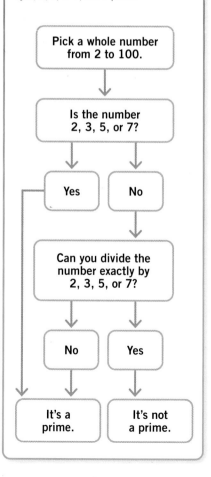

Pick a whole number from 2 to 100.

Is the number 2, 3, 5, or 7?

Yes — No

Can you divide the number exactly by 2, 3, 5, or 7?

No — Yes

It's a prime. — It's not a prime.

Prime factorization

Prime numbers are the building blocks of numbers. That's because every whole number is either a prime or a composite (the product of multiplying together primes). Prime factors are the primes that are multiplied together to make a composite number.

Making a factor tree

Every whole number that's not a prime can be broken down into a string of prime factors. Finding the prime factors of any whole number is called prime factor decomposition, or prime factorization. An easy method of prime factorization is to make a factor tree.

Different tree, same result
Often there is more than one way to create a factor tree. Every composite number has a unique set of prime factors.

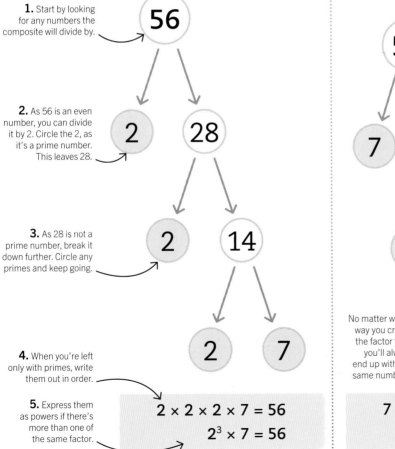

1. Start by looking for any numbers the composite will divide by.

2. As 56 is an even number, you can divide it by 2. Circle the 2, as it's a prime number. This leaves 28.

3. As 28 is not a prime number, break it down further. Circle any primes and keep going.

4. When you're left only with primes, write them out in order.

5. Express them as powers if there's more than one of the same factor.

$2 \times 2 \times 2 \times 7 = 56$

$2^3 \times 7 = 56$

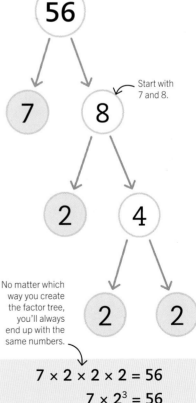

Start with 7 and 8.

No matter which way you create the factor tree, you'll always end up with the same numbers.

$7 \times 2 \times 2 \times 2 = 56$

$7 \times 2^3 = 56$

Common factors and multiples

When two or more numbers have the same factors in common, we call the factors they share common factors. When two or more numbers have the same multiples in common, the multiples they share are called common multiples.

Common factors

All the factors of 12 and 16 are shown in the diagrams below. The common factors are highlighted in yellow. The highest number that will divide into both numbers is called the greatest common factor (GCF).

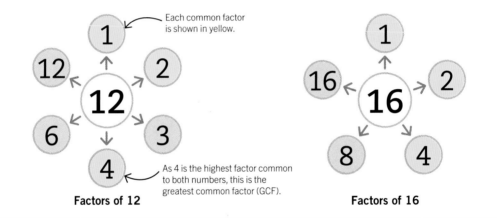

Each common factor is shown in yellow.

As 4 is the highest factor common to both numbers, this is the greatest common factor (GCF).

Factors of 12

Factors of 16

Common multiples

You can use number lines to list the multiples of two or more numbers, then identify the common multiples. The smallest number common to both lists is called the least common multiple (LCM). Here, we've listed the multiples of 4 and 6 up to 36.

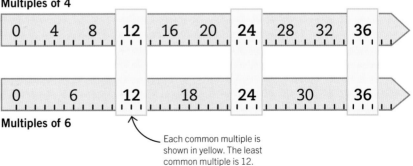

Multiples of 4

Multiples of 6

Each common multiple is shown in yellow. The least common multiple is 12.

Finding the GCF and LCM using a factor tree

For smaller numbers, you can work out the GCF and LCM by listing the factors, but for larger numbers, it helps to make a factor tree. Here, we are finding the GCF and LCM of 36 and 120.

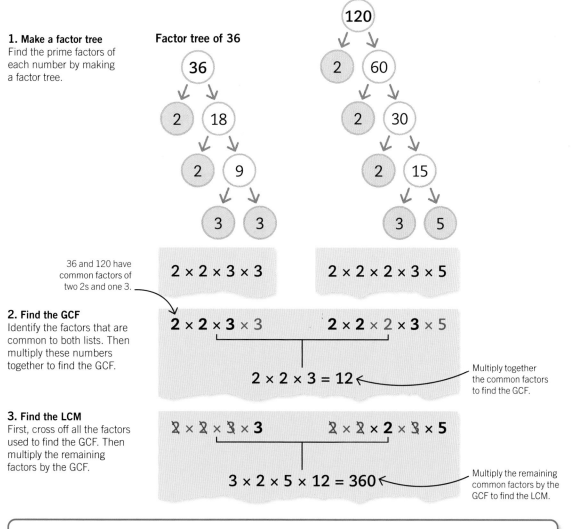

Factor tree of 120

1. Make a factor tree
Find the prime factors of each number by making a factor tree.

Factor tree of 36

36 and 120 have common factors of two 2s and one 3.

$2 \times 2 \times 3 \times 3$

$2 \times 2 \times 2 \times 3 \times 5$

2. Find the GCF
Identify the factors that are common to both lists. Then multiply these numbers together to find the GCF.

$2 \times 2 \times 3 \times 3$ $2 \times 2 \times 2 \times 3 \times 5$

$2 \times 2 \times 3 = 12$

Multiply together the common factors to find the GCF.

3. Find the LCM
First, cross off all the factors used to find the GCF. Then multiply the remaining factors by the GCF.

$\cancel{2} \times \cancel{2} \times \cancel{3} \times 3$ $\cancel{2} \times \cancel{2} \times 2 \times \cancel{3} \times 5$

$3 \times 2 \times 5 \times 12 = 360$

Multiply the remaining common factors by the GCF to find the LCM.

🔍 **Using a Venn diagram**

An alternative way to find the GCF and LCM, once you have listed all the factors, is to use a Venn diagram (see page 217). Here, we are showing how to find the GCF and LCM of 36 and 120 using this method.

1. Write the common factors in the overlap between the circles and the rest of the numbers outside the intersection.

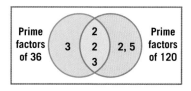

Prime factors of 36   3   2 2 3   2, 5   Prime factors of 120

2. Find the GCF by multiplying together the numbers in the intersection.

$2 \times 2 \times 3 = 12$

3. To find the LCM, multiply together the numbers in all three sections.

$3 \times 2 \times 2 \times 3 \times 2 \times 5 = 360$

Order of operations

When you work out a calculation with more than one operation, such as $2 + 20 \div 4$, you will get a different answer depending on which part of the calculation you tackle first. That is why we follow a conventional order of operations.

PEMDAS

There's a handy acronym that tells you the order in which operations need to be performed: PEMDAS.

1. **P** stands for Parentheses
Always work out the things in parentheses first.

Work out the calculation in parentheses first, then multiply.

$$4 \times (5 + 2)$$
$$= 4 \times 7$$
$$= 28$$

If you calculate 4×5 first, then add 2, you end up with the answer 22, which is wrong.

2. **E** stands for Exponents
Exponents is another name for powers or indices (see page 22). Work out any squares, cubes, or higher powers before moving on to the next operation.

Square the 5 first, then multiply.

$$4 \times 5^2$$
$$= 4 \times 25$$
$$= 100$$

If you work out 4×5 first, then square, you end up with 400, which is wrong.

3. **MD** stands for Multiplication/Division
Always multiply and/or divide before adding or subtracting. Neither takes precedence: if there are two similar operations, start from the left.

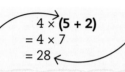

$$7 + 5 \times 4$$
$$= 7 + 20 = 27$$

Do the multiplication before the addition.

Start from the left with similar operations.

$$8 \div 2 \times 4$$
$$= 4 \times 4 = 16$$

4. **AS** stands for Addition/Subtraction
Addition and subtraction are always the last operations. Again, neither takes precedence, but you must work from left to right.

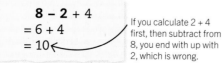

$$8 - 2 + 4$$
$$= 6 + 4$$
$$= 10$$

If you calculate $2 + 4$ first, then subtract from 8, you end with up with 2, which is wrong.

Angles
and shapes

Angles

Angles are found everywhere, from roads and buildings to furniture and machinery. Angles are a measurement of the turn, or rotation, between two rays that share a common point, called the vertex. This turn is measured in units called degrees (°).

Types of angles

The size of an angle depends on the size of the turn between two lines. A full turn, or a circle, is 360° and a half turn, or straight line, is 180°. There are four other types of angles: right angle, acute angle, obtuse angle, and reflex angle.

Key facts

✓ Acute angles are between 0° and 90°.

✓ A right angle is 90°, which is a quarter of a full turn.

✓ Obtuse angles are between 90° and 180°.

✓ A straight line, or straight angle, is 180°, which is half a full turn.

✓ Reflex angles are greater than 180°.

✓ A circle is 360°, which is a full turn.

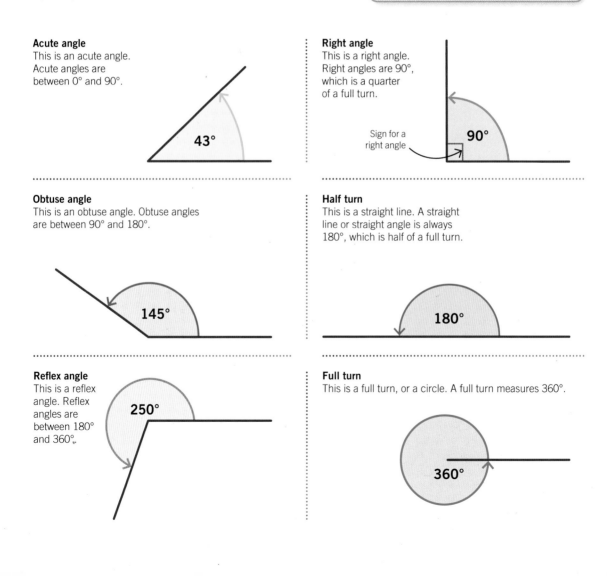

Acute angle
This is an acute angle. Acute angles are between 0° and 90°.

43°

Right angle
This is a right angle. Right angles are 90°, which is a quarter of a full turn.

Sign for a right angle

90°

Obtuse angle
This is an obtuse angle. Obtuse angles are between 90° and 180°.

145°

Half turn
This is a straight line. A straight line or straight angle is always 180°, which is half of a full turn.

180°

Reflex angle
This is a reflex angle. Reflex angles are between 180° and 360°.

250°

Full turn
This is a full turn, or a circle. A full turn measures 360°.

360°

Angle facts

Sometimes we can work out the sizes of unknown angles using the information we know about the number of degrees in a full turn, on a straight line, or in a right angle.

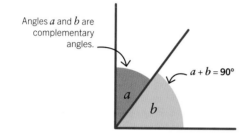

Angles a and b are complementary angles.

$a + b = 90°$

a

b

Angles in a right angle

If a right angle is split into two or more angles, the sum of these angles is always 90°, because there are 90° in a right angle. Any two angles that add up to 90° are called complementary angles.

Angles on a straight line

If a straight line is split into two or more angles, the sum of these angles is always 180°, because there are 180° on a straight line. When two angles are created by one line meeting another, the angles are called a linear pair of angles or supplementary angles.

Angles a and b are called a linear pair of angles or supplementary angles.

$a + b = 180°$

a

b

Angles around a point

Angles around a point, or vertex, add up to 360°, because they make up a full turn and there are 360° in a full turn. The sum of angles around a point will always be 360°.

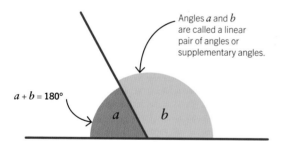

$a + b + c + d = 360°$

a

b

d

c

Angles a, b, c, and d together make a full turn.

Angles and parallel lines

Multiple lines that have the same direction are called parallel lines. They are always the same distance apart and never meet. When another line intersects a pair of parallel lines, it creates pairs of congruent angles.

Key facts

✓ When two lines intersect, the angles vertically opposite each other are congruent.

✓ Alternate angles are congruent angles on different (alternate) sides of a line crossing a pair of parallel lines.

✓ Corresponding angles are congruent angles on the same (corresponding) sides of a line crossing a pair of parallel lines.

Parallel and transversal lines

When another line intersects two or more parallel lines, it is called a transversal. This line creates pairs of angles that are congruent. These angles have different names depending on their relationship: vertically opposite, alternate, and corresponding.

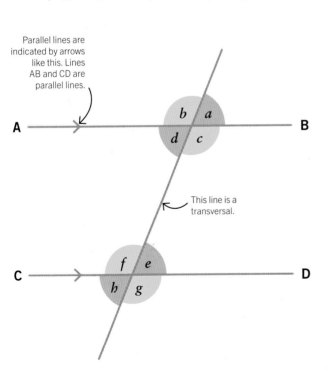

Parallel lines are indicated by arrows like this. Lines AB and CD are parallel lines.

This line is a transversal.

Vertically opposite angles

Angles on the opposite sides of two lines that cross each other are congruent. They are called vertically opposite angles. Four pairs of vertically opposite angles are created by a transversal crossing a pair of parallel lines.

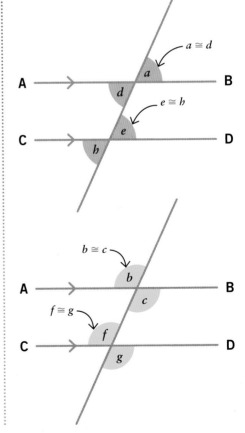

$a \cong d$

$e \cong b$

$b \cong c$

$f \cong g$

📑 Calculating angles

Question

Find the degree measure of angle x.

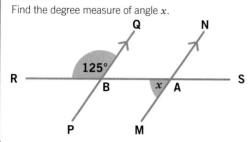

Answer

We can use the rules we know about angles and lines to find x. Angles in a straight line add up to 180°, so we can find the degree measure of angle RBP.

This means "angle." → $\angle$**RBP = 180° − 125° = 55°**

Angle RBP and angle x are corresponding angles, so they are congruent. Angle x is 55°.

Alternate angles

Angles on different (alternate) sides of a transversal line crossing a pair of parallel lines are congruent. They are known as alternate angles. Two pairs of alternate angles are created when a transversal crosses a pair of parallel lines.

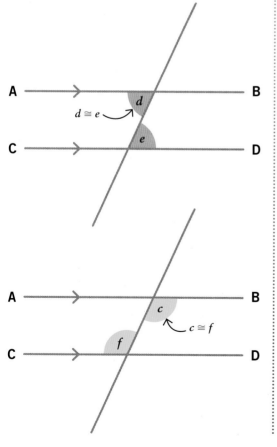

Corresponding angles

When a transversal line intersects a pair of parallel lines, the angles on the same (corresponding) sides of the lines, and either both above or below the parallel lines, are congruent. These are called corresponding angles. Four pairs of corresponding angles are created when a transversal crosses a pair of parallel lines.

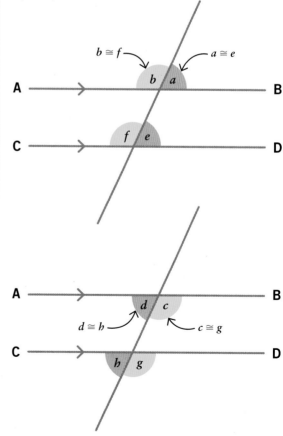

Measuring and drawing angles

Angles are measured in increments called degrees (°). A tool called a protractor has a scale showing degrees around its curved edge that can be used to measure and draw angles.

✓ Angles are measured in degrees (°).

✓ Angles can be measured and drawn using a tool called a protractor.

✓ Position the protractor so its center sits at the vertex of the angle.

Measuring angles

A protractor has two scales that run in opposite directions so angles can be read from the baseline in both directions.

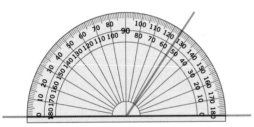

1. Position the protractor over the angle so the center aligns with the vertex of the angle and the baseline of the angle lines up with 0° on the protractor.

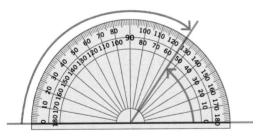

2. Use the outer scale to measure the angle up from 0° from the left. Use the inner scale to measure the angle up from 0° from the right.

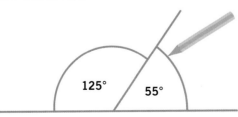

3. Mark and label the angles. Remember to include the units. These angles are 125° and 55°.

Drawing angles

When you are asked to draw an angle of a given size, you can use a protractor to measure and draw the angle.

1. Draw a straight line with a ruler and mark the point where you want the angle to start.

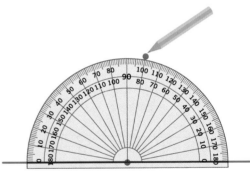

2. Position the protractor so the center is over the point and the line aligns with 0°. Read the degrees from 0° on the scale and mark the position of the angle you want with a point.

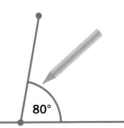

3. Remove the protractor. Use a ruler to draw a line between the two points and mark the angle.

Symmetry

Some shapes possess a property called symmetry. There are two types of symmetry: line and rotational. A shape with no symmetry is asymmetrical.

Line symmetry

A two-dimensional (2D) shape has line symmetry when it can be divided by a line into two equal parts. This line is called the line of symmetry and can occur more than once in one shape. A shape that has line symmetry can be folded in half and both sides come together exactly.

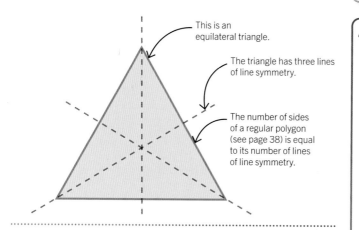

This is an equilateral triangle.

The triangle has three lines of line symmetry.

The number of sides of a regular polygon (see page 38) is equal to its number of lines of line symmetry.

Rotational symmetry

A 2D shape is also symmetrical if it can be rotated clockwise or counterclockwise and still look exactly the same in other positions. This is called rotational symmetry and can occur in a shape more than once. The number of positions in which the shape looks the same is called the order. If a shape has no rotational symmetry, we say it has rotational symmetry order 1.

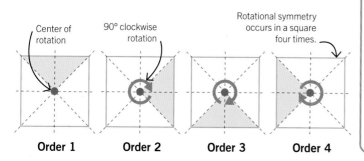

Center of rotation

90° clockwise rotation

Rotational symmetry occurs in a square four times.

Order 1   Order 2   Order 3   Order 4

Key facts

✓ A 2D shape has line symmetry if it can be divided by a line into two equal parts.

✓ A 2D shape has rotational symmetry if it can be rotated clockwise or counterclockwise and still look exactly the same in other positions.

✓ Regular polygons have the same number of lines of symmetry and the same order of rotational symmetry as the number of sides.

Triangle symmetry

Question
Are the following statements true, sometimes true, or false?
a) A right triangle has one line of line symmetry.
b) A right triangle has rotational symmetry order 2.

Answer
a) Sometimes true. An isosceles right triangle has one line of symmetry.

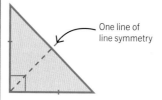

One line of line symmetry

b) Never true. All right triangles have rotational symmetry order 1 (no rotational symmetry).

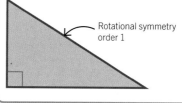

Rotational symmetry order 1

Properties of triangles

A triangle is a polygon that has three sides, three points where the sides meet (called vertices), and three angles. Each vertex is often labeled with a capital letter. A triangle with vertices A, B, and C is known as ΔABC. The symbol Δ can be used to represent the word "triangle."

Equilateral triangles

An equilateral triangle has three equal sides, three equal angles, three lines of line symmetry, and rotational symmetry of order 3 (see page 35).

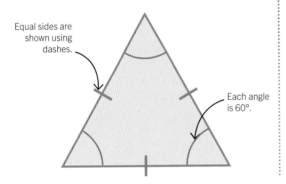

Equal sides are shown using dashes.

Each angle is 60°.

Isosceles triangles

An isosceles triangle has two equal sides, two equal angles, one line of line symmetry, and no rotational symmetry.

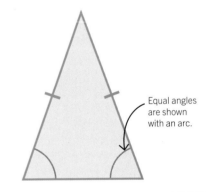

Equal angles are shown with an arc.

Right triangles

A right triangle has one angle that is 90°. The sides can all be different lengths, or two sides can be the same, but they can never all be the same length. A right triangle will only have symmetry if it has two sides of the same length.

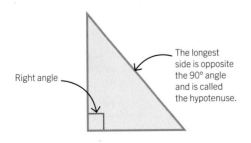

Right angle

The longest side is opposite the 90° angle and is called the hypotenuse.

Scalene triangles

A scalene triangle has three sides of different length and three angles of different size. It has no line or rotational symmetry.

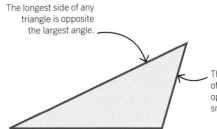

The longest side of any triangle is opposite the largest angle.

The shortest side of any triangle is opposite the smallest angle.

Properties of quadrilaterals

Quadrilaterals are shapes that have four sides, vertices, and angles. They can be either regular or irregular. A regular quadrilateral has equal sides and angles. An irregular quadrilateral has sides and angles of different sizes.

Key facts

✓ A quadrilateral has four sides, four vertices, and four angles.

✓ Squares, rectangles, parallelograms, rhombuses, trapezoids, and kites are all quadrilaterals.

✓ Regular quadrilaterals have sides and angles that are equal in size. Irregular quadrilaterals have sides and angles that are not equal in size.

Square
A square has four sides of equal length, four equal angles, four lines of line symmetry, and rotational symmetry (see page 35) of order 4. Opposite sides are parallel and diagonals bisect (divide into two equal parts) each other at right angles.

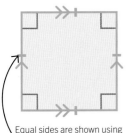

Equal sides are shown using a single or double line.

Rectangle
A rectangle has two pairs of sides of equal lengths. Each pair of sides is parallel and the diagonals are congruent. It has four equal angles, two lines of line symmetry, and rotational symmetry of order 2.

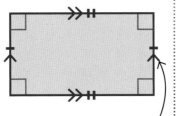

Parallel sides are shown using an arrow or a double arrow.

Parallelogram
A parallelogram has two pairs of sides of equal length. Each pair of sides is parallel and the diagonals bisect each other. A parallelogram also has two pairs of equal angles, no line symmetry, and rotational symmetry of order 2.

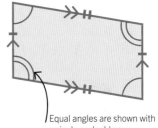

Equal angles are shown with a single or double arc.

Rhombus
A rhombus is a type of parallelogram that has sides that are all the same length. It has two pairs of equal angles and opposite sides that are parallel. Diagonals are perpendicular. It also has two lines of line symmetry and rotational symmetry of order 2.

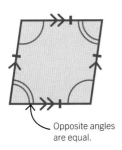

Opposite angles are equal.

Trapezoid
A trapezoid has one pair of parallel sides of unequal length. When the two nonparallel sides are the same length, called an isosceles trapezoid, it will have one line of line symmetry.

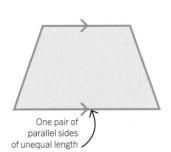

One pair of parallel sides of unequal length

Kite
A kite has two pairs of sides of equal length, one pair of equal angles, one line of line symmetry, and no rotational symmetry. The diagonals bisect each other at 90°.

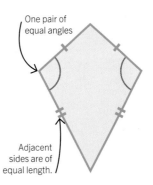

One pair of equal angles

Adjacent sides are of equal length.

Properties of polygons

A polygon is a 2D shape that has three or more straight sides and has as many sides as it does angles. Polygons are named for the number of sides and angles they have. A polygon with seven sides and angles is called a heptagon, because "hept" means seven.

Regular polygons
In a regular polygon, the lengths of the sides and the sizes of the angles are always equal. Although a polygon must have at least three sides and angles, it can have any number of sides and angles above this number. A myriagon has 10000 sides and angles.

Key facts

✓ A regular polygon has sides of equal length and angles of equal size.

✓ An irregular polygon has at least two sides or two angles that are different.

✓ A concave polygon has at least one reflex angle.

✓ A convex polygon only has acute and obtuse angles.

Triangle
(3 sides and angles)

Quadrilateral
(4 sides and angles)

Pentagon
(5 sides and angles)

Hexagon
(6 sides and angles)

Heptagon
(7 sides and angles)

Octagon
(8 sides and angles)

Nonagon
(9 sides and angles)

Decagon
(10 sides and angles)

Hendecagon
(11 sides and angles)

Dodecagon
(12 sides and angles)

Pentadecagon
(15 sides and angles)

Icosagon
(20 sides and angles)

Irregular polygons
A polygon with at least two sides or angles that are different from each other is called an irregular polygon. There are two types of irregular polygon: concave and convex.

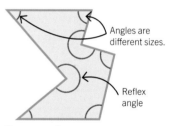

Angles are different sizes.

Reflex angle

Concave polygons
A concave polygon has at least one angle greater than 180° (a reflex angle).

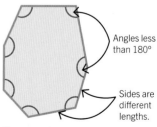

Angles less than 180°

Sides are different lengths.

Convex polygons
A convex polygon has no angles greater than 180°. Its angles are always either acute or obtuse.

Angles in a triangle

A triangle is one of the most basic 2D shapes.
It always has three sides, which create three angles.
No matter the lengths of these sides or how different
the angles are, when you add them up, the interior
angles of a triangle will always equal 180°.

📌 **Key facts**

✓ Interior angles in a triangle add up to 180°.

✓ Exterior angles of a triangle add up to 360°.

Interior angles

We can see how the angles in a triangle will
always add up to 180° by rearranging them
to form a straight line.

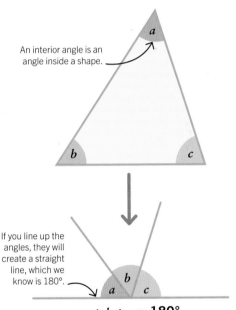

An interior angle is an angle inside a shape.

If you line up the angles, they will create a straight line, which we know is 180°.

$$a + b + c = 180°$$

Exterior angles

Exterior angles of a triangle are found by extending
each side. The sum of an exterior angle and its
adjacent interior angle is 180°, because angles on
a straight line add up to 180°. Each exterior angle
is equal to the sum of the two interior angles it
does not touch. The sum of all three exterior
angles is 360°.

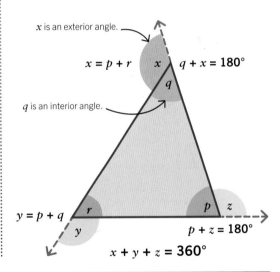

x is an exterior angle.

$x = p + r$

$q + x = 180°$

q is an interior angle.

$y = p + q$

$p + z = 180°$

$$x + y + z = 360°$$

📑 Find the missing angles

Question
Using what you know about interior and
exterior angles of triangles, what are the
degree measures of angles a and b in
this triangle?

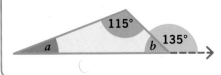

115°

a

b 135°

Answer
1. The sum of an exterior angle and its adjacent interior angle is
   180°, so we find b by subtracting 135° from 180°.
   $$b = 180° - 135° = 45°$$

2. The interior angles of a triangle add to 180°, so angle a must be
   180° minus the two known angles.
   $$a = 180° - 115° - 45° = 20°$$

Angles in a quadrilateral

A quadrilateral has four sides, which create four angles where they meet. When put together, these angles will make up a full turn, or 360°.

Interior angles of a quadrilateral

We can see how there are 360° in a quadrilateral by breaking one down into two triangles or by rearranging the corners of the shape around a point.

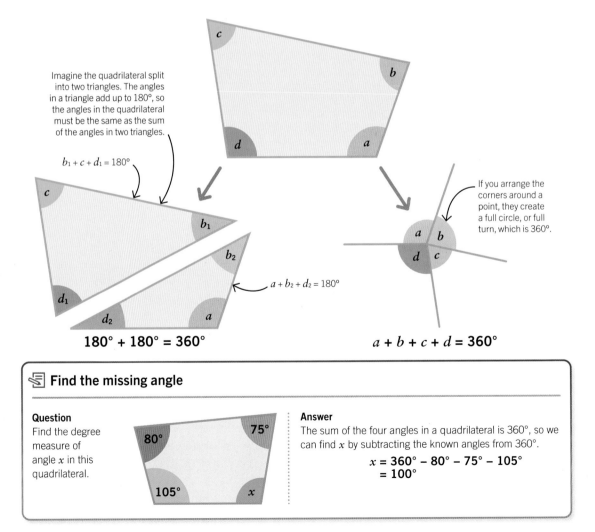

Imagine the quadrilateral split into two triangles. The angles in a triangle add up to 180°, so the angles in the quadrilateral must be the same as the sum of the angles in two triangles.

$b_1 + c + d_1 = 180°$

$a + b_2 + d_2 = 180°$

If you arrange the corners around a point, they create a full circle, or full turn, which is 360°.

$$180° + 180° = 360°$$

$$a + b + c + d = 360°$$

📰 Find the missing angle

Question
Find the degree measure of angle x in this quadrilateral.

80°   75°

105° x

Answer
The sum of the four angles in a quadrilateral is 360°, so we can find x by subtracting the known angles from 360°.

$$x = 360° - 80° - 75° - 105°$$
$$= 100°$$

Exterior angles of a polygon

An exterior angle is the angle formed on the outside of a polygon when you extend one of its sides outward. If you add together all of the exterior angles in any polygon, they will always add up to 360°.

Irregular polygon
We can see how the exterior angles in any polygon will always add up to 360° by rearranging the angles around a point.

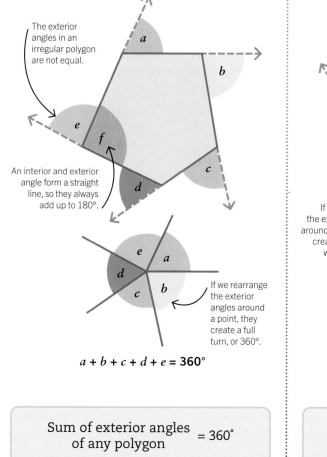

The exterior angles in an irregular polygon are not equal.

An interior and exterior angle form a straight line, so they always add up to 180°.

If we rearrange the exterior angles around a point, they create a full turn, or 360°.

$$a + b + c + d + e = 360°$$

Sum of exterior angles of any polygon $= 360°$

Regular polygon
The exterior angles of a regular polygon will also add up to 360°. We can use this to find the size of a single exterior angle.

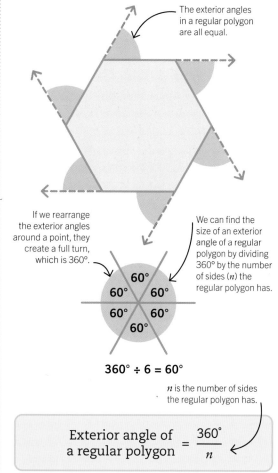

The exterior angles in a regular polygon are all equal.

If we rearrange the exterior angles around a point, they create a full turn, which is 360°.

We can find the size of an exterior angle of a regular polygon by dividing 360° by the number of sides (n) the regular polygon has.

$$360° ÷ 6 = 60°$$

n is the number of sides the regular polygon has.

Exterior angle of a regular polygon $= \dfrac{360°}{n}$

Interior angles of a polygon

Although the sum of the exterior angles of a polygon is always 360°, the sum of the interior angles varies depending on how many sides the polygon has.

Interior angles of a convex polygon
All angles in a convex polygon are less than 180°. We can find the sum of any convex polygon's interior angles by dividing the polygon into triangles. The angles in a triangle add to 180°, so the sum of the polygon's angles can be found by multiplying the number of triangles it can be split into by 180°.

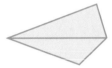

Quadrilateral
This quadrilateral can be split into two triangles. We can find the sum of the quadrilateral's interior angles by finding the sum of the angles in the two triangles:

$$2 \times 180° = 360°$$

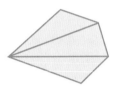

Pentagon
This pentagon can be split into three triangles. The sum of its interior angles is equal to the sum of the angles in the three triangles:

$$3 \times 180° = 540°$$

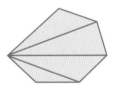

Hexagon
This hexagon can be split into four triangles. The sum of the interior angles is equal to the sum of the angles in the four triangles:

$$4 \times 180° = 720°$$

Heptagon
This heptagon can be split into five triangles. The sum of its interior angles is equal to the sum of the angles in the five triangles:

$$5 \times 180° = 900°$$

A formula for any convex polygon
The number of triangles a polygon can be split into is always two fewer than the number of sides the polygon has. This pattern means we can use a formula to find the sum of the interior angles of any convex polygon.

n stands for the number of sides the polygon has.

Sum of interior angles of a convex polygon $= (n - 2) \times 180°$

Interior angles of a regular polygon
The size of an interior angle of a regular polygon can be calculated by dividing the sum of all the interior angles by the number of sides the polygon has. This can't be done for an irregular polygon, because the angles are not equal.

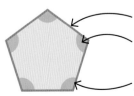

Regular pentagon

1. A pentagon has 5 sides.

2. Use the formula to find the sum of the interior angles:
$(5 - 2) \times 180° = 540°$

3. To find the size of one angle, we divide the sum by the number of sides: $540° \div 5 = 108°$

Properties of a circle

A circle is a set of points equidistant from a fixed point (the center). Together, these points form the circumference of a circle. Every part of this line is at an equal distance from the center point.

Parts of a circle

A circle can be folded into two identical halves. The line of this fold is its diameter. A circle may also be rotated around its center. This means that a circle has infinite line symmetry, because any diameter line could be the line of symmetry, and infinite rotational symmetry, because it will look the same no matter how much you rotate it (see page 35). A circle can be divided into many different parts, each with a specific name.

(see page 35)

Key facts

✓ The circumference is the distance around the outside edge of the circle.

✓ Every point in the circumference is at an equal distance from the center.

✓ The radius is the distance from the center to any point on the circle's circumference.

✓ The diameter is any straight line that passes through the center from one side of the circle to the other.

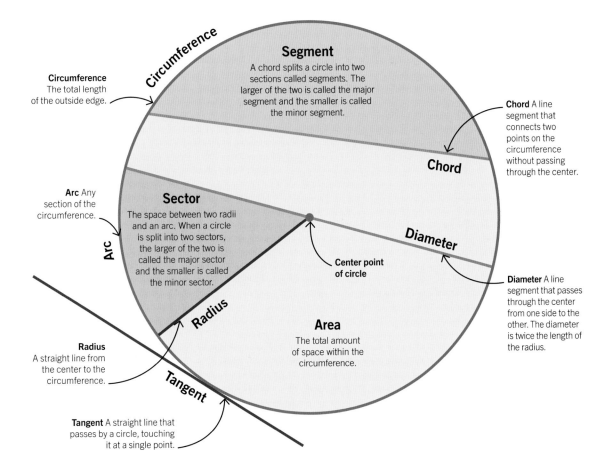

Circumference

Circumference
The total length of the outside edge.

Segment
A chord splits a circle into two sections called segments. The larger of the two is called the major segment and the smaller is called the minor segment.

Chord A line segment that connects two points on the circumference without passing through the center.

Chord

Arc Any section of the circumference.

Sector
The space between two radii and an arc. When a circle is split into two sectors, the larger of the two is called the major sector and the smaller is called the minor sector.

Arc

Center point of circle

Diameter

Diameter A line segment that passes through the center from one side to the other. The diameter is twice the length of the radius.

Radius

Area
The total amount of space within the circumference.

Radius
A straight line from the center to the circumference.

Tangent

Tangent A straight line that passes by a circle, touching it at a single point.

Practice question
Working with angles

We can use rules about numbers and shapes to solve complicated problems. Using the rules of geometry to solve problems is known as geometrical reasoning.

See also

31 Angle facts
38 Properties of polygons
41 Exterior angles of a polygon
42 Interior angles of a polygon

Question
The blue lines here are part of a regular polygon. How many sides does the complete blue polygon have and what is the shape's name?

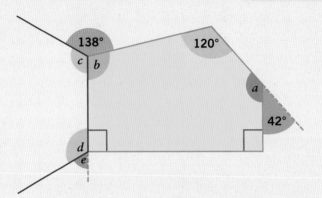

Answer
1. We can answer this question by applying what we know about angles to the diagram. We can find angle a, because angles on a straight line add up to 180°.

$$a = 180° - 42° = 138°$$

2. Next, we can find the sum of the interior angles of the orange pentagon, which will help us find angle b.

$$\text{Sum of interior angles of a convex polygon} = (n - 2) \times 180°$$

$$= (5 - 2) \times 180°$$
$$= 540°$$

3. We can now find angle b by subtracting the angles we know from 540°.

$$b = 540° - 120° - 138° - 90° - 90°$$
$$= 102°$$

4. Knowing angle b means we can find the size of angle c, because angles at a point add up to 360°.

$$c = 360° - 138° - 102°$$
$$= 120°$$

5. We know that angles in a regular polygon are equal, so angle d must also be 120°.

$$d = c = 120°$$

6. To find the number of sides in the regular polygon, we need to know one of the exterior angles, so we need to find angle e. We can use the rule that angles on a straight line add to 180°.

$$e = 180° - 120°$$
$$= 60°$$

7. We can now find the number of sides of the blue shape. The exterior angles of a regular polygon add up to 360°, so we divide this number by the value of the exterior angle to find the number of sides.

$$\text{Number of sides} = \frac{360°}{60°} = 6$$

The blue polygon has 6 sides, so it is a regular hexagon.

Fractions, decimals, and percentages

Fractions

A fraction is a way of showing a quantity that is a part of a whole number. All fractions are shown as two numbers, one written above the other.

Key facts

✓ A fraction represents a part of a whole number.
✓ The top number of a fraction is the numerator.
✓ The bottom number is the denominator.
✓ Equivalent fractions look different from each other but represent the same value.

What is a fraction?

A fraction describes how many parts of a whole there are—for example, one-half, five-eighths, and three-quarters. Here, the fraction shows three-quarters of a whole.

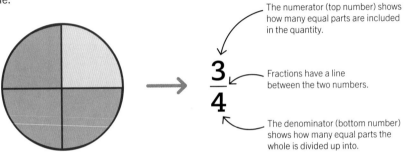

The numerator (top number) shows how many equal parts are included in the quantity.

Fractions have a line between the two numbers.

The denominator (bottom number) shows how many equal parts the whole is divided up into.

Equivalent fractions

The same fraction can be written in different ways and still refer to the same quantity. Even though they look different, they are equivalent ("equal") fractions.

Scaling down

A fraction with many parts can be scaled down or "simplified" to a simpler equivalent fraction by dividing the numerator and denominator by the same number.

Scaling up

To scale up the fraction into an equivalent fraction with more parts, we multiply both the numerator and denominator by the same number.

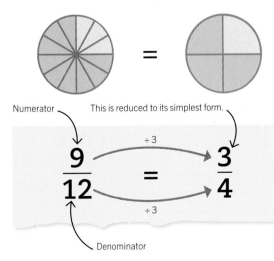

Numerator

This is reduced to its simplest form.

$$\frac{9}{12} \xrightarrow{\div 3} \frac{3}{4}$$

Denominator

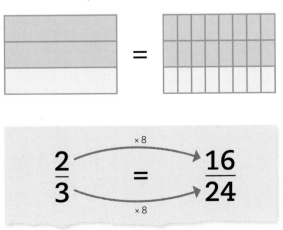

$$\frac{2}{3} \xrightarrow{\times 8} \frac{16}{24}$$

Improper fractions and mixed numbers

Fractions aren't always less than a whole. A fraction that is larger than 1 can be represented as either an improper fraction, also known as a top-heavy fraction, or as a mixed number, which combines a whole number with a proper fraction.

Types of fraction
There are three ways in which fractions can be represented.

Proper fractions
Fractions with a value less than 1 are called proper fractions.

$\dfrac{1}{4}$

The numerator is smaller than the denominator.

Improper fractions
Fractions with a value greater than 1 are called improper fractions.

$\dfrac{35}{4}$

The numerator is larger than the denominator.

Mixed numbers
Fractions that combine a whole number with a proper fraction are called mixed numbers.

$8\dfrac{3}{4}$

Converting improper fractions to mixed numbers
A fraction is simply a division. So when you convert an improper fraction to a mixed number, you just divide the numerator by the denominator.

1. Divide the numerator by the denominator.

2. The division results in a whole number with 3 left over (a remainder of 3).

$$\frac{11}{4} = 11 \div 4 = 2 \text{ r.}3 = 2\frac{3}{4}$$

3. The result is a mixed number with a whole number 2 and a fraction of ¾.

Converting mixed numbers to improper fractions
When converting a mixed number to an improper fraction, you multiply the whole number by the denominator and then add the result to the numerator.

1. Multiply the whole number by the denominator.

2. Add the numerator.

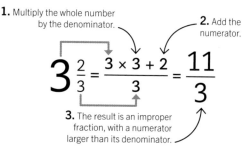

$$3\frac{2}{3} = \frac{3 \times 3 + 2}{3} = \frac{11}{3}$$

3. The result is an improper fraction, with a numerator larger than its denominator.

Visualizing fractions
You can visualize ¹¹/₄ as 2³/₄ by drawing three groups of four numbers each. The fraction is two whole numbers with ³/₄ left over.

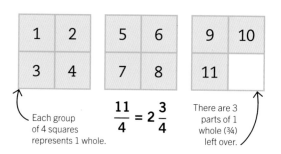

Each group of 4 squares represents 1 whole.

$$\frac{11}{4} = 2\frac{3}{4}$$

There are 3 parts of 1 whole (¾) left over.

Visualizing fractions
By grouping the fraction into four groups of three numbers each, you can count the parts: 3 wholes with ²/₃ left over is the same as ¹¹/₃.

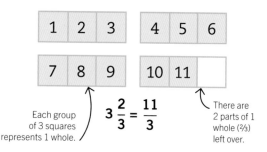

Each group of 3 squares represents 1 whole.

$$3\frac{2}{3} = \frac{11}{3}$$

There are 2 parts of 1 whole (²/₃) left over.

Comparing fractions

It's difficult to compare the sizes of fractions with different denominators, such as $\frac{8}{11}$ and $\frac{5}{7}$. So we convert each one into an equivalent fraction with the same denominator.

Ordering fractions
To put fractions in order of size, you need to find a denominator that is common to each fraction. List the common multiples of each denominator to find the least common denominator (LCD; see page 26). The LCD will become the common denominator of each fraction.

Key facts

✓ The least common denominator (LCD) is a number that can be divided by all original denominators.

✓ The LCD is a good way of comparing the sizes of different fractions.

✓ The LCD can be found by listing the multiples of all the original denominators.

1. List the multiples of the denominators of each of the fractions you want to compare in order to find the LCD.

The LCD of each denominator is 24.

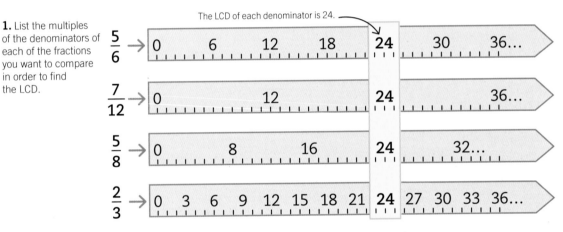

2. Now that you know the common denominator, convert each fraction so that they share a denominator of 24. Multiply the numerator and denominator by the amount needed to create an equivalent fraction.

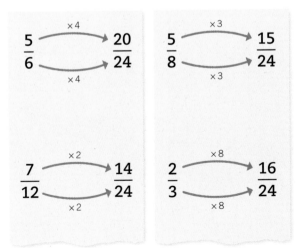

3. It's now much easier to compare the fractions. Put them in order from greatest to smallest.

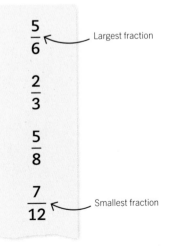

$\frac{5}{6}$ — Largest fraction

$\frac{2}{3}$

$\frac{5}{8}$

$\frac{7}{12}$ — Smallest fraction

Adding and subtracting fractions

Just like whole numbers, fractions can be added or subtracted. If the denominators are different, it helps to convert them to the same denominator.

Fractions with the same denominator

To add or subtract proper fractions with the same denominator, simply add or subtract the numerators to find the result. The denominators stay the same.

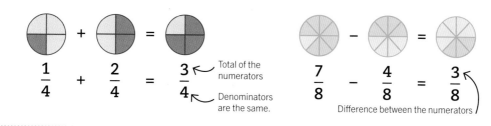

$$\frac{1}{4} + \frac{2}{4} = \frac{3}{4}$$

Total of the numerators

Denominators are the same.

$$\frac{7}{8} - \frac{4}{8} = \frac{3}{8}$$

Difference between the numerators

Fractions with different denominators

If fractions have different denominators, it helps to convert them to the same denominator before adding or subtracting. It is sometimes useful to convert mixed numbers to improper fractions first. Alternatively, you can calculate the integers and the fraction parts separately.

1. Calculate $1\frac{1}{2} + 2\frac{2}{3}$.

$$1\frac{1}{2} + 2\frac{2}{3} = ?$$

2. Convert the mixed numbers into improper fractions.

$$1\frac{1}{2} = \frac{3}{2} \qquad 2\frac{2}{3} = \frac{8}{3}$$

3. Using the LCD, convert each fraction so that they share a common denominator.

$$\frac{3}{2} \overset{\times 3}{\underset{\times 3}{=}} \frac{9}{6} \qquad \frac{8}{3} \overset{\times 2}{\underset{\times 2}{=}} \frac{16}{6}$$

4. Now that they have the same denominators, add together the numerators.

$$\frac{9}{6} + \frac{16}{6} = \frac{25}{6}$$

5. Convert the resulting improper fraction back into a mixed number.

$$\frac{25}{6} = 4\frac{1}{6}$$

1. Calculate $1\frac{3}{4} - \frac{1}{8}$.

$$1\frac{3}{4} - \frac{1}{8} = ?$$

2. Remove the 1 from the mixed number (to add back in later) and scale up $\frac{3}{4}$ so that both fractions share the same denominator.

$$\frac{3}{4} \overset{\times 2}{\underset{\times 2}{=}} \frac{6}{8}$$

3. Subtract one numerator from the other.

$$\frac{6}{8} - \frac{1}{8} = \frac{5}{8}$$

4. Then add back in the 1.

$$\frac{5}{8} + 1 = 1\frac{5}{8}$$

Fraction of an amount

A fraction such as ¼ represents the number of parts of a whole. When that whole is an amount, such as the amount of flour in a bag, finding a fraction of that amount gives you the quantity in that part of the whole. The part or parts can be a whole number. There is a simple method for calculating a fraction of an amount.

Key facts

✓ Calculate a fraction of an amount by multiplying the total amount by the fraction's numerator, then dividing the result by its denominator.

✓ You can also divide the total amount by the denominator, then multiply by the numerator.

Calculating a fraction of an amount
What is ⅘ of an 800 g bag of flour? To find out, you need to calculate ⅘ × 800. To do this, you can work out ⅕ of 800, then multiply by 4.

⅘ × 800 g = ?

Total amount of flour: 800 g

1. First, work out ⅕ by dividing the total amount by the denominator of the fraction.

$$800 \div 5 = 160$$

2. Then multiply by the numerator to find ⅘.

$$160 \times 4 = 640 \text{ g}$$

3. It doesn't matter in which order you perform these operations. You can multiply the total amount by the numerator of the fraction first, then divide the result by the denominator.

$$800 \times 4 = 3200$$
$$3200 \div 5 = 640 \text{ g}$$

Dividing treasure

Question
A pirate captain divides up 220 gold coins unequally between the ship's crew. Crewmate 1 gets ½. Crewmate 2 gets ¼. Crewmate 3 gets ⅕. Crewmate 4 gets ¹⁄₂₀. What is each one's share?

....

Answer
1. Multiply the total treasure by the numerator, then divide the result by the denominator to find each share.

Crewmate 1:
$$1 \times 220 \div 2 = 110 \text{ gold coins}$$

Crewmate 2:
$$1 \times 220 \div 4 = 55 \text{ gold coins}$$

Crewmate 3:
$$1 \times 220 \div 5 = 44 \text{ gold coins}$$

Crewmate 4:
$$1 \times 220 \div 20 = 11 \text{ gold coins}$$

2. Add up each share to check that the total comes to 220.
$$110 + 55 + 44 + 11 = 220$$

Multiplying fractions

Fractions can be multiplied just like any other number. Just as multiplying a number by 2 results in two times that number, multiplying it by ½ results in half the number. In this way, multiplying a number by a fraction can also be understood as finding the fraction of that number.

Multiplying a fraction by a whole number
When you multiply a fraction by a whole number, it is like adding that fraction to itself that number of times.

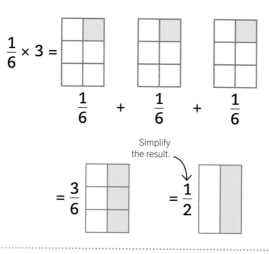

$$\frac{1}{6} \times 3 =$$

$$\frac{1}{6} + \frac{1}{6} + \frac{1}{6}$$

Simplify the result.

$$= \frac{3}{6} \qquad = \frac{1}{2}$$

Multiplying two proper fractions
The method for multiplying proper fractions is very simple. You multiply the numerators together, then the denominators. If you multiply ⅔ by ¾, it's useful to think of this as finding ⅔ of ¾. The result will be a smaller fraction.

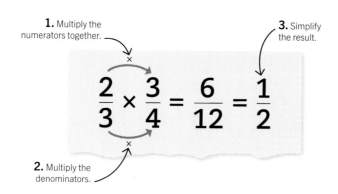

1. Multiply the numerators together.

3. Simplify the result.

$$\frac{2}{3} \times \frac{3}{4} = \frac{6}{12} = \frac{1}{2}$$

2. Multiply the denominators.

Key facts

✓ Multiplying a number by a fraction is the same as finding that fraction of the number.

✓ When multiplying, the numerators are multiplied together and so are the denominators.

✓ The result from multiplying fractions can often be simplified.

Multiplying mixed numbers

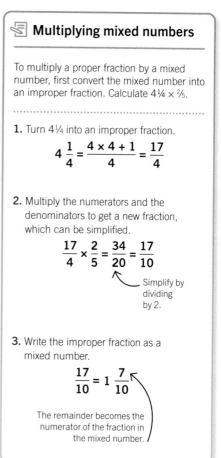

To multiply a proper fraction by a mixed number, first convert the mixed number into an improper fraction. Calculate 4¼ × ⅖.

1. Turn 4¼ into an improper fraction.

$$4\frac{1}{4} = \frac{4 \times 4 + 1}{4} = \frac{17}{4}$$

2. Multiply the numerators and the denominators to get a new fraction, which can be simplified.

$$\frac{17}{4} \times \frac{2}{5} = \frac{34}{20} = \frac{17}{10}$$

Simplify by dividing by 2.

3. Write the improper fraction as a mixed number.

$$\frac{17}{10} = 1\frac{7}{10}$$

The remainder becomes the numerator of the fraction in the mixed number.

Dividing fractions

When dividing one whole number by another, it is helpful to think of the process as finding out how many times the second number fits into the first. The same applies to fractions. So if you are working out $\frac{1}{4} \div \frac{1}{2}$, you are finding out how many times $\frac{1}{2}$ fits into $\frac{1}{4}$. There are some simple rules for dividing fractions.

Dividing a whole number by a fraction

When you divide a whole number by a fraction, such as $3 \div \frac{3}{4}$, you are finding out how many times that fraction fits into the whole number.

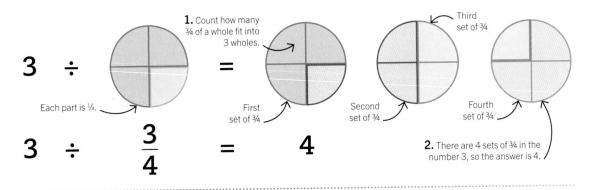

1. Count how many $\frac{3}{4}$ of a whole fit into 3 wholes.

Each part is $\frac{1}{4}$.

First set of $\frac{3}{4}$

Second set of $\frac{3}{4}$

Third set of $\frac{3}{4}$

Fourth set of $\frac{3}{4}$

2. There are 4 sets of $\frac{3}{4}$ in the number 3, so the answer is 4.

$$3 \div \frac{3}{4} = 4$$

Dividing a fraction by a whole number

When you divide a fraction by a whole number, you are splitting the fraction into that many parts. So if you calculate $\frac{3}{4} \div 2$, you are splitting $\frac{3}{4}$ into twice as many parts.

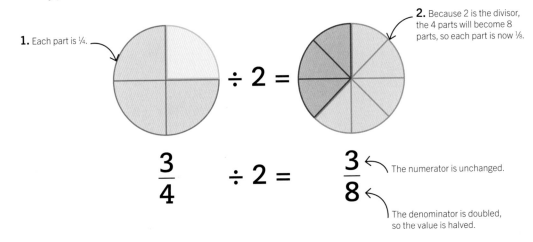

1. Each part is $\frac{1}{4}$.

2. Because 2 is the divisor, the 4 parts will become 8 parts, so each part is now $\frac{1}{8}$.

$$\frac{3}{4} \div 2 = \frac{3}{8}$$

The numerator is unchanged.

The denominator is doubled, so the value is halved.

Inverse operations

When ¾ is divided by 2, the value of ¾ is halved (see opposite). So dividing the fraction by 2 is equivalent to multiplying the fraction by ½. Dividing and multiplying are inverse (opposite) operations, and there's an easy technique involving multiplication you can use to divide a fraction by a whole number. You convert the whole number into an improper fraction, turn it upside down, and multiply the two fractions together. When you turn a fraction upside down, you are finding the reciprocal of that fraction.

1. Convert 2 into an improper fraction. The whole number becomes the numerator, with a denominator of 1.

2. Change the ÷ sign to a × sign and turn ²/₁ upside down so that the numerator becomes the denominator and vice versa.

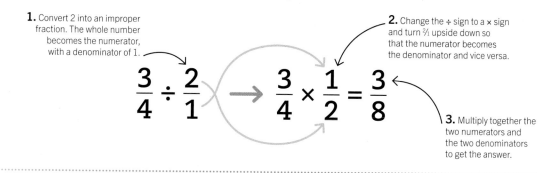

3. Multiply together the two numerators and the two denominators to get the answer.

Dividing two fractions

The technique of dividing fractions by multiplying the first fraction by the reciprocal of the second fraction can be applied to dividing any fraction by another. Here, we are dividing two proper fractions: ¼ ÷ ⅓.

1. Visualize ¼ ÷ ⅓ by scaling up both fractions so that they are out of the same number of parts.

2. Count how much of ³/₁₂ fits into ⁴/₁₂.

3. ³/₁₂ ÷ ⁴/₁₂ is the same as 3 ÷ 4 or ¾.

4. A much quicker method is to turn the second fraction upside down and multiply the two fractions together.

³/₁ is the reciprocal of ⅓.

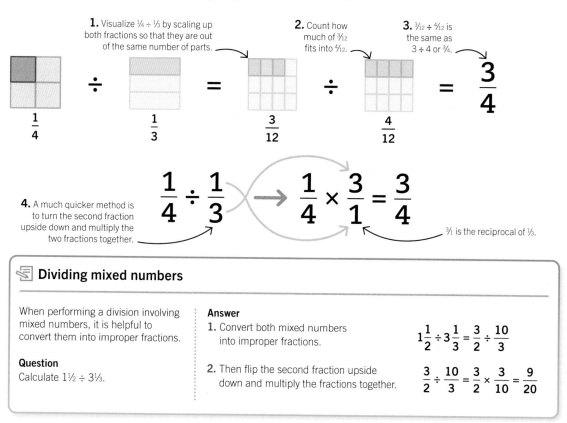

📎 Dividing mixed numbers

When performing a division involving mixed numbers, it is helpful to convert them into improper fractions.

Question
Calculate 1½ ÷ 3⅓.

Answer
1. Convert both mixed numbers into improper fractions.

$$1\frac{1}{2} \div 3\frac{1}{3} = \frac{3}{2} \div \frac{10}{3}$$

2. Then flip the second fraction upside down and multiply the fractions together.

$$\frac{3}{2} \div \frac{10}{3} = \frac{3}{2} \times \frac{3}{10} = \frac{9}{20}$$

Percentages

Percent means "per hundred." A percentage represents an amount as a number out of 100 and can be a useful way to compare two or more quantities. The symbol % is used to indicate a percentage.

Key facts

✓ **A percentage is a way of representing an amount out of 100.**

✓ **Percentages are represented by the symbol %.**

✓ **Fractions and decimals can be expressed as percentages.**

Parts of 100

Percentages can be thought of as an amount divided into 100 equal parts, so that 10% is 10 parts out of 100.

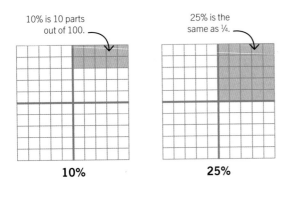

10% is 10 parts out of 100.

25% is the same as ¼.

10%   **25%**

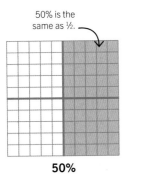

50% is the same as ½.

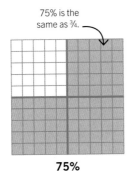

75% is the same as ¾.

50%   **75%**

Percentages and fractions

To convert a fraction into a percentage, change it to a decimal, then multiply by 100.

1. Divide the numerator by the denominator.

$$\frac{3}{4} = 3 \div 4 = 0.75$$

2. Multiply by 100.

$$0.75 \times 100 = 75\%$$

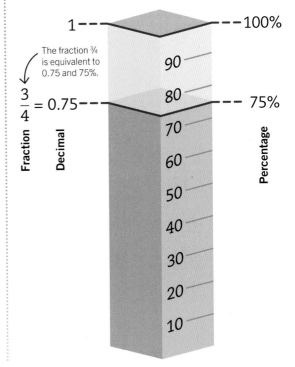

The fraction ¾ is equivalent to 0.75 and 75%.

$$\frac{3}{4} = 0.75$$

1 -- 100%

$\frac{3}{4}$ = 0.75 -- 75%

Fraction   Decimal

90
80
70
60
50
40
30
20
10

Percentage

Fractions, decimals, and percentages

Any number can be expressed as a fraction, a decimal, or a percentage. They each have different common uses in math.

Conversion methods

The fraction, decimal, and percentage form of the same number may look different, but they are equal. The three are interchangeable and can be converted from one to the other using the following methods.

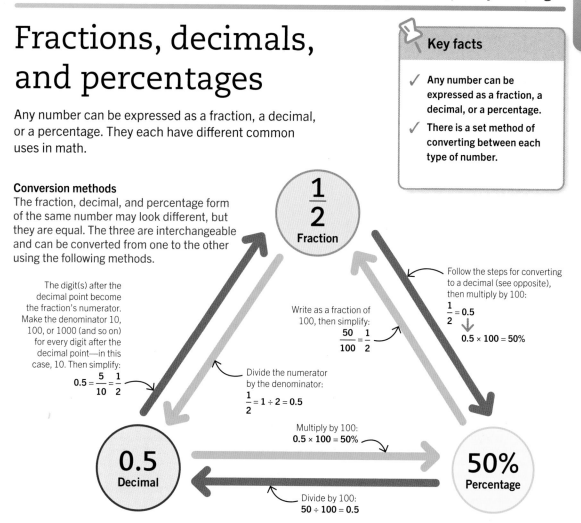

The digit(s) after the decimal point become the fraction's numerator. Make the denominator 10, 100, or 1000 (and so on) for every digit after the decimal point—in this case, 10. Then simplify:

$$0.5 = \frac{5}{10} = \frac{1}{2}$$

Write as a fraction of 100, then simplify:

$$\frac{50}{100} = \frac{1}{2}$$

Follow the steps for converting to a decimal (see opposite), then multiply by 100:

$$\frac{1}{2} = 0.5$$
$$\downarrow$$
$$0.5 \times 100 = 50\%$$

Divide the numerator by the denominator:

$$\frac{1}{2} = 1 \div 2 = 0.5$$

Multiply by 100:
$$0.5 \times 100 = 50\%$$

Divide by 100:
$$50 \div 100 = 0.5$$

$\frac{1}{2}$ **Fraction**

0.5 **Decimal**

50% **Percentage**

🔍 Everyday numbers to remember

Various simple decimals, fractions, and percentages are used in daily life. Some common ones are listed here.

Decimal	Fraction	Percentage	Decimal	Fraction	Percentage
0.1	$\frac{1}{10}$	10%	0.5	$\frac{1}{2}$	50%
0.25	$\frac{1}{4}$	25%	0.666...	$\frac{2}{3}$	66.7%
0.333...	$\frac{1}{3}$	33.3%	0.75	$\frac{3}{4}$	75%

Percentage of an amount

Just like calculating a fraction of an amount (see page 50), working out a percentage of an amount tells you how much of the whole amount that percentage represents.

> **Key facts**
>
> ✓ To find the value of a given percentage, convert the percentage into a decimal and multiply by the total amount.
>
> ✓ You can also convert the percentage to a fraction, then multiply by the total amount.

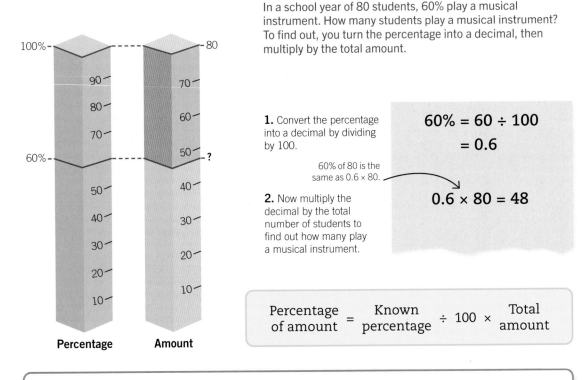

Percentage   **Amount**

Calculating a percentage of an amount
In a school year of 80 students, 60% play a musical instrument. How many students play a musical instrument? To find out, you turn the percentage into a decimal, then multiply by the total amount.

1. Convert the percentage into a decimal by dividing by 100.

$$60\% = 60 \div 100$$
$$= 0.6$$

60% of 80 is the same as 0.6 × 80.

2. Now multiply the decimal by the total number of students to find out how many play a musical instrument.

$$0.6 \times 80 = 48$$

$$\frac{\text{Percentage}}{\text{of amount}} = \frac{\text{Known}}{\text{percentage}} \div 100 \times \frac{\text{Total}}{\text{amount}}$$

⚙ Calculating a percentage of an amount using a fraction

You can also work out the calculation above by converting the percentage into a fraction instead of a decimal.

1. Write the percentage as a fraction out of 100, then simplify.

$$60\% = \frac{60}{100} = \frac{3}{5}$$

2. Write 80 as a fraction, then multiply the two fractions together and simplify.

$$\frac{3}{5} \times \frac{80}{1} = \frac{240}{5} = \frac{48}{1} = 48$$

Mental percentage calculations

Percentages are most commonly used in calculations that multiply or divide a quantity, such as a price. There are some simple tricks to make it easier to calculate percentages.

Simplifying
Complex percentages can be broken down in your head to make calculations simpler. For example, a bike is sold in a shop for $600. The buyer then sells the bike for 21% more. What is the new price of the bike with the percentage increase?

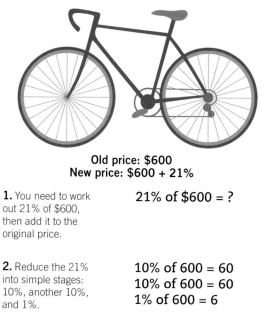

Old price: $600
New price: $600 + 21%

1. You need to work out 21% of $600, then add it to the original price.

$$21\% \text{ of } \$600 = ?$$

2. Reduce the 21% into simple stages: 10%, another 10%, and 1%.

$$10\% \text{ of } 600 = 60$$
$$10\% \text{ of } 600 = 60$$
$$1\% \text{ of } 600 = 6$$

3. Add together 10%, 10%, and 1% to work out 21% of 600.

$$60 + 60 + 6 = 126$$

4. Add the calculated amount to the original price to get the new, increased price.

$$\$126 + \$600 = \$726$$

Switching
A percentage and an amount can be switched so that they produce the same result. This switching trick can be used to simplify calculations.

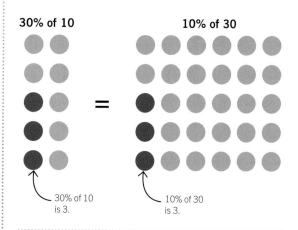

30% of 10   **10% of 30**

=

30% of 10 is 3.   10% of 30 is 3.

Doubling and halving
Another way of making calculations more straightforward is by "doubling and halving." You double the percentage and halve the amount, or vice versa, to make the numbers easier. However, you can use any scaling factor as long as one side is scaled up and the other is scaled down.

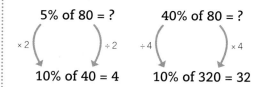

5% of 80 = ?   40% of 80 = ?

×2   ÷2   ÷4   ×4

10% of 40 = 4   10% of 320 = 32

Finding the percentage change

Sometimes you need to calculate the percentage change when a quantity has increased or decreased. Calculating percentage change is helpful in many real-life situations, such as calculating profit, loss, or a change in population.

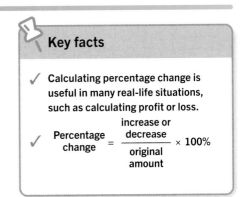

Key facts

✓ Calculating percentage change is useful in many real-life situations, such as calculating profit or loss.

✓ $\text{Percentage change} = \dfrac{\text{increase or decrease}}{\text{original amount}} \times 100\%$

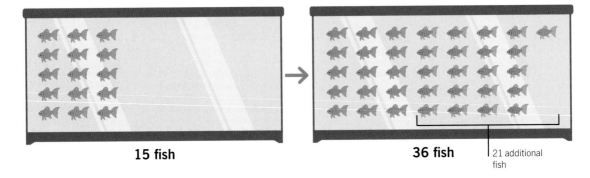

15 fish

36 fish

21 additional fish

Calculating a percentage increase or decrease

The population of fish in an aquarium increases from 15 to 36. What's the percentage change? To answer questions like this, we can use a formula. Don't forget to include the percentage symbol % in your answer.

$$\text{Percentage change} = \dfrac{\text{increase or decrease}}{\text{original amount}} \times 100\%$$

$$\text{Percentage change} = \dfrac{21}{15} \times 100\%$$

$$= 140\%$$

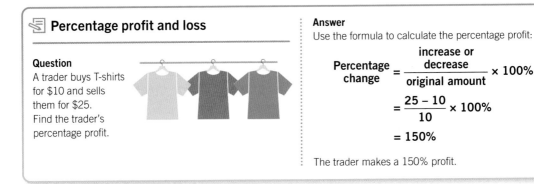

📑 **Percentage profit and loss**

Question
A trader buys T-shirts for $10 and sells them for $25.
Find the trader's percentage profit.

Answer
Use the formula to calculate the percentage profit:

$$\text{Percentage change} = \dfrac{\text{increase or decrease}}{\text{original amount}} \times 100\%$$

$$= \dfrac{25 - 10}{10} \times 100\%$$

$$= 150\%$$

The trader makes a 150% profit.

Percentage increase and decrease

Percentages are used a lot in everyday life to describe how quantities change, such as when prices rise or fall. To calculate the new value after a percentage increase or decrease, use the following methods.

Key facts

✓ Calculate the new total after a percentage increase by adding to the original amount.

✓ Calculate the new total after a percentage decrease by subtracting from the original amount.

Percentage increase

Suppose cookies normally come in 380 g packages. If packages with a special offer include 25% extra free, how much do they weigh? You can work out the answer in two steps.

1. First, calculate 25% of 380 g. Write the percentage as a fraction out of 100 and multiply by 380.

$$\frac{25}{100} \times 380 \text{ g} = 95 \text{ g}$$

2. Then add the result to the original weight.

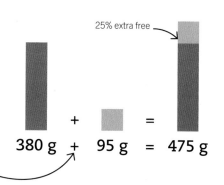

25% extra free

$$380 \text{ g} + 95 \text{ g} = 475 \text{ g}$$

Percentage decrease

Shops often have discounts, such as 15% off a $12 T-shirt. To calculate the price after the discount, use the same method as for percentage increase but subtract from the original amount instead of adding.

1. Write the percentage as a fraction out of 100 and multiply by the price.

$$\frac{15}{100} \times \$12 = \$1.80$$

2. Subtract the result from the original price to find the discounted price.

15% discount

$$\$12 - \$1.80 = \$10.20$$

One-step method

You can use a shortcut to work out percentage increases and decreases in a single step. To do this, turn the percentage increase into a decimal to create a multiplier, and then use this to find the answer on a calculator. For instance, a 25% increase (100% + 25% = 125%) is 1.25 as a decimal. Multiply the price by 1.25 on a calculator to find the answer. Similarly, for a 15% reduction (100% − 15% = 85%), multiply by 0.85.

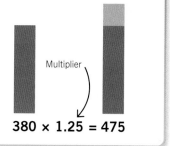

Multiplier

$$380 \times 1.25 = 475$$

Reverse percentages

If you're 20% taller than you were five years ago, how tall were you then? Sometimes we need to work backward to find an original amount before a percentage change. This is particularly useful when dealing with money.

Percentage increase

The value of houses tends to change over time. If a house that now costs $351,000 has increased in price by 30% in the last five years, what was it worth five years ago?

1. To answer the question, sketch two bars representing the original and the new price.

2. The bars show that $351,000 is 130% of the original price. Use this to work out how much 1% is.

$$1\% = \$351\,000 \div 130$$
$$= \$2700$$

3. Multiply $2,700 by 100 to work out what the price was five years ago.

$$100\% = 100 \times \$2700$$
$$= \$270\,000$$

Five years ago, the house was worth $270,000.

Percentage decrease

You can apply the same technique to percentage decreases. For example, if sales of DVDs fell by 75% between 2011 and 2021, how many were sold in 2011 if 32 million DVDs were sold in 2021?

1. Sketch two bars representing the original and the new sales figures.

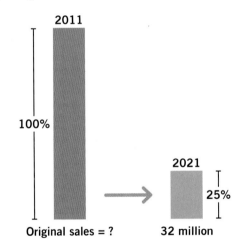

2. The bars show that 32 million is 25% of sales in 2011. Use this to work out how much 1% is.

$$1\% = 32\,000\,000 \div 25$$
$$= 1\,280\,000$$

3. Multiply 1,280,000 by 100 to work out how many DVDs were sold in 2011.

$$100\% = 100 \times 1\,280\,000$$
$$= 128\,000\,000$$

In 2011, 128 million DVDs were sold.

Growth and decay

The cost of food tends to rise year after year, but the value of a car tends to decrease as it gets older. Patterns of repeated increase or decrease are known as growth and decay. If the quantity changes by the same percentage each time, you can use a percentage multiplier to predict the outcome.

Key facts

✓ Repeated percentage increase produces a pattern called exponential growth.

✓ Decay is a pattern of repeated decrease.

✓ To calculate the result of a repeated percentage change, multiply the initial quantity by a percentage multiplier raised to a power:
$$N = N_0 \times (\text{multiplier})^n$$

Growth

A movie streaming service starts with 10,000 subscribers in its first year. Each year, the number of subscribers increases by 15% of the previous year, as shown on the chart below. The pattern forms an upward curve called an exponential growth curve.

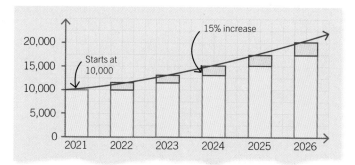

Suppose you want to predict how many subscribers there will be after three years. Instead of drawing a chart, you can use a formula. To use the formula, turn the percentage increase into a decimal and use this as the multiplier. For example, a 15% increase (100% + 15%) equals 115%, which is 1.15 as a decimal.

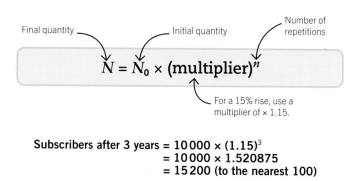

Final quantity — Initial quantity — Number of repetitions

$$N = N_0 \times (\text{multiplier})^n$$

For a 15% rise, use a multiplier of × 1.15.

Subscribers after 3 years = $10\,000 \times (1.15)^3$
$= 10\,000 \times 1.520875$
$= 15\,200$ **(to the nearest 100)**

Decay

You can also use a percentage multiplier for a pattern of repeated decrease. We call this decay or depreciation.

Question
A new car costs $9,000. If its value falls by 20% each year, what will it be worth after two years to the nearest $100?

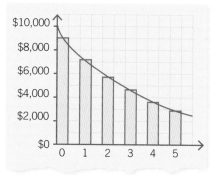

Answer
1. Turn the percentage change into a multiplier. For a 20% fall, use a multiplier of × 0.8.

2. Put all the numbers into the formula to find the answer.

Final value of car = $N_0 \times (\text{multiplier})^n$
$= 9000 \times (0.8)^2$
$= 9000 \times 0.64$
$= 5760$

The car will be worth $5,800 (to the nearest $100) after two years.

Compound interest

When you save money in a bank, it earns interest each year. Unlike simple interest, where the amount added is the same every year, compound interest rises each year. Over a long period, savings that earn compound interest grow far more than savings that earn simple interest.

Compound vs simple interest
The graph here compares how $10,000 in a savings account would grow if it earned 10% compound interest (orange) rather than 10% simple interest (purple). Compound interest is calculated at regular intervals, such as once a year. The payment calculated is a percentage of the total in the account at that point rather than a percentage of the original sum (simple interest). As a result, if you leave the interest invested in the account, the interest paid increases every year.

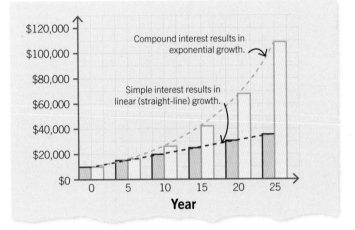

Using a percentage multiplier
To calculate the outcome of growth from compound interest, you can use the percentage multiplier formula from the previous page (see page 61).

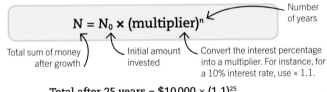

$$N = N_0 \times (\text{multiplier})^n$$

Number of years

Total sum of money after growth

Initial amount invested

Convert the interest percentage into a multiplier. For instance, for a 10% interest rate, use × 1.1.

Total after 25 years = $10\,000 \times (1.1)^{25}$
= $108\,347.06$

Interest on loans

If you borrow money from a bank, you pay interest on the loan. Like the interest on savings, the interest on a loan is calculated as compound interest. It can mount quickly if a borrower doesn't make regular repayments back to the bank.

Question
A man wants to buy a motorcycle but has no savings. He borrows $5,000 from his bank at a compound interest rate of 18% per year. If he doesn't pay back anything for three years, how much will his total debt be?

Answer
Total debt = $5000 \times (1.18)^3$
= 8215.16

After three years, the total debt will be $8,215.16.

Recurring decimals

Terminating decimals are numbers that have a finite set of digits (they come to an end), such as 0.5, 0.01, or 0.00003. A recurring decimal never ends with a final digit. Instead, the number repeats a set of digits forever.

⅓ as a decimal

As a decimal, the fraction one-third, or ⅓, is 0.3333 ….. You can demonstrate this by dividing 1 by 3, where at every decimal place the same remainder has to be carried over to the next digit. You can also see it on a calculator display.

The decimal repeats forever.

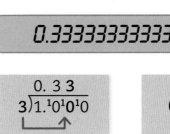

$1 \div 3 =$ 0.33333333333

1. 3 does not divide into 1, so add a decimal point and carry the 1.

2. 10 divided by 3 gives 3 with a remainder of 1, so you need to carry this to the next zero.

3. This process is repeated infinitely, because the decimal never ends.

4. The number is written as 0.3 with a bar (or a dot) over the recurring digit.

⅐ as a decimal

Not all recurring decimals only repeat a single digit.

The decimal has a repeating pattern of six digits: 142857.

$1 \div 7 =$ 0.142857142857

When the recurring decimal is written out, a bar is drawn over the repeating digits.

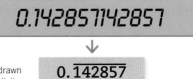

$0.\overline{142857}$

⚙ Prime factor clues

All terminating decimals will convert to a fraction that in its simplest form has a denominator with prime factors (see page 25) of 2 or 5. If the denominator of the fraction does not have one of these prime factors, then the decimal will always be recurring.

	Terminating decimals			Recurring decimals		
Fraction	$\frac{1}{5}$	$\frac{1}{25}$	$\frac{1}{200}$	$\frac{1}{6}$	$\frac{1}{9}$	$\frac{4}{11}$
Equivalent decimals	0.2	0.04	0.005	$0.1\overline{6}$	$0.\overline{1}$	$0.\overline{36}$

Recurring decimals and fractions

Although a recurring decimal is infinitely long and so can never be written down in full, it can always be turned into a fraction. The fraction is another way of representing the value precisely.

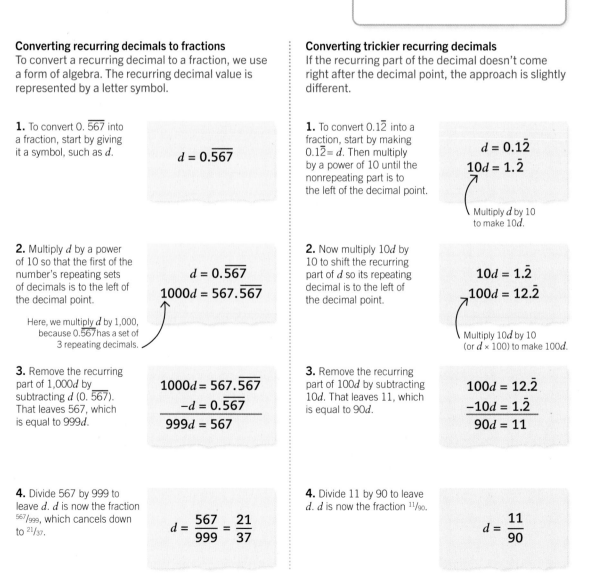

Converting recurring decimals to fractions
To convert a recurring decimal to a fraction, we use a form of algebra. The recurring decimal value is represented by a letter symbol.

1. To convert $0.\overline{567}$ into a fraction, start by giving it a symbol, such as d.

$$d = 0.\overline{567}$$

2. Multiply d by a power of 10 so that the first of the number's repeating sets of decimals is to the left of the decimal point.

$$d = 0.\overline{567}$$
$$1000d = 567.\overline{567}$$

Here, we multiply d by 1,000, because $0.\overline{567}$ has a set of 3 repeating decimals.

3. Remove the recurring part of $1{,}000d$ by subtracting d ($0.\overline{567}$). That leaves 567, which is equal to $999d$.

$$1000d = 567.\overline{567}$$
$$-d = 0.\overline{567}$$
$$999d = 567$$

4. Divide 567 by 999 to leave d. d is now the fraction $567/999$, which cancels down to $21/37$.

$$d = \frac{567}{999} = \frac{21}{37}$$

Converting trickier recurring decimals
If the recurring part of the decimal doesn't come right after the decimal point, the approach is slightly different.

1. To convert $0.1\bar{2}$ into a fraction, start by making $0.1\bar{2} = d$. Then multiply by a power of 10 until the nonrepeating part is to the left of the decimal point.

$$d = 0.1\bar{2}$$
$$10d = 1.\bar{2}$$

Multiply d by 10 to make $10d$.

2. Now multiply $10d$ by 10 to shift the recurring part of d so its repeating decimal is to the left of the decimal point.

$$10d = 1.\bar{2}$$
$$100d = 12.\bar{2}$$

Multiply $10d$ by 10 (or $d \times 100$) to make $100d$.

3. Remove the recurring part of $100d$ by subtracting $10d$. That leaves 11, which is equal to $90d$.

$$100d = 12.\bar{2}$$
$$-10d = 1.\bar{2}$$
$$90d = 11$$

4. Divide 11 by 90 to leave d. d is now the fraction $11/90$.

$$d = \frac{11}{90}$$

Measure

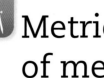

Metric units of measure and time

The metric system is used for measuring length, mass, and capacity. Every unit in the metric system is based on 10, 100, or 1,000, which often makes calculations simple.

Key facts

✓ Millimeters, centimeters, meters, and kilometers are the standard metric units of length.

✓ Milligrams, grams, kilograms, and metric tons are the standard metric units of mass.

✓ Milliliters, centiliters, liters, and kiloliters are the standard metric units of capacity.

Units of length
Length is the distance between two points. It is typically measured in millimeters (mm), centimeters (cm), meters (m), and kilometers (km). Millimeters are useful for measuring very small things, while kilometers are useful for measuring large distances.

10 millimeters (mm) = 1 centimeter (cm)
100 centimeters (cm) = 1 meter (m)
1000 meters (m) = 1 kilometer (km)

Units of mass
Mass is the amount of matter in an object. It can be measured in milligrams (mg), grams (g), kilograms (kg), and tons (t). Very light things are measured in milligrams and extremely heavy things are measured in metric tons.

1000 milligrams (mg) = 1 gram (g)
1000 grams (g) = 1 kilogram (kg)
1000 kilograms (kg) = 1 metric ton (t)

Units of capacity
Capacity is the amount of space within a container. It can be measured in milliliters (ml), centiliters (cl), liters (l), and kiloliters (kl). Milliliters are used for measuring very small capacities and kiloliters are used for measuring very large capacities.

1000 milliliters (ml) = 1 liter (l)
100 centiliters (cl) = 1 liter (l)
1000 liters (l) = 1 kiloliter (kl)

🔍 Units of time

Unlike metric units, units of time are not based on the number 10, so they are not a metric unit. Divisions of the day and year were established in ancient times and are typically based on the numbers 60 and 12.

60 seconds = 1 minute
60 minutes = 1 hour
24 hours = 1 day
7 days = 1 week
12 months = 1 year

Imperial units of measure

Some countries, such as the US, typically use units called imperial units. Unlike the metric system, these units are not based on the number 10.

Key facts

✓ Inches, feet, yards, and miles are the standard imperial units of length.

✓ Ounces, pounds, stone, hundredweights, and tons are the standard imperial units of mass.

✓ Fluid ounces, cups, pints, quarts, and gallons are the standard imperial units of capacity.

Units of length

Length is the distance between two points. It can be measured in inches (in), feet (ft), yards (yd), and miles. Shorter lengths are measured in inches and longer lengths are measured in miles.

12 inches (in) = 1 foot (ft)

3 feet (ft) = 1 yard (yd)

1760 yards (yd) = 1 mile

Units of mass

Mass is the amount of matter in an object. It can be measured in ounces (oz), pounds (lb), stone, hundredweights (cwt), and tons (t). Very light things are measured in ounces and extremely heavy things are measured in tons.

16 ounces (oz) = 1 pound (lb)

14 pounds (lb) = 1 stone

112 pounds (lb) = 1 hundredweight (cwt)

2240 pounds (lb) = 1 ton

20 hundredweight (cwt) = 1 ton

Units of capacity

Capacity is the amount of space within a container. It can be measured in fluid ounces (fl oz), cups, pints (pt), quarts (qt), and gallons (gal). Small capacities are measured in fluid ounces and very large capacities are measured in gallons.

8 fluid ounces (fl oz) = 1 cup

20 fluid ounces (fl oz) = 1 pint (pt)

2 pints (pt) = 1 quart (qt)

8 pints (pt) = 1 gallon (gal)

4 quarts (qt) = 1 gallon (gal)

🔍 Measuring using the body

Since ancient times, many different units of measurement have been used. Some units of length were based on parts of the human body.

A cubit is 18 inches and is based on the length of the arm from the elbow to the tip of the middle finger.

A span is 9 inches and is based on the distance from the end of the thumb to the end of the little finger of a spread hand.

Cubit

Span

Yard

Hand

A hand is 4 inches and is based on the width of the four fingers of one hand.

A yard is based on the distance from the tip of the nose to the middle fingertip.

A foot is based on the length of a foot.

Foot

Converting units of measure

Sometimes measurements are given in one unit when you need them in a different unit. To convert from one unit to another, you multiply or divide by a number called a conversion factor.

Key facts

✓ To convert between two units of measurement, we multiply or divide by the conversion factor for those units.

✓ To convert between metric and imperial units, we can use approximate conversions.

Conversion factors
A conversion factor is the number you need to multiply or divide a measurement by to change it from one unit to another. For example, there are 100 cm in 1 m, so the conversion factor for converting between the two units is 100. You can use the tables on page 66 to convert from one metric unit to another or the tables on page 67 to convert from one imperial unit to another.

This elephant weighs 2,600 kg. To convert this measurement to metric tons, we divide it by 1,000, because there are 1,000 kg in 1 t: 2600 ÷ 1000 = 2.6 t.

This mouse is 4.3 cm long. To convert this measurement to millimeters, we multiply by the conversion factor of 10, because there are 10 mm in 1 cm: 4.3 × 10 = 43 mm.

Metric–imperial conversion
Sometimes it is necessary to convert a measurement from a metric unit to an imperial unit, or vice versa. To do this, we use these approximate metric–imperial conversions.

Metric	Imperial
2.5 centimeters (cm)	1 inch (in)
30 centimeters (cm)	1 foot (ft)
1 meter (m)	1 1/10 yards (yd)
1.6 kilometers (km)	1 mile
8 kilometers (km)	5 miles
1 kilogram (kg)	2 1/4 pounds (lb)
1 metric ton (t)	1 imperial ton (t)
1 liter (l)	1 3/4 pints (pt)
4.5 liters (l)	1 gallon (gal)

Converting units of area and volume

To convert units of measurement involving area and volume, we need to remember that area and volume represent measurements of two or three dimensions. It is helpful to convert each dimension separately first.

📌 **Key facts**

✓ Area and volume measurements represent measurements in two or three dimensions respectively.

✓ To convert units of area or volume, convert each dimension separately, then multiply together.

Converting area

To convert the area of a shape, it is best to convert each dimension separately, then multiply them together using the area formula for that shape. Remember: 1 cm² does not equal 10 mm², and 1 m² does not equal 100 cm².

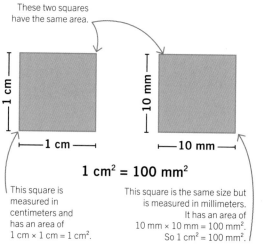

These two squares have the same area.

$$1 \text{ cm}^2 = 100 \text{ mm}^2$$

This square is measured in centimeters and has an area of 1 cm × 1 cm = 1 cm².

This square is the same size but is measured in millimeters. It has an area of 10 mm × 10 mm = 100 mm². So 1 cm² = 100 mm².

Converting volume

When converting volumes, it is best to convert each dimension separately, then multiply them together using the volume formula for that shape. Remember: 1 cm³ does not equal 10 mm³, and 1 m³ does not equal 100 cm³.

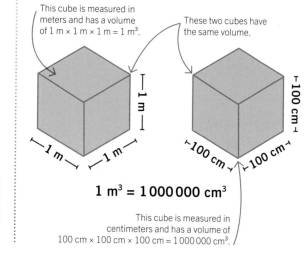

This cube is measured in meters and has a volume of 1 m × 1 m × 1 m = 1 m³.

These two cubes have the same volume.

$$1 \text{ m}^3 = 1\,000\,000 \text{ cm}^3$$

This cube is measured in centimeters and has a volume of 100 cm × 100 cm × 100 cm = 1 000 000 cm³.

📑 **Volume of a box**

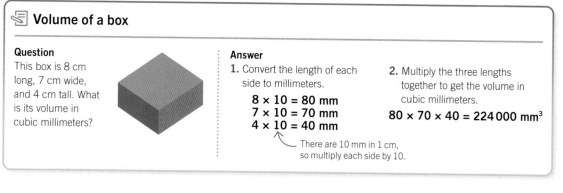

Question
This box is 8 cm long, 7 cm wide, and 4 cm tall. What is its volume in cubic millimeters?

Answer
1. Convert the length of each side to millimeters.

8 × 10 = 80 mm
7 × 10 = 70 mm
4 × 10 = 40 mm

There are 10 mm in 1 cm, so multiply each side by 10.

2. Multiply the three lengths together to get the volume in cubic millimeters.

80 × 70 × 40 = 224 000 mm³

Compound units of measure

A compound unit of measure combines two or more different units. Speed, pressure, and density are all compound measures.

Formula triangles

When you have a formula in the form $A = {}^B/c$, you can use a formula triangle to help you remember the relationship between the three variables A, B, and C. The dividend, in this case B, is written at the top of the triangle, with the other two variables, A and C, beneath. The position of each variable in the triangle tells you whether to divide or multiply it by another variable.

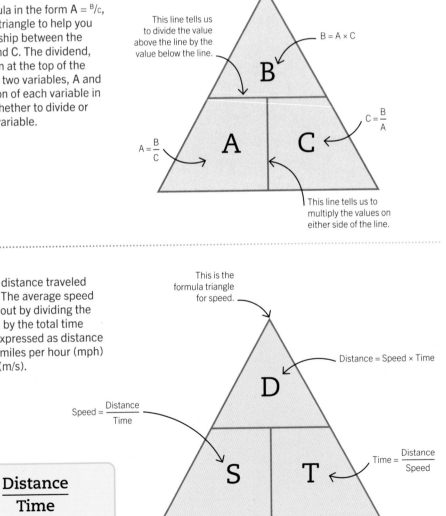

This line tells us to divide the value above the line by the value below the line.

$B = A \times C$

$C = \dfrac{B}{A}$

$A = \dfrac{B}{C}$

This line tells us to multiply the values on either side of the line.

Units of speed

Speed is a measure of distance traveled over a particular time. The average speed of an object is worked out by dividing the total distance traveled by the total time taken. The answer is expressed as distance per time unit, such as miles per hour (mph) or meters per second (m/s).

This is the formula triangle for speed.

$Distance = Speed \times Time$

$Speed = \dfrac{Distance}{Time}$

$Time = \dfrac{Distance}{Speed}$

$$Speed = \frac{Distance}{Time}$$

Units of pressure

Pressure is the force applied to a particular surface area. This is calculated by dividing the total force (in Newtons) by the total surface area. Pressure is measured in N/m^2, or in pascals (Pa).

$$\text{Pressure} = \frac{\text{Force}}{\text{Area}}$$

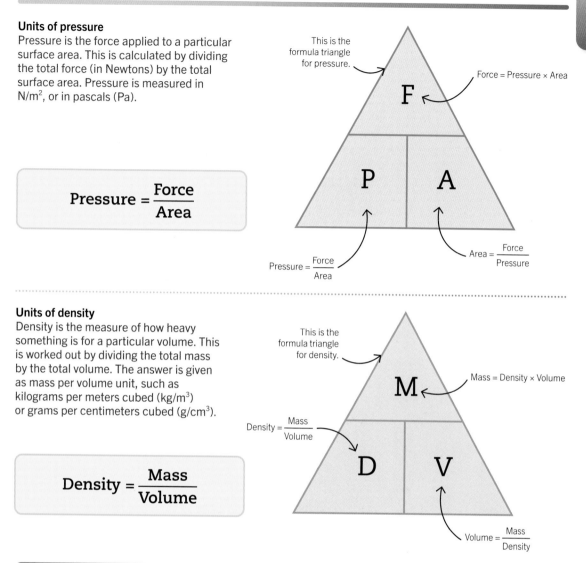

This is the formula triangle for pressure.

Force = Pressure × Area

$$\text{Pressure} = \frac{\text{Force}}{\text{Area}}$$

$$\text{Area} = \frac{\text{Force}}{\text{Pressure}}$$

Units of density

Density is the measure of how heavy something is for a particular volume. This is worked out by dividing the total mass by the total volume. The answer is given as mass per volume unit, such as kilograms per meters cubed (kg/m^3) or grams per centimeters cubed (g/cm^3).

$$\text{Density} = \frac{\text{Mass}}{\text{Volume}}$$

This is the formula triangle for density.

Mass = Density × Volume

$$\text{Density} = \frac{\text{Mass}}{\text{Volume}}$$

$$\text{Volume} = \frac{\text{Mass}}{\text{Density}}$$

🔍 Population density

To get an idea of how crowded a place is, we can calculate its population density. Unlike density, which refers to the weight of an object per unit of volume, population density refers to the number of people living in a particular area. New York City is one of the most densely populated places in the US, where approximately 8,400,000 people are crammed into an area of 784 km^2. To work out the city's population density, we divide the population by the area, which equals 10,714 people per km^2.

Practice questions
Working with compound units

See also

70–71 Compound units of measure

109 Formulas

110 Rearranging formulas

To use the formulas for speed, density, and pressure, we substitute the measurements that we know into the relevant formula and calculate the result.

Calculating speed

Question
The distance from London to New York is roughly 5,600 km, and a plane takes 7 hours to complete the journey. What is its average speed in mph?

Answer
1. To calculate the answer, we can use the formula for speed.

$$\text{Speed} = \frac{\text{Distance}}{\text{Time}}$$

2. Substitute the known measurements into the formula and evaluate to find the answer.

$$\text{Speed} = \frac{5600}{7} = 800 \text{ mph}$$

Calculating volume

Question
If a solid gold ring weighs 5 g and the density of gold is 20 g/cm³, what is the volume of the ring in cm³?

Answer
1. For this calculation, we can use the formula for density.

$$\text{Density} = \frac{\text{Mass}}{\text{Volume}}$$

2. To find the volume instead of density, we need to rearrange the formula. Use a formula triangle to remember the relationship between the values.

This line means divide. So to find the volume, divide mass by density.

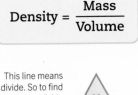

3. Substitute the measurements into the formula and evaluate to find the answer.

$$\text{Volume} = \frac{\text{Mass}}{\text{Density}}$$
$$= \frac{5}{20}$$
$$= 0.25 \text{ cm}^3$$

Calculating force

Question
A bookcase with a 0.1 m² base exerts a pressure of 8,500 N/m² on the ground. What force does it exert in Newtons?

Answer
1. For this calculation, we can use the formula for pressure.

$$\text{Pressure} = \frac{\text{Force}}{\text{Area}}$$

2. To work out how to rearrange the formula, we can use a formula triangle.

This line means multiply. So to find the force, multiply pressure by area.

3. Substitute the measurements into the formula and evaluate to find the answer.

$$\text{Force} = \text{Pressure} \times \text{Area}$$
$$= 8500 \times 0.1$$
$$= 850 \text{ N}$$

Perimeter and area

Every closed 2D shape, whether it has straight edges or curved sides, can be described by its perimeter and area. The perimeter is the distance around the outside of a shape, while the area is a measure of the space inside the perimeter.

Perimeter
The perimeter of a shape is calculated by finding the sum of the lengths of all its sides. Each side is measured one at a time and then added together.

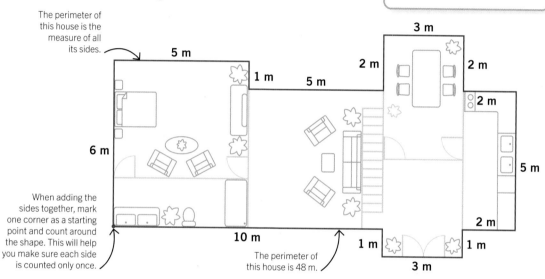

The perimeter of this house is the measure of all its sides.

When adding the sides together, mark one corner as a starting point and count around the shape. This will help you make sure each side is counted only once.

The perimeter of this house is 48 m.

5 m 1 m 5 m 3 m 2 m 2 m 2 m 5 m 6 m 10 m 1 m 3 m 2 m 1 m

Area
The amount of space enclosed within a 2D shape is called its area. It is measured in square units. We could find the area of this rectangle by simply counting up the number of square units it covers, but this can be time-consuming. It is usually much quicker to find the area using a formula, which involves calculating the area using the known lengths.

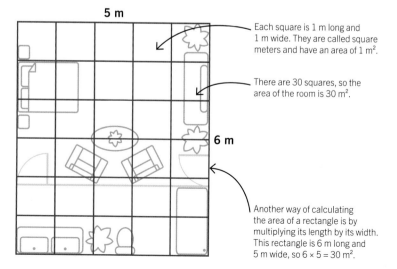

Each square is 1 m long and 1 m wide. They are called square meters and have an area of 1 m².

There are 30 squares, so the area of the room is 30 m².

Another way of calculating the area of a rectangle is by multiplying its length by its width. This rectangle is 6 m long and 5 m wide, so 6 × 5 = 30 m².

5 m 6 m

Area formulas

Counting the squares inside a 2D shape to find its area can be time-consuming. Instead, we can use formulas to work out the area of some simple polygons more quickly. To use an area formula, we simply substitute the known measurements of a shape into the formula.

Area of a rectangle
The area of a rectangle is found by multiplying its length (l) by its width (w).

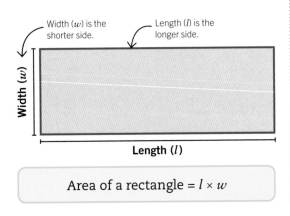

Width (w) is the shorter side.

Length (l) is the longer side.

Width (w)

Length (l)

$$\text{Area of a rectangle} = l \times w$$

Area of a parallelogram
The area of a parallelogram is calculated by multiplying the length of its base (b) by the vertical height (h).

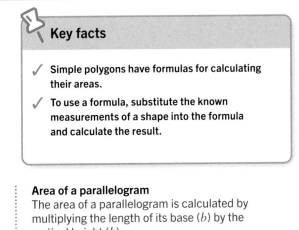

The vertical height (h) is the perpendicular distance from the base to the side that is parallel to it.

Height (h)

Base (b)

$$\text{Area of a parallelogram} = b \times h$$

Area of a triangle
The area of a triangle is calculated by halving the base (b) and multiplying it by the vertical height (h). The base can be any side of the triangle.

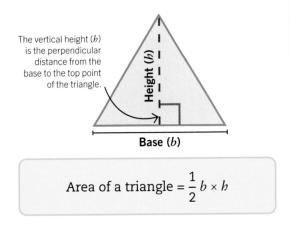

The vertical height (h) is the perpendicular distance from the base to the top point of the triangle.

Height (h)

Base (b)

$$\text{Area of a triangle} = \frac{1}{2} b \times h$$

Area of a trapezoid
The area of a trapezoid is found by multiplying the average length of its parallel sides by the vertical height (h).

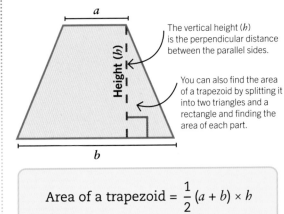

a

The vertical height (h) is the perpendicular distance between the parallel sides.

You can also find the area of a trapezoid by splitting it into two triangles and a rectangle and finding the area of each part.

Height (h)

b

$$\text{Area of a trapezoid} = \frac{1}{2}(a + b) \times h$$

How area formulas work

We can see how and why the formulas for finding the area of triangles and parallelograms work by rearranging the shapes.

Triangles

Two identical triangles can always be rearranged into a rectangle or parallelogram. That means the area of a triangle is always half of a rectangle or parallelogram, so the formula for the area of a triangle is half of a rectangle or parallelogram's formula: ½ $b \times h$.

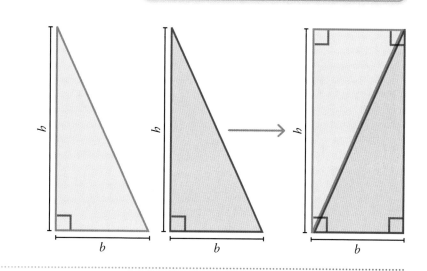

Parallelograms

A parallelogram can be split into a rectangle and two triangles. If one triangle is moved to the other side, the shape becomes a rectangle. The rectangle on the right has a length and a width that are equal to the vertical height and base length of the parallelogram, so the area formula of a rectangle ($l \times w$) is the same as $b \times h$ of a parallelogram.

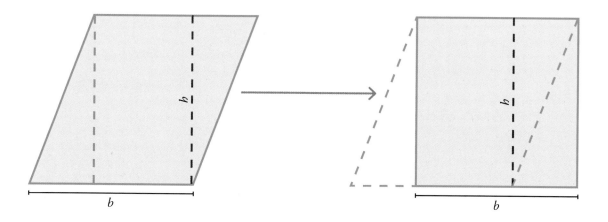

Circumference and area of a circle

The circumference of a circle is the distance around its outside edge. The area of a circle is the amount of space inside the circumference. We calculate the circumference and area of a circle using formulas that involve a special number called π, or "pi."

The number pi
In all circles, the relationship between the circumference and diameter is always the same. The circumference of a circle will always be approximately 3.14 times larger than its diameter. This number is called π, or "pi." It is used in many formulas associated with circles.

$$\pi = 3.14$$

The numbers after the decimal point in π go on forever, but we usually round it to two decimal places.

Calculating circumference
There are two formulas that can be used to find the circumference of a circle—using π and the diameter (the length from one side of the circle to the other through the center point), or using π and the radius (the distance from the center to the circumference).

This is the formula we use when we are given the diameter.

$$\text{Circumference } (C) = \pi d$$
$$\text{Circumference } (C) = 2\pi r$$

This is the formula we use when we are given the radius.

The radius is half the length of the diameter, so the formula involves multiplying the radius by 2.

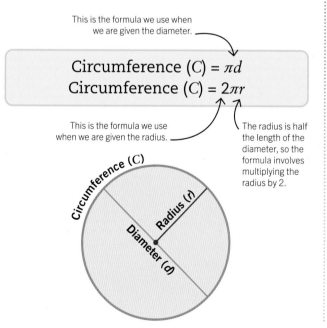

Calculating area
The area of a circle is given in square units. To calculate the area of a circle, we use a simple formula involving the length of the radius and π.

$$\text{Area of a circle} = \pi r^2$$

To calculate the area, we need to know the radius.

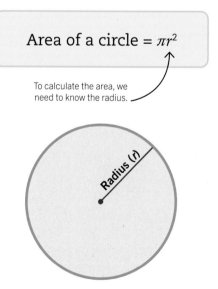

Length of an arc and area of a sector

An arc is a section of a circle's circumference and a sector is a wedge of a circle, like a pizza slice. We can calculate the length of an arc and the area of a sector using two simple formulas.

Finding the length of an arc
We calculate the length of an arc using its related angle at the center of the circle and the total length of the circle's circumference.

$$\text{Arc length} = \frac{\text{angle between radii}}{360°} \times \text{circumference}$$

Substituting the angle between the radii and the circumference of the circle into the formula will give the length of the arc:

$$\frac{120°}{360°} \times 12 = 4 \text{ cm}$$

Circumference = 12 cm

120°

Finding the area of a sector
A sector is made up of two radii and an arc. If you know the area of the circle and the angle between the radii, you can work out the sector's area.

$$\text{Area of a sector} = \frac{\text{angle between radii}}{360°} \times \text{area of a circle}$$

Substituting the known values into the formula will give the area of the sector:

$$\frac{60°}{360°} \times 24 = 4 \text{ cm}^2$$

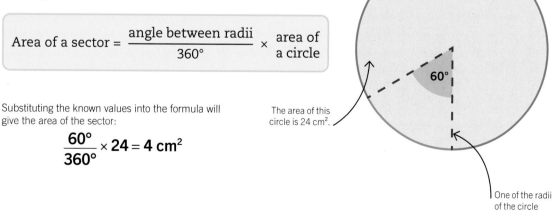

The area of this circle is 24 cm².

60°

One of the radii of the circle

Practice questions
Compound 2D shapes

A compound or composite shape is a shape that is made up of two or more simpler shapes, such as rectangles or triangles. To work out the total area of a compound shape, you need to identify the different simple shapes that form it and work out the area of each.

See also

74 Area formulas

76 Circumference and area of a circle

Question

What is the area of the compound shape below? Give the answer in cm² to two decimal places.

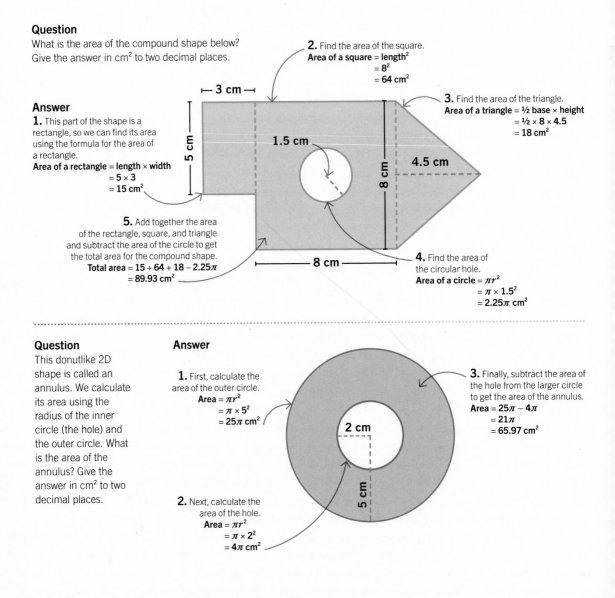

2. Find the area of the square.
Area of a square = length²
$$= 8^2$$
$$= 64 \text{ cm}^2$$

Answer

1. This part of the shape is a rectangle, so we can find its area using the formula for the area of a rectangle.
Area of a rectangle = length × width
$$= 5 \times 3$$
$$= 15 \text{ cm}^2$$

3. Find the area of the triangle.
Area of a triangle = ½ base × height
$$= \tfrac{1}{2} \times 8 \times 4.5$$
$$= 18 \text{ cm}^2$$

5. Add together the area of the rectangle, square, and triangle and subtract the area of the circle to get the total area for the compound shape.
Total area = 15 + 64 + 18 − 2.25π
$$= 89.93 \text{ cm}^2$$

4. Find the area of the circular hole.
Area of a circle = πr^2
$$= \pi \times 1.5^2$$
$$= 2.25\pi \text{ cm}^2$$

Question

This donutlike 2D shape is called an annulus. We calculate its area using the radius of the inner circle (the hole) and the outer circle. What is the area of the annulus? Give the answer in cm² to two decimal places.

Answer

1. First, calculate the area of the outer circle.
Area = πr^2
$$= \pi \times 5^2$$
$$= 25\pi \text{ cm}^2$$

2. Next, calculate the area of the hole.
Area = πr^2
$$= \pi \times 2^2$$
$$= 4\pi \text{ cm}^2$$

3. Finally, subtract the area of the hole from the larger circle to get the area of the annulus.
Area = 25π − 4π
$$= 21\pi$$
$$= 65.97 \text{ cm}^2$$

3D shapes

A three-dimensional (3D) shape has length, width, and height. 3D shapes are often referred to as solids. If they are closed, made up of flat surfaces, and have only straight edges, they are also called polyhedrons.

Key facts

✓ All 3D shapes have length, width, and height.

✓ A prism is a 3D shape with an identical face at either end and the same cross-section the whole way through.

✓ Closed 3D shapes with flat faces and straight edges are called polyhedrons.

✓ Closed solid shapes that have curved surfaces, like a cone, are not polyhedrons.

Types of solid

There is a never-ending variety of 3D shapes. They differ from one another in the numbers of faces, edges, and vertices they have. A face is a surface of a 3D shape. Where two faces meet, they create an edge. Where three or more edges meet, they make a vertex.

A prism is a solid that has an identical face at either end and the same cross-section the whole way through the shape.

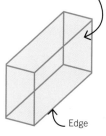

Edge

Face

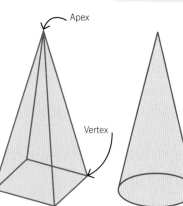

Apex

Vertex

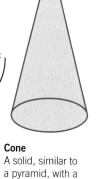

A solid with a curved surface is not a polyhedron.

Rectangular prism
A six-sided prism made up of rectangular faces. A cube is a type of rectangular prism with all edges of equal lengths.

Cylinder
A prism with circular end faces that are connected by a single curved surface.

Pyramid
A polyhedron made up of triangles that connect to a base and all meet at a single upper vertex, or apex. The base can be any polygon.

Cone
A solid, similar to a pyramid, with a circular base and curved surface that rises to a single point, or apex.

Sphere
A rounded solid with only one surface. Every point on the surface is the same distance from the sphere's central point.

🔍 Platonic solids

Named after Plato, the Greek philosopher, Platonic solids are regular polyhedrons—shapes with faces that are identical regular polygons of the same size. There are only five such regular polyhedrons. Plato believed the Universe was made up of tiny Platonic solids.

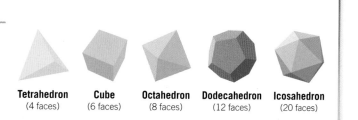

Tetrahedron
(4 faces)

Cube
(6 faces)

Octahedron
(8 faces)

Dodecahedron
(12 faces)

Icosahedron
(20 faces)

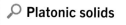

3D cross-sections

Key facts

A cross-section is the 2D shape that is created by a plane slicing through a 3D shape such as a rectangular prism or a pyramid. The shape of a cross-section depends on the angle of the slice.

- ✓ A cross-section is the 2D shape made by a plane slicing through a 3D solid.
- ✓ The shape of a cross-section varies according to the direction of the slice.

Cross-sections of rectangular prisms

Slicing through a rectangular prism at right angles to its faces will give a rectangular cross-section. Slicing through a rectangular prism at a slant can give a cross-section in the shape of a parallelogram, triangle, trapezoid, pentagon, or hexagon, depending on the number of faces you cut through.

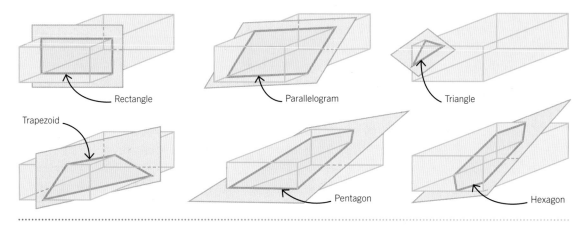

Right-rectangular pyramid

Slicing through a pyramid with a rectangular base can create a variety of shapes depending on the angle and position of the slice. A horizontal slice will give the same shape as the base but smaller. A vertical slice through the apex gives a triangular cross-section, but vertical slices at other positions give trapezoids.

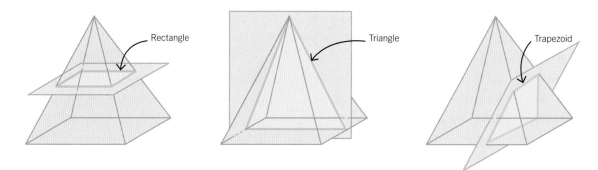

Plans and elevations

Sometimes it is useful to be able to draw an accurate 2D representation of a 3D shape. These drawings are called plans and elevations.

Key facts

✓ Plans and elevations give a 2D representation of a 3D shape.

✓ Plan view is a look from above.

✓ Elevations look from the front and the side.

2D representations

A 3D shape can be drawn on special graph paper, called isometric paper, to give a good sense of its shape. However, the shape's angles, edge lengths, and surface area cannot be accurately represented this way. Instead we draw plans and elevations to show the shape from above, the side, and the front more accurately.

A shape can be drawn on isometric paper to give it a 3D appearance.

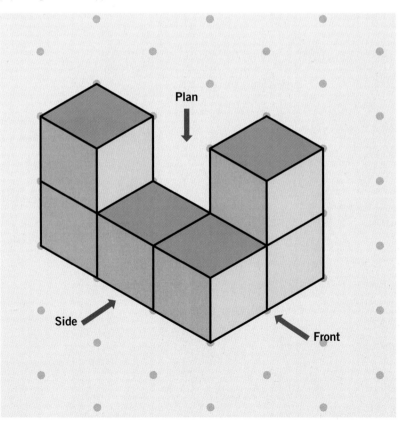

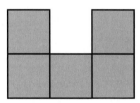

The **plan** looks at the shape directly from above.

The side elevation shows the shape from the side. The view from the other side would be a mirror image.

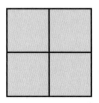

The front elevation shows the shape directly from the front. From the back, the elevation would be a mirror image.

Volume of a rectangular prism

The volume of a 3D shape is a measure of the space within its surfaces. The volume of any rectangular prism can be calculated by using a simple formula.

Rectangular prism
Volume is measured in cube units. We can find the volume of a rectangular prism by counting the number of cube units that make it up, but this can be time-consuming. Instead we use a formula, which involves multiplying its length, width, and height together.

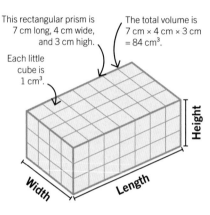

This rectangular prism is 7 cm long, 4 cm wide, and 3 cm high.

Each little cube is 1 cm³.

The total volume is 7 cm × 4 cm × 3 cm = 84 cm³.

Height

Width

Length

> Volume of a rectangular prism = length × width × height

Cube
A cube is a regular rectangular prism with six square faces, so a cube's edges all have the same length. To calculate a cube's volume, this length is multiplied by itself twice. This process is also known as cubing.

All edges are the same length.

Each little cube is 1 cm³.

All faces are identical squares.

The total volume is 3 cm × 3 cm × 3 cm = 27 cm³.

Length

> Volume of a cube = length × length × length
> = length³

📌 **Key facts**

✓ The volume of a rectangular prism is the space within the shape.

✓ To find the volume of a rectangular prism, use the formula:
  Volume = **length** × **width** × **height**

✓ To find the volume of a cube, use the formula:
  Volume = **length³**

🗐 **How much will fit?**

Question
The back of a truck is 6 m long, 3 m wide, and 4 m high. How many identical cubic boxes with a side length of 50 cm can be loaded into the truck?

Answer
1. First, we work out the volume of the truck.
  6 × 3 × 4 = 72 m³

2. Next, we find the volume of one box. Remember to convert the units from centimeters to meters first to match the units used for the truck.
  50 cm = 0.5 m
  0.5 × 0.5 × 0.5 = 0.125 m³

3. Finally, we divide the volume of the truck by the volume of one box to find out how many boxes will fit in the truck.
  72 ÷ 0.125 = 576

576 boxes can be loaded into the truck.

Surface area of a rectangular prism

The surface area of a 3D shape is the sum of the areas of each of its faces. There is a simple formula for calculating the surface area of a rectangular prism and a cube, both of which have six sides.

Key facts

✓ The surface area of a rectangular prism or cube is the total area of its six faces.

✓ The formula for the surface area of a rectangular prism is:
Surface area = $2(lw + wh + lh)$

✓ The formula for the surface area of a cube is:
Surface area = $6a^2$

Rectangular prism

Rectangular prisms have three matching pairs of rectangular faces. The faces in each pair are parallel to each other. Each pair forms two of the rectangular prism's six parallel faces. The area of a face is length × width (lw), width × height (wh), or length × height (lh).

Cube

A cube has six identical faces, each with the same area. The area of one face is calculated by squaring the length of its edge. The surface area of the cube is therefore six times the area of one face.

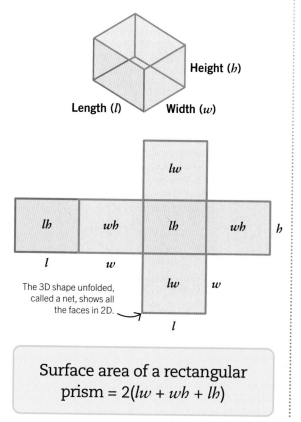

The 3D shape unfolded, called a net, shows all the faces in 2D.

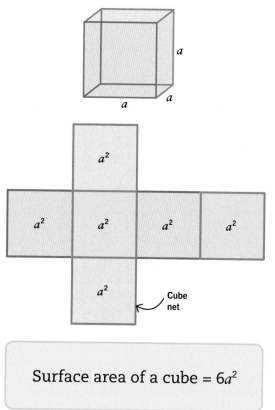

Cube net

Surface area of a rectangular prism = $2(lw + wh + lh)$

Surface area of a cube = $6a^2$

Volume and surface area of a prism

A prism is a 3D shape with identical faces at each end. When you make a cut through the prism parallel to these faces, you create a shape called a cross-section. Knowing the cross-section and length of a prism, we can use simple formulas to calculate volume and surface area.

Calculating volume

The volume of a prism is calculated by multiplying its length by the area of its cross-section. To find the volume of this triangular prism, we would need to find the area of the triangular face and multiply it by the length.

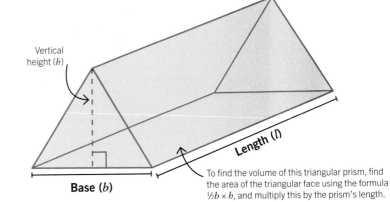

Vertical height (h)

Length (l)

Base (b)

To find the volume of this triangular prism, find the area of the triangular face using the formula ½b × h, and multiply this by the prism's length.

> Volume of a prism = area of cross-section × length

Calculating surface area

To calculate the surface area of a prism, add together the areas of its faces. First, find the area of its two end faces. Next, find the area of each of its other faces. Add all of these areas together. You can work this out easily using a net of the shape.

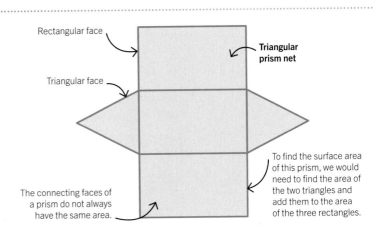

Rectangular face

Triangular prism net

Triangular face

The connecting faces of a prism do not always have the same area.

To find the surface area of this prism, we would need to find the area of the two triangles and add them to the area of the three rectangles.

> Surface area of a prism = sum of the areas of its faces

Volume and surface area of a cylinder

The faces of a cylinder are two parallel circles connected by a curved surface. The volume and surface area of a cylinder are calculated using the same methods that we use to find those of a prism.

Calculating volume
The volume of a cylinder is calculated by multiplying the area of its circular cross-section by its height. The area of the circular cross-section is calculated like any other circle (see page 76).

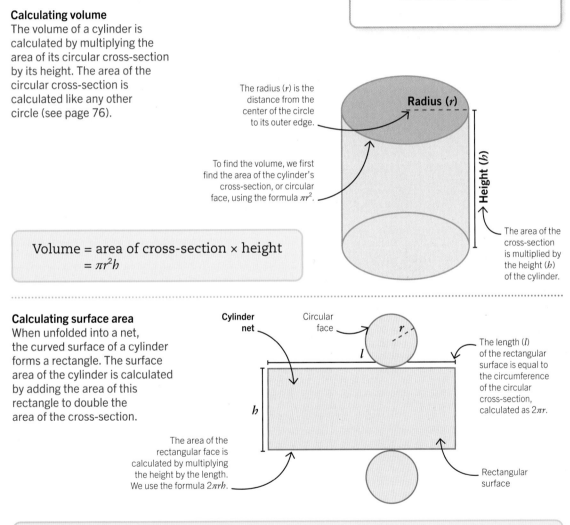

The radius (r) is the distance from the center of the circle to its outer edge.

Radius (r)

To find the volume, we first find the area of the cylinder's cross-section, or circular face, using the formula πr^2.

Height (h)

The area of the cross-section is multiplied by the height (h) of the cylinder.

$$\text{Volume} = \text{area of cross-section} \times \text{height}$$
$$= \pi r^2 h$$

Calculating surface area
When unfolded into a net, the curved surface of a cylinder forms a rectangle. The surface area of the cylinder is calculated by adding the area of this rectangle to double the area of the cross-section.

Cylinder net

Circular face

The length (l) of the rectangular surface is equal to the circumference of the circular cross-section, calculated as $2\pi r$.

The area of the rectangular face is calculated by multiplying the height by the length. We use the formula $2\pi rh$.

Rectangular surface

$$\text{Surface area of a cylinder} = \text{area of rectangular face} + (2 \times \text{area of circular face})$$
$$= 2\pi rh + 2\pi r^2$$

Volume and surface area of a pyramid

A pyramid is a solid with a polygon for a base that is connected by triangular sides to a single point, or apex, at the top. The number of triangular sides is equal to the number of edges on the base. All pyramids, regardless of the number of sides, share the same basic formula for volume and surface area.

Calculating volume
The volume of a pyramid is calculated by multiplying the area of the base by the vertical height, then multiplying the resulting value by $\tfrac{1}{3}$. This formula works for any pyramid with a base of any shape.

The area of the base (B) for this rectangular-based pyramid is length × width.

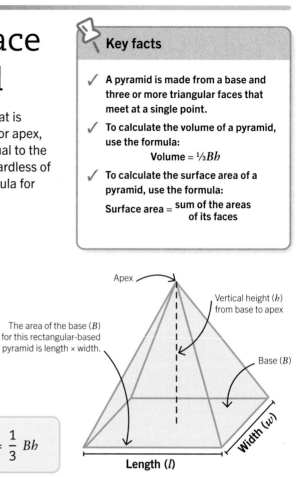

Apex

Vertical height (h) from base to apex

Base (B)

Width (w)

Length (l)

$$\text{Volume of a pyramid} = \frac{1}{3} \times \text{area of base} \times \text{vertical height} = \frac{1}{3}Bh$$

Calculating surface area
To find the surface area of a pyramid, calculate the area of each of its faces using the formula for each shape (see page 74), then add each area together.

This triangular-based pyramid is made up of four triangular faces. To find its surface area, we calculate the area of each face using the formula $\tfrac{1}{2}bh$, where b is the width of the base of the triangle and h is the height from its base.

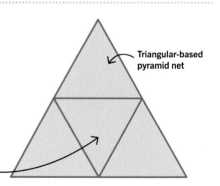

Triangular-based pyramid net

Surface area of a pyramid = sum of the areas of its faces

Volume and surface area of a cone

A cone has a circular base and a curved surface that connects the base to the point (apex). We can use formulas to calculate the volume and surface area of a cone.

Key facts

✓ To calculate the volume of a cone, the formula is:
Volume = $\frac{1}{3} \times \pi r^2 h$

✓ To calculate the surface area of a cone, the formula is:
Surface area = $\pi r^2 + \pi rs$

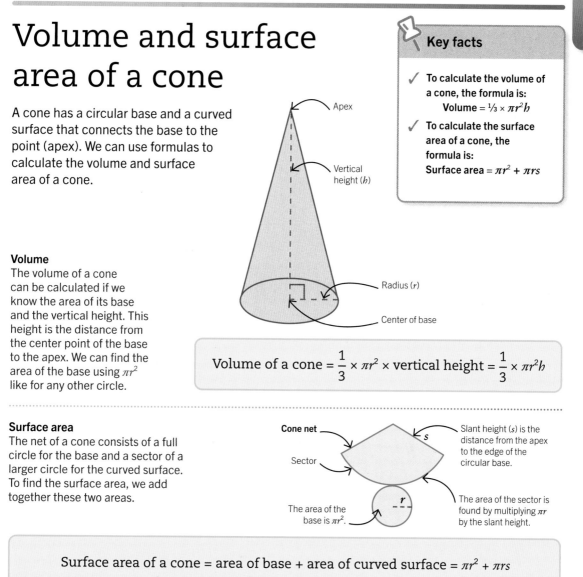

Apex

Vertical height (h)

Radius (r)

Center of base

Volume
The volume of a cone can be calculated if we know the area of its base and the vertical height. This height is the distance from the center point of the base to the apex. We can find the area of the base using πr^2 like for any other circle.

$$\text{Volume of a cone} = \frac{1}{3} \times \pi r^2 \times \text{vertical height} = \frac{1}{3} \times \pi r^2 h$$

Surface area
The net of a cone consists of a full circle for the base and a sector of a larger circle for the curved surface. To find the surface area, we add together these two areas.

Cone net

Sector

The area of the base is πr^2.

Slant height (s) is the distance from the apex to the edge of the circular base.

The area of the sector is found by multiplying πr by the slant height.

$$\text{Surface area of a cone} = \text{area of base} + \text{area of curved surface} = \pi r^2 + \pi rs$$

🔍 Frustums

A frustum is the 3D shape that is created by slicing off the tip of a cone parallel to the base. It's easy to find the volume of a frustum if we imagine the volume of the full cone and subtract the tip that has been removed.

Finding the volume of a frustum
1. Imagine the frustum is a cone and calculate its volume.
2. Find the volume of the conical tip that has been removed.
3. Subtract the volume of the tip from the volume of the cone.

Volume and surface area of a sphere

A sphere is a 3D shape with only one curved surface. Every point on the surface is the same distance from the sphere's center point.

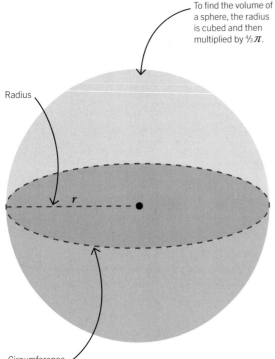

To find the volume of a sphere, the radius is cubed and then multiplied by $\tfrac{4}{3}\pi$.

Radius

r

Circumference

Calculating volume

The volume of a sphere is the amount of space inside its single curved face. The volume of a sphere is calculated using the number π, which is the ratio between the circumference and the diameter. The only measurement needed to find the volume is the sphere's radius or diameter.

$$\text{Volume of a sphere} = \frac{4}{3}\pi r^3$$

Calculating surface area

Unlike some 3D shapes, a sphere cannot be unfolded or unrolled into a net, so we calculate its surface area with a formula instead. The surface area of any sphere will always be four times the area of a circle with the same radius.

$$\text{Surface area of a sphere} = 4\pi r^2$$

📧 **Surface area of a globe**

Question
A globe has a radius of 3.5 cm and is a perfect sphere. What is its surface area in cm² to one decimal place?

Answer
Calculate the surface area of the globe using the formula.

$$\begin{aligned}\text{Surface area of a sphere} &= 4\pi r^2 \\ &= 4 \times \pi \times 3.5^2 \\ &= 153.9 \text{ cm}^2\end{aligned}$$

Practice questions
Compound 3D shapes

A shape made up of two or more different shapes is called a compound shape. The surface area or volume of a compound 3D shape can be worked out by tackling each of its component shapes one by one.

See also

82 Volume of a rectangular prism

85 Volume and surface area of a cylinder

86 Volume and surface area of a pyramid

88 Volume and surface area of a sphere

Question

This compound shape is made up of half a sphere, called a hemisphere, and a cylinder. What is the total surface area of the shape? Give your answer in cm² to two decimal places.

Answer

1. To find the surface area of the hemisphere, use the formula for the surface area of a sphere and divide it by 2.

Surface area of a hemisphere $= \dfrac{4\pi r^2}{2}$

$= \dfrac{4 \times \pi \times 10^2}{2}$

$= \dfrac{400\pi}{2}$

$= 200\pi$ cm²

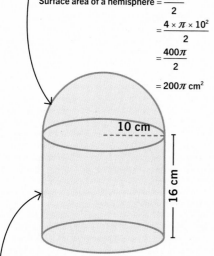

10 cm

16 cm

2. The surface area of the cylindrical part of the shape only includes one of its end faces, so we use the formula to find the surface area of one circular face and the rectangular face.

Surface area of a cylinder $= 2\pi rh + \pi r^2$

$= (2 \times \pi \times 10 \times 16) + (\pi \times 10^2)$

$= 320\pi + 100\pi$

$= 420\pi$ cm²

3. Add together the two results for the total surface area of the compound shape.

Total surface area $= 200\pi + 420\pi$

$= 1947.79$ cm²

Question

This compound shape is made up of a rectangular prism and a pyramid. What is the total volume of the shape? Give your answer in m³ to two decimal places.

Answer

1. Use the formula for the volume of a pyramid to find the volume of the top part of the shape.

Volume of a pyramid $= \frac{1}{3} \times$ area of base $\times$ vertical height

$= \frac{1}{3} \times (6.7 \times 2.9) \times 2.8$

$= \frac{1}{3} \times 19.43 \times 2.8$

$= 18.135$ m³

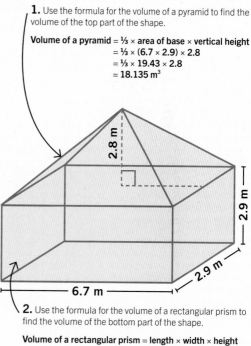

2.8 m

2.9 m

2.9 m

6.7 m

2. Use the formula for the volume of a rectangular prism to find the volume of the bottom part of the shape.

Volume of a rectangular prism $=$ length $\times$ width $\times$ height

$= 6.7 \times 2.9 \times 2.9$

$= 56.347$ m³

3. Add these two volumes together to get the total volume of the compound shape.

Total volume $= 18.135 + 56.347$

$= 74.48$ m³

Rounding and estimating

When dealing with numbers, such as measurements, you don't always need to be exact. Numbers can be rounded to give a simpler figure to work with and calculations may be estimated to give an approximate (rough) result.

Key facts

✓ Numbers that are on or above the midpoint of an interval are rounded up. Numbers below the midpoint are rounded down.

✓ Numbers with decimals can be rounded up or down to a chosen number of decimal places.

✓ The first significant figure in a number is the first digit that is not zero.

✓ Estimation involves rounding the figures in a calculation to work out an approximate answer.

Rounding
Sometimes it is necessary to adjust numbers, such as measurements, to a more sensible or useful figure. This is called rounding. Numbers can be rounded up or rounded down.

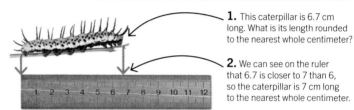

1. This caterpillar is 6.7 cm long. What is its length rounded to the nearest whole centimeter?

2. We can see on the ruler that 6.7 is closer to 7 than 6, so the caterpillar is 7 cm long to the nearest whole centimeter.

This symbol means "approximately equal to."

6.7 cm ≈ 7 cm

Up or down?
Whether a number is rounded up or down depends on where it falls within an interval of numbers. Generally, if the number is on or above the midpoint of the interval group, you round it up. If it is below the midpoint, you round it down. This number line shows how some of the numbers between 30 and 40 are rounded to the nearest 10.

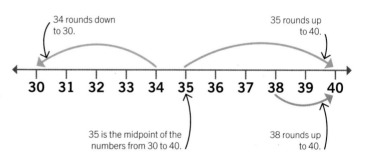

34 rounds down to 30.

35 rounds up to 40.

35 is the midpoint of the numbers from 30 to 40.

38 rounds up to 40.

Decimal places
Decimals can be rounded to a chosen number of decimal places. Once you have chosen the number of places, you round up when the next digit to be omitted is 5 or above, and down when it's 4 or below.

1. The exact length of a year on Earth is 365.2421875 days. We can round this long number to a certain number of decimal places depending on how accurate we want it to be.

365.2421875

2. To round it to four decimal places, look at the digit after the fourth decimal place. It's 8, so we round up the 1 to 2.

365.2422

3. To round it to two decimal places, look at the digit after the second decimal place. It's 2, so we round down, meaning that the 4 stays the same.

365.24

Significant figures

One common way of rounding is to use "significant figures" (often abbreviated to "s.f."), especially with very large or very small numbers. To round to any number of significant figures, start from the first nonzero digit from the left, then count each digit that follows as another significant figure.

1. This number has 6 significant figures.

320,014

2. This is the number rounded to 5 significant figures.

320,010

The zeros between the 2 and 1 are significant figures.

We write a 0 in place of the 4.

3. This is the number rounded to 2 significant figures.

320,000

The 3 and the 2 are significant figures. We write zeros in place of the other digits.

1. This number has 4 significant figures.

0.004712

These zeros are not significant figures.

The first significant figure is 4.

2. This is the number rounded to 3 significant figures.

0.00471

3. This is the number rounded to 1 significant figure.

0.005

The 4 has been rounded up to 5.

Estimation

Sometimes it is useful to quickly check whether your result for a tricky calculation is sensible by rounding the numbers up or down and calculating an approximate result. Working with approximate numbers like this is called estimation. It is particularly useful for checking the answer you get from a calculator.

1. The easiest way to calculate the volume of this box would be to use a calculator. But if you want to know if the answer it gives you (547.96 cm³) is sensible, you can estimate the volume.

2. First, round each of the side measurements up or down to make them easier to work with.

$$3.5 \text{ cm} \approx 4 \text{ cm}$$
$$10.3 \text{ cm} \approx 10 \text{ cm}$$
$$15.2 \text{ cm} \approx 15 \text{ cm}$$

3. Now multiply these numbers together to estimate the volume of the box.

$$4 \times 10 \times 15 = 600 \text{ cm}^3$$

4. 600 cm³ is close to the result given by the calculator, so 547.96 cm³ is correct.

Bounds of accuracy

When we measure something, our measurement is only as accurate as the instrument we use. A set of scales may round a measurement to the nearest 0.1 kg, so it can be useful to know how far out the measurement could be. The lowest and highest possible values are called the bounds of accuracy.

Upper and lower bounds

This cat weighs 4.3 kg to the nearest 0.1 kg. Because measurements are not exact, but rounded to a certain degree, the real weight could actually be higher or lower. The smallest number that could be rounded up to the given number is called the lower bound. The lowest number that would round up to the next estimated value is called the upper bound.

Key facts

✓ A measurement's bounds of accuracy are its lowest or highest possible values.

✓ The lower bound is the lowest value that would round up to the given value.

✓ The upper bound is the lowest value that would round up to the next estimated value.

1. If the cat weighed 4.24 kg, the scales would have rounded it down to 4.2 kg.

2. 4.25 kg is the lowest value that rounds up to 4.3 kg, so this is the lower bound.

3. 4.35 kg is the lowest value that rounds up to 4.4 kg, so this is the upper bound.

| 4.24 | 4.25 | 4.26 | 4.27 | 4.28 | 4.29 | 4.30 | 4.31 | 4.32 | 4.33 | 4.34 | 4.35 |

4. Whatever the unit of accuracy that a measurement is taken to, the upper and lower bounds are half a unit either way of the measurement. The cat's weight was given to the nearest 0.1 kg, so the bounds of accuracy are 0.05 kg higher or lower.

The error interval

The range of possible values for a measurement is known as the error interval. We can express the error interval using inequality notation (see page 154).

$$4.25 \text{ kg} \leq \text{weight of cat} < 4.35 \text{ kg}$$

This means the weight is greater than or equal to 4.25 kg.

This means the weight is less than 4.35 kg.

Arithmetic with bounds

If you calculate with rounded numbers, there will be errors in the result of the calculation. If you work out the bounds of each part of the calculation, you can find the bounds of the result.

Operation	Upper bound of result	Lower bound of result
Addition **A + B**	Upper bound of A + Upper bound of B	Lower bound of A + Lower bound of B
Subtraction **A − B**	Upper bound of A − Lower bound of B	Lower bound of A − Upper bound of B
Multiplication **A × B**	Upper bound of A × Upper bound of B	Lower bound of A × Lower bound of B
Division **A ÷ B**	Upper bound of A ÷ Lower bound of B	Lower bound of A ÷ Upper bound of B

Subtracting the largest of B from the smallest of A gives the smallest possible answer.

Dividing the largest of A by the smallest of B gives the largest possible answer.

Bounds of a division

Question

The weights in this calculation are given to the nearest 10 kg. What are the upper and lower bounds of the result to two decimal places?

$$5400 \text{ kg} \div 300 \text{ kg} = ?$$

Answer

1. First, find the bounds of each part of the calculation.

$$5395 \text{ kg} \leq \text{weight 1} < 5405 \text{ kg}$$
$$295 \text{ kg} \leq \text{weight 2} < 305 \text{ kg}$$

2. To find the upper bound for the result of the calculation, divide the upper bound of the first weight by the lower bound of the second weight.

$$5405 \div 295 = 18.32$$

3. To find the lower bound, divide the lower bound of the first weight by the upper bound of the second weight.

$$5395 \div 305 = 17.69$$

4. This gives us the bounds of accuracy for the result of the calculation.

$$17.69 \leq \text{result} < 18.32$$

Introducing algebra

Algebraic terms

Sometimes we don't know all of the numbers needed to work something out. Algebra is the branch of mathematics that uses letters as symbols to stand for numbers that we don't know or that might change. Using letters in this way allows us to work with values that we don't know and understand the relationship between numbers. The building blocks of algebra are called terms.

Key facts

✓ In algebra, a number, letter, or combination of both is called a term.

✓ Expressions and equations are built from terms.

✓ The rules of arithmetic work in the same way with terms as with ordinary numbers.

✓ Letters represent values that are unknown or values that aren't fixed.

Building blocks

In algebra, expressions and equations (see pages 96 and 130) are built from terms. A term can be a number, a letter representing a number, or a combination of numbers and letters.

Letters are used as symbols for values that are not known or values that can change. These terms are called variables.

This means $3 \times n$, or $n + n + n$. The number 3 is called the coefficient of n.

This means $y \times y$.

This means $4 \times b \div c$.

Terms that are numbers are called constants.

2 x c^3 b^2 $3n$ a^2 $9tu$ $x^2 y^3$ $\dfrac{c}{2}$ y^2 ab -5 $\dfrac{4b}{c}$

How terms are written

Mathematicians follow set rules to make sure their algebra can be understood. The rules of arithmetic apply to algebraic terms in the same way as to ordinary numbers.

Term	Explanation
x	When letters are used in terms, they are usually lowercase letters of the alphabet.
$-b$	Terms can be positive or negative. If there is no + or − sign written before a term, it is positive.
ab	The multiplication sign isn't used in terms: "a multiplied by b" is written as "ab." Letters in terms appear in alphabetical order.
$3b$	When multiplying numbers and letters to make a term, the number is written first.
$\dfrac{a}{2}$	Terms where one value is divided by another are written as fractions.
y^2	Like ordinary numbers, terms can be squared.

Expressions

Expressions are used in algebra to represent relationships between values. They are built up from a combination of terms and symbols. To make complicated expressions easier to read and understand, we can simplify them by combining together any terms that are the same. These are called "like" terms.

Key facts

✓ Expressions are made from terms, the building blocks of algebra.

✓ You simplify an expression by combining like terms.

✓ Like terms have exactly the same letters or contain no letters.

Building expressions from terms

Expressions are made up of at least two terms with operator symbols, such as + or −, between them. They don't have equals signs in them, so they can't be solved like equations (see page 130).

This expression is made up of five terms.

Each term is separated from the next by either a + or a − sign. These symbols are called "operators."

$$2x + 5y - y + 6z - 2$$

Varieties of expression

An expression can be built from any combination of terms. It can be made up entirely of letter terms, just number terms, or a combination of the two.

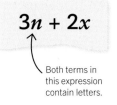

$$3n + 2x$$

Both terms in this expression contain letters.

$$4 + 3 - 1$$

This expression is made up of numbers.

$$7ab - y + 12$$

This expression has a combination of numbers and letters.

Combining like terms

Terms are "like" if they share exactly the same letters or if they contain no letters. Terms with the same combination of letters can also be combined.

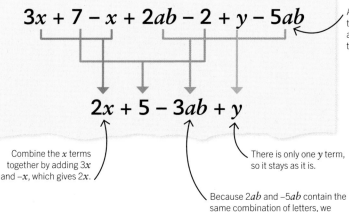

$$3x + 7 - x + 2ab - 2 + y - 5ab$$

Always read the sign before a term. This term is −5ab.

$$2x + 5 - 3ab + y$$

Combine the x terms together by adding 3x and −x, which gives 2x.

There is only one y term, so it stays as it is.

Because 2ab and −5ab contain the same combination of letters, we can combine them to give −3ab.

Substitution

The letters within terms and expressions can typically have any value. If we are given the value of a letter, we can replace that letter to find the total of, or evaluate, a term or expression. This is called substitution.

Substituting a number for a letter
When we are given the value of a letter in a term, we can substitute the letter with that value and evaluate the expression. Each time that letter appears in the same expression, we swap it for the same value.

x could be substituted with any value.

If we are told that x is 8, we can put 8 in place of the x in the term.

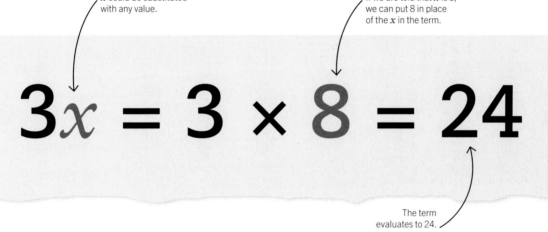

$$3x = 3 \times 8 = 24$$

The term evaluates to 24.

Substituting numbers into expressions

Question
Evaluate the expression $x - 3y + 5$, if $x = 7$ and $y = 2$.

Answer
1. To evaluate the expression, we will need to substitute the given values into the expression.

$$x - 3y + 5$$

$$7 - 3 \times 2 + 5$$

2. According to the order of operations (see page 28), we first carry out the multiplication, then the subtraction and addition.

$$7 - 3 \times 2 + 5$$
$$= 7 - 6 + 5$$
$$= 6$$

The value of the expression is 6 when $x = 7$ and $y = 2$.

Exponents in algebra

An exponent (or power) is an instruction to multiply a number, term, or expression by itself a certain number of times. In algebra, any term can have an exponent, and an exponent can be any number.

y to the power of 4

Exponents work with terms and expressions in the same way as they do with ordinary numbers (see page 22). An exponent with a term or expression tells us how many times we need to multiply that value by itself.

The exponent tells us how many times to multiply y.

$$y^4 = y \times y \times y \times y$$

⚙ Parentheses and exponents

Remember the order of operations (see page 28) when dealing with parentheses and exponents. Parentheses must be dealt with before exponents, so when an exponent is applied to parentheses, it tells us to multiply everything inside the parentheses that number of times.

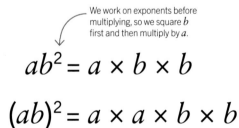

We work on exponents before multiplying, so we square b first and then multiply by a.

$$ab^2 = a \times b \times b$$

$$(ab)^2 = a \times a \times b \times b$$

Parentheses tell us we need to square both a and b.

🔍 Squared terms

When an expression contains a term with an exponent of two, it is called a quadratic expression (see page 100). Typically, quadratic expressions contain a squared variable, such as x, a number that is multiplied by that variable, and a constant (a number without a variable).

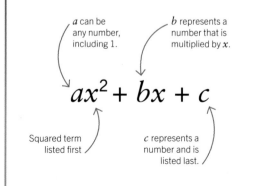

a can be any number, including 1.

b represents a number that is multiplied by x.

$$ax^2 + bx + c$$

Squared term listed first

c represents a number and is listed last.

Expanding parentheses

In algebra, expressions may have unknown values, or variables, inside parentheses. Expanding an expression means rewriting it with the parentheses removed. It can be useful to expand parentheses to separate the terms so they can be combined and simplified.

How to expand parentheses

We expand parentheses by multiplying each of the values inside the parentheses by the value outside the parentheses. This is known as the distributive property.

The parentheses have been expanded.

$$2(x + y) = 2x + 2y$$

Visualizing expansion of parentheses

We can see how the expansion of parentheses works by visualizing the expressions as the areas of rectangles.

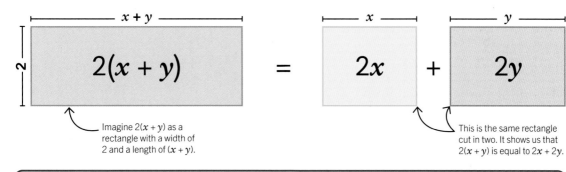

Imagine $2(x + y)$ as a rectangle with a width of 2 and a length of $(x + y)$.

This is the same rectangle cut in two. It shows us that $2(x + y)$ is equal to $2x + 2y$.

⚙ **Multiplying by negative terms**

Remember the rules of multiplying negative numbers when expanding parentheses that involve negative terms (see page 14). A negative term multiplied by a positive term gives a negative result. Two negative terms multiplied together give a positive result.

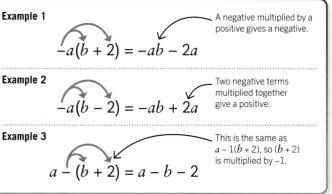

Example 1

A negative multiplied by a positive gives a negative.

$$-a(b + 2) = -ab - 2a$$

Example 2

Two negative terms multiplied together give a positive.

$$-a(b - 2) = -ab + 2a$$

Example 3

This is the same as $a - 1(b + 2)$, so $(b + 2)$ is multiplied by -1.

$$a - (b + 2) = a - b - 2$$

Expanding quadratics

Sometimes expressions contain more than one set of parentheses, which you may need to multiply together. When the same unknown value appears in both parentheses, expanding them will often result in a squared term, such as x^2. An expression that contains a term with a highest exponent of 2 is called a quadratic expression.

Key facts

✓ The distributive property allows us to expand multiple parentheses. Multiply each term in the first parentheses by each term in the second parentheses.

✓ If the same unknown appears in both sets of parentheses, it will give a squared term, such as x^2.

✓ A quadratic expression is one containing a term with a highest exponent of 2.

How to expand multiple parentheses
To expand two sets of parentheses, we multiply each term in the first set of parentheses by each term in the second set of parentheses and then combine like terms.

$$(x + 2)(x + 1) = x^2 + x + 2x + 2$$
$$= x^2 + 3x + 2$$

This is the quadratic expression in its standard form.

Visualizing the quadratic expression
We can better understand how to expand multiple parentheses by imagining the expression as the area of a rectangle.

We can split up the rectangle into smaller parts to help us see how to expand the parentheses.

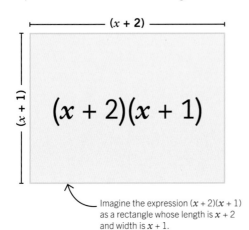

Imagine the expression $(x + 2)(x + 1)$ as a rectangle whose length is $x + 2$ and width is $x + 1$.

The smaller rectangles show that $(x + 2)(x + 1)$ is equal to $x^2 + x + 2x + 2$.

Factoring

Just as we can expand parentheses, sometimes it is useful to do the opposite, called factoring. It involves putting parentheses into an expression by dividing each term in the expression by a common factor, which is then placed outside the set of parentheses.

Key facts

✓ Factoring is the opposite of expanding.

✓ To factor an expression, find a common factor of its terms and take it outside a set of parentheses.

✓ Check that the factoring is correct by expanding the parentheses back out.

Factoring simple expressions

If the terms in a linear expression (an expression where the power of each variable is 1) share a common factor, we can divide the terms by that factor to factor the expression. The result of dividing the terms is enclosed by parentheses and the factor goes on the outside.

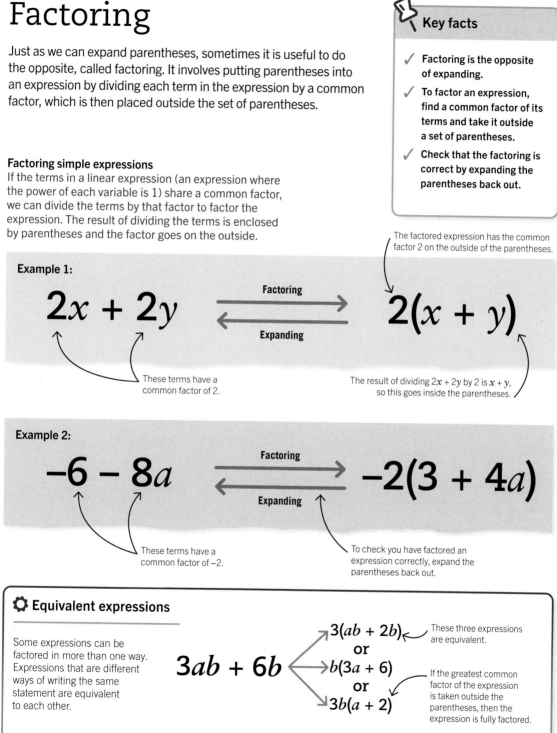

The factored expression has the common factor 2 on the outside of the parentheses.

Example 1:

$$2x + 2y \xrightleftharpoons[\text{Expanding}]{\text{Factoring}} 2(x + y)$$

These terms have a common factor of 2.

The result of dividing $2x + 2y$ by 2 is $x + y$, so this goes inside the parentheses.

Example 2:

$$-6 - 8a \xrightleftharpoons[\text{Expanding}]{\text{Factoring}} -2(3 + 4a)$$

These terms have a common factor of −2.

To check you have factored an expression correctly, expand the parentheses back out.

⚙ Equivalent expressions

Some expressions can be factored in more than one way. Expressions that are different ways of writing the same statement are equivalent to each other.

$$3ab + 6b \longleftrightarrow \begin{cases} 3(ab + 2b) \\ \text{or} \\ b(3a + 6) \\ \text{or} \\ 3b(a + 2) \end{cases}$$

These three expressions are equivalent.

If the greatest common factor of the expression is taken outside the parentheses, then the expression is fully factored.

Factoring quadratics

Some quadratic expressions can be factored as two sets of parentheses multiplied together. Knowing how to factor a quadratic expression can be useful when you need to solve a quadratic equation.

Factoring using rectangles

Factoring quadratics is the opposite of expanding quadratics (see page 100). One way to factor a quadratic expression is to visualize each part of the expression as the area of a rectangle.

1. We can factor $x^2 + 3x + 2$ by imagining each of the terms in the expression as the area of a rectangle.

$$x^2 \quad + \quad 3x \quad + \quad 2$$

2. The term x^2 can be drawn as a square with sides x units long and x units high. The term $3x$ can be broken down into three rectangles and 2 can be broken down into two squares.

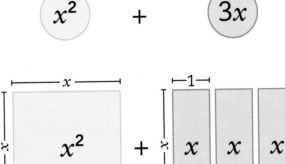

3. If we rearrange these shapes into one big rectangle, we can find its length and height.

The length is $(x + 2)$ and the height is $(x + 1)$.

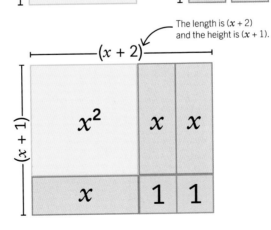

4. The length and height of the rectangle give us the parentheses to factor the quadratic. The factored quadratic is $(x + 1)(x + 2)$.

$$(x + 1)(x + 2)$$

We know that the area of a rectangle is found by multiplying its sides, so multiplying the expressions for the sides of the rectangle will give the expression we started with.

Checking your answer

Multiplying out factored parentheses is a useful way to check you have correctly factored an expression, because expanding is the opposite of factoring.

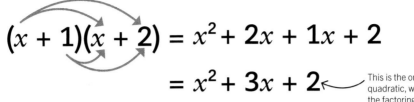

$$(x + 1)(x + 2) = x^2 + 2x + 1x + 2$$
$$= x^2 + 3x + 2$$

This is the original quadratic, which proves the factoring is correct.

Factoring without using rectangles

Quadratic expressions are typically in the form $ax^2 + bx + c$. To factor a simple expression where the value of a is 1, we simply need to look for a pair of numbers with a sum equal to b and a product equal to c. These will be the numbers that go in the parentheses.

In this expression c, called the constant, is −10.

1. To factor this expression, we need to find two numbers with a sum of 3 and a product of −10.

$$x^2 + 3x - 10$$

This means $1x^2$, so here the value of a, the coefficient of x^2, is 1.

The value of b, the coefficient of x, is 3.

2. One of the numbers we're looking for must be negative and the other positive, because we need a negative c and positive b.

Numbers with a product of −10	Sum
−1, 10	9 ✗
−5, 2	−3 ✗
−2, 5	3 ✔

The numbers −2 and 5 multiply to give −10 and add to give 3, so these are the factors we need.

3. We put these numbers into the parentheses with the x terms to give the factored expression $(x - 2)(x + 5)$.

$$(x - 2)(x + 5)$$

This is the factored expression.

4. We can check they are correct by expanding the parentheses out again.

$$= x^2 + 5x - 2x - 10$$
$$= x^2 + 3x - 10$$

Expand the parentheses to check the answer.

Factoring harder quadratic expressions

Sometimes quadratic expressions in the form $ax^2 + bx + c$ have a value for a that is not 1. Not all of these expressions can be factored, but some trial and error will reveal if they can.

Factoring when a is not 1

To work out if we can factor a quadratic expression when a is not 1, we first find a pair of terms that multiply together to give the x^2 term and put each of these in a set of parentheses. We then try different factor pairs for the other values in the parentheses until we find a factorization that matches the original expression.

1. Here is a quadratic expression where the value of a is 3.

a is 3.   *b* is 11.

$$3x^2 + 11x + 6$$

c is 6.

2. To factor the expression, you need to find a pair of terms that multiply together to give $3x^2$. As 3 is a prime number, the two terms must be $3x$ and x.

$$(3x + ?)(x + ?)$$

3. To find the other numbers for the factorization, we look for two numbers that will multiply together to equal the value of c. In this expression c is 6, so we write out the factor pairs of 6.

4. To work out which numbers are correct, we try each factor pair in the parentheses and expand them to see which gives the original quadratic expression. The different orders of the factor pair change the result, so we try them both ways around.

Factor pairs of 6	
1	6
2	3
−1	−6
−2	−3

The numbers we're looking for will be positive, because a and b are positive, so we can disregard these negative pairs.

Factor pairs	Expansion	
$(3x + 1)(x + 6)$	$3x^2 + 19x + 6$	✗
$(3x + 6)(x + 1)$	$3x^2 + 9x + 6$	✗
$(3x + 3)(x + 2)$	$3x^2 + 9x + 6$	✗
$(3x + 2)(x + 3)$	$3x^2 + 11x + 6$	✓

This matches the original quadratic expression, so it must be the correct factorization.

5. The correct factorization is $(3x + 2)(x + 3)$.

$$3x^2 + 11x + 6 = (3x + 2)(x + 3)$$

The difference of two squares

Some quadratic expressions don't have a middle, x, term and consist of just an x^2 term and a number. In some special situations, we can still factor the expression using the rule of the difference of two squares.

Key facts

✓ The difference of two squares is a method of factoring for some quadratic equations.

✓ You can use the rule of the difference of two squares to factor a quadratic expression in the form:
$$p^2 - q^2$$

✓ The factoring will always have the form:
$$(p + q)(p - q)$$

Visualizing the difference of two squares
When we have a quadratic expression that consists of one square value subtracted from another square value, such as $x^2 - 16$, we call it the difference of two squares. These expressions are in the form $p^2 - q^2$. Their factoring will always have the form $(p + q)(p - q)$.

1. We can factor the expression $9x^2 - 4$ using the difference of two squares, as it consists of one square value subtracted from another.

$$9x^2 - 4$$

This quadratic expression is in the form $p^2 - q^2$.

2. We can visualize the expression as a shape. Because 9 is equal to 3×3, we can imagine $9x^2$ as a square with sides $3x$ units long. The full expression we need to factor is $9x^2 - 4$, so we imagine the -4 as a square with sides 2 units long that is cut away from the larger square.

3. We can split up the shape and rearrange it to form a rectangle. This allows us to find the lengths of its sides and, therefore, the factors of the expression $9x^2 - 4$.

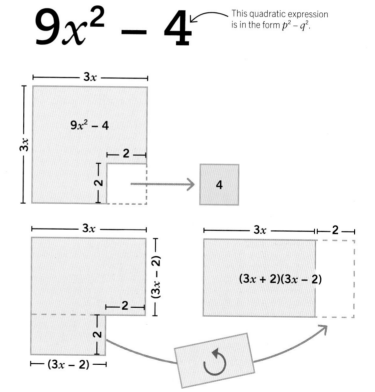

4. The rectangle has sides $(3x + 2)$ and $(3x - 2)$, so the factored expression is $(3x + 2)(3x - 2)$.

The factored expression has the form $(p + q)(p - q)$.

$$9x^2 - 4 = (3x + 2)(3x - 2)$$

Algebraic fractions

Sometimes algebraic expressions have fractions containing unknown values in them. These fractions follow the same rules as fractions composed of numbers. It is often useful to simplify algebraic fractions to make them easier to work with.

Simplifying algebraic fractions

If the numerator and denominator of an algebraic fraction share a common factor, we can simplify the fraction by canceling out the common factors in the numerator and denominator.

If a number appears in both the numerator and the denominator, it cancels itself out.

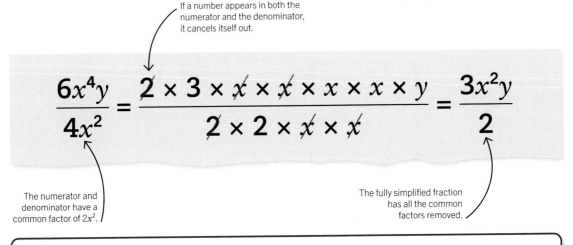

$$\frac{6x^4y}{4x^2} = \frac{2 \times 3 \times \not{x} \times \not{x} \times x \times x \times y}{2 \times 2 \times \not{x} \times \not{x}} = \frac{3x^2y}{2}$$

The numerator and denominator have a common factor of $2x^2$.

The fully simplified fraction has all the common factors removed.

🔍 Factoring to simplify

Sometimes expressions in algebraic fractions need to be factored to reveal a common factor.

1. In this algebraic fraction, both the numerator and denominator contain + and − signs, and there's no obvious common factor.

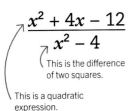

$$\frac{x^2 + 4x - 12}{x^2 - 4}$$

This is the difference of two squares.

This is a quadratic expression.

2. To simplify the fraction, we can factor the numerator and denominator (see pages 102–103 and 105).

$$\frac{(x - 2)(x + 6)}{(x - 2)(x + 2)}$$

Now we can see the numerator and denominator have a common factor of $(x - 2)$.

3. The common factor of $(x - 2)$ cancels itself out in the numerator and denominator, leaving the fully simplified fraction.

$$\frac{x + 6}{x + 2}$$

There are no more common factors, because the remaining values are part of an addition.

Adding and subtracting algebraic fractions

Algebraic fractions can be added and subtracted, but they often need to be manipulated first. Problems involving algebraic fractions sometimes look complicated, but the rules are the same as for numerical fractions (see page 49).

see page 49

Key facts

✓ When doing arithmetic with algebraic fractions, follow the same rules as for numerical fractions.

✓ To add or subtract two algebraic fractions, they first need a common denominator.

✓ One way to find a common denominator is to multiply the denominators by each other.

Fractions with different denominators

Fractions with the same denominator can be added or subtracted just like numerical fractions. To add or subtract fractions with different denominators, we need to give them a common denominator.

Method 1
These fractions don't have a common denominator, so we need to change at least one of them to add the two fractions together.

1. Since x is a factor of $3x$, we can easily find a common denominator for these two fractions.

$$\frac{1}{x} + \frac{2}{3x}$$

2. Multiply the numerator and denominator of the first fraction by 3.

$$= \frac{3 \times 1}{3 \times x} + \frac{2}{3x}$$

3. Now that the two fractions have a common denominator, they can be added.

$$= \frac{3}{3x} + \frac{2}{3x}$$

4. Add the numerators. The denominator stays as it is.

$$= \frac{3 + 2}{3x}$$

5. This gives us the sum of the two algebraic fractions.

$$= \frac{5}{3x}$$

Method 2
If it isn't easy to spot a common denominator for two fractions, multiplying the denominators by each other will always work.

1. Subtracting fractions is similar to adding them. In this case, there is no obvious common denominator.

$$\frac{3}{x + 2} - \frac{2}{x}$$

2. Multiply the numerator and denominator of each fraction by the denominator of the other to give them both a common denominator.

$$= \frac{3x}{x(x + 2)} - \frac{2(x + 2)}{x(x + 2)}$$

3. The denominators are now the same, so the two fractions can be subtracted. Expand the parentheses in the numerator.

$$= \frac{3x - 2(x + 2)}{x(x + 2)}$$

4. Simplify the numerator by combining the like terms.

$$= \frac{3x - 2x - 4}{x(x + 2)}$$

5. This gives us the difference of the two original fractions.

$$= \frac{x - 4}{x(x + 2)}$$

Multiplying and dividing algebraic fractions

Sometimes we need to multiply and divide fractions that contain unknown values. Algebraic fractions can be multiplied and divided in the same way as numerical fractions.

Multiplication

To multiply two algebraic fractions together, follow the same steps as you would for numerical fractions (see page 51).

1. To multiply these algebraic fractions, we follow the same steps as for multiplying ordinary numerical fractions.

$$\frac{2a}{3} \times \frac{a}{3b}$$

2. Multiply each numerator together. Multiply each denominator together.

$$= \frac{2a \times a}{3 \times 3b}$$

3. This gives us the product of the multiplication.

$$= \frac{2a^2}{9b}$$

Division

To divide two algebraic fractions, find the reciprocal of the second fraction by flipping the fraction upside down, then multiply the numerators and denominators.

1. To divide these fractions, we follow the same steps as for numerical fractions.

$$\frac{2a}{3} \div \frac{a}{3b}$$

2. Flip the second fraction upside down and replace the division symbol with a multiplication symbol.

$$= \frac{2a}{3} \times \frac{3b}{a}$$

3. Multiply the numerators together and multiply the denominators together.

$$= \frac{2a \times 3b}{3 \times a}$$

4. The numerator and denominator in this fraction have a common factor of $3a$, so we divide both by $3a$ to simplify.

$$= \frac{6ab}{3a}$$

5. Any number divided by 1 is itself, so the result of the division is $2b$.

$$= \frac{2b}{1} = 2b$$

🔍 Factoring first

It can be a good idea to simplify a complex algebraic fraction before multiplying or dividing. Numerators and denominators can be factored in the same way as normal algebraic expressions (see pages 101–104).

$$\frac{x^2 + 2x - 8}{3x + 12} = \frac{(x + 4)(x - 2)}{3(x + 4)} = \frac{(x - 2)}{3}$$

Formulas

A formula describes the fixed mathematical relationship between two or more values. It can be useful when you want to find out the value of one variable and know the other variables. Formulas exist for all sorts of situations, such as finding lengths in geometry or working out an object's speed in physics.

Distance around a Ferris wheel
Having a general formula for the circumference of a circle (see page 76) means we can work out the distance around any circle if we know its radius.

The circumference (C) is the subject of the formula. It is the value we are trying to work out.

Calculating $2 \times \pi \times$ radius will give us the circumference.

$$C = 2\pi r$$

The radius (r) of the Ferris wheel is the distance from its center to the edge.

This formula can be used to find the circumference of any circle. You just need to know the circle's radius.

The circumference (C) is the distance around the outer edge.

Using formulas

To use a formula, we swap in, or substitute, known values for letters in the formula and evaluate the expression. This gives us the value of the subject.

Question
The formula for the area (A) of a trapezoid is:

$$A = \frac{1}{2}(a + b) \times h$$

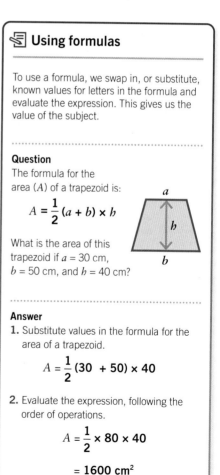

What is the area of this trapezoid if $a = 30$ cm, $b = 50$ cm, and $h = 40$ cm?

Answer
1. Substitute values in the formula for the area of a trapezoid.

$$A = \frac{1}{2}(30 + 50) \times 40$$

2. Evaluate the expression, following the order of operations.

$$A = \frac{1}{2} \times 80 \times 40$$

$$= 1600 \text{ cm}^2$$

Rearranging formulas

A formula describes the relationship between variables. If the value of the subject of a formula is known but we want to find out the value of one of the other variables, we can rearrange the formula to make the unknown the subject.

Key facts

✓ Rearranging a formula allows us to change the subject.

✓ A new subject is isolated by removing the operations around it in reverse order.

✓ Actions taken to rearrange a formula must be done to both sides of the formula.

Unpacking a formula
To make a variable the subject of a formula, we remove the operations around it in the reverse order that they would be applied, according to the order of operations (see page 28). By always making any changes to both sides at once, the formula is kept balanced and remains true.

1. Suppose we know that the temperature is 86°F. We can convert this measurement from Fahrenheit to Celsius by using a formula for converting between the two units.

2. This formula for converting temperature has Fahrenheit (F) as the subject. To make Celsius (C) the subject, we need to rearrange the formula.

$$F = 1.8C + 32$$

3. According to the order of operations, + 32 would be the last operation performed on C. So we remove this first by subtracting 32 from both sides.

$$F - 32 = 1.8C + 32 - 32$$
$$F - 32 = 1.8C$$

These two terms cancel each other out.

4. Now we need to do the opposite of multiplying by 1.8 to isolate C. So we divide both sides by 1.8.

$$\frac{(F - 32)}{1.8} = \frac{1.8C}{1.8}$$
$$\frac{(F - 32)}{1.8} = C$$

Dividing by 1.8 cancels out multiplying by 1.8.

5. We can write the formula the other way around to show that C is now the subject of the formula.

$$C = \frac{(F - 32)}{1.8}$$

6. Finally, we can substitute our measurement of F into the formula to find C. 86°F is 30°C.

$$C = \frac{(86 - 32)}{1.8} = 30$$

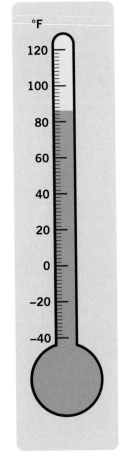

Functions

A function is a mathematical expression that takes an input value, such as a single number; processes the input according to a specific rule; and gives an output value. It is often represented as $f(x)$.

Function machines

Functions work a little like machines—you put something into a machine and the machine produces an output. When we work with functions, we put an input, such as a number, into the function. The function operates on the number and produces an output.

> **Key facts**
>
> ✓ A function has an input and an output.
>
> ✓ A function works like a machine, operating on an input to give an output.
>
> ✓ We use the notation $f(x)$ to represent functions, where f is the name of the function and x is the input value, or variable.

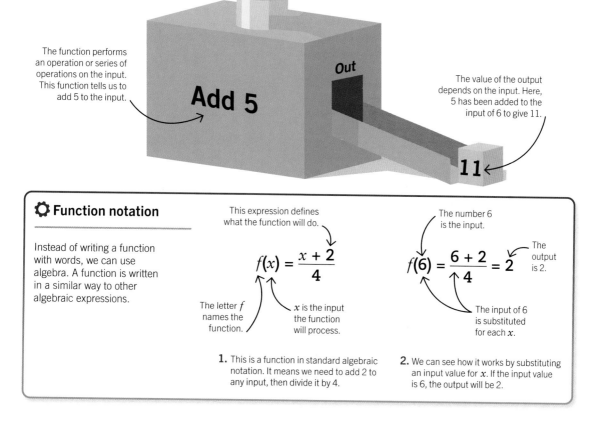

We can put a number into the function input. Here, we are using the number 6 as an input.

6

In

The function performs an operation or series of operations on the input. This function tells us to add 5 to the input.

Add 5

Out

The value of the output depends on the input. Here, 5 has been added to the input of 6 to give 11.

11

⚙ Function notation

Instead of writing a function with words, we can use algebra. A function is written in a similar way to other algebraic expressions.

This expression defines what the function will do.

$$f(x) = \frac{x + 2}{4}$$

The letter f names the function.

x is the input the function will process.

The number 6 is the input.

$$f(6) = \frac{6 + 2}{4} = 2$$

The output is 2.

The input of 6 is substituted for each x.

1. This is a function in standard algebraic notation. It means we need to add 2 to any input, then divide it by 4.

2. We can see how it works by substituting an input value for x. If the input value is 6, the output will be 2.

Inverse functions

A function takes an input, x, and gives an output, y. If we know the output of a function and want to work out what the input is, we perform the opposite of the function. This reversed version of the original function gives you the inverse function.

Reversing the machine
Applying the inverse of a function is like sending a number backward through a function machine. If going forward through the machine is the function f, the name of the inverse function is f^{-1}.

The input of this function is 2.

To see how the inverse of the function, f, works, we can use the output of f as the input of the inverse function, f^{-1}.

Using the output of f as the input of f^{-1} gives the original input to f.

This is the equation that defines the inverted function. It is the reverse of the original function.

$$f(x) = \frac{x + 2}{4}$$

The output of the function is 1.

$$f^{-1}(x) = 4x - 2$$

Function

Inverse function

⚙ **Finding an inverse function**

Because an inverse function "swaps" the input, x, with the output, y, to find the equation of an inverse function, we simply swap the variables in the equation of the original function.

1. First, we take the original function, f.

$$f(x) = \frac{x + 2}{4}$$

2. Use y as the name of the output of f.

$$\frac{x + 2}{4} = y$$

3. To find the inverse function, swap each x for a y, and each y for an x.

$$\frac{y + 2}{4} = x$$

4. Cross-multiply, then rewrite the equation to make y the subject of the equation (see page 110).

$$y + 2 = 4x$$
$$y = 4x - 2$$

5. This gives the new inverse function and is written as f^{-1}.

$$f^{-1}(x) = 4x - 2$$

The inverse of the function f

Composite functions

When the output of one function is fed into a second function as an input, we call it a composite function. The whole combined process can be written as a single composite function.

Building a composite function

A composite function where two functions are carried out can be written $f(g(x))$ or $(f \circ g)(x)$. A composite function $f(g(x))$ is like a machine that performs function g, then function f.

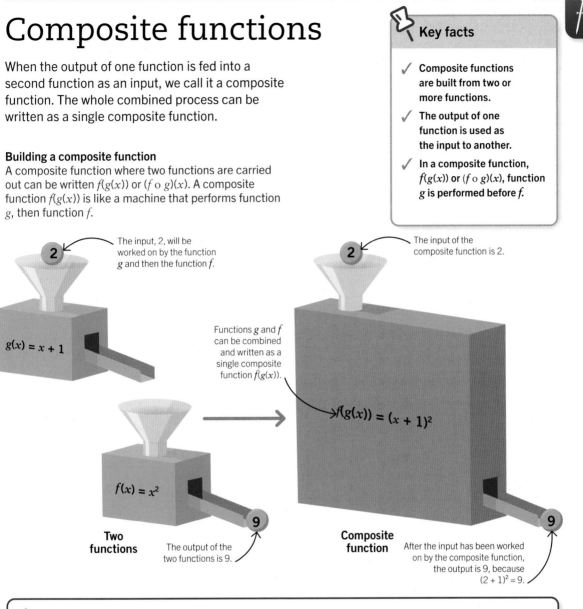

The input, 2, will be worked on by the function g and then the function f.

$g(x) = x + 1$

Functions g and f can be combined and written as a single composite function $f(g(x))$.

$f(x) = x^2$

Two functions

The output of the two functions is 9.

9

The input of the composite function is 2.

$f(g(x)) = (x + 1)^2$

Composite function

After the input has been worked on by the composite function, the output is 9, because $(2 + 1)^2 = 9$.

9

⚙ Order of functions

The name of the composite function shows which function is performed first, so the order of letters is important. The function written next to the variable, x, must be carried out first. When $f(x) = x^2$ and $g(x) = x + 1$, is $f(g(x))$ equal to $g(f(x))$?

1. First, we work out the composite function for $f(g(x))$.
$$f(g(x)) = f(x + 1) = (x + 1)^2 = x^2 + 2x + 1$$

2. Next, work out the composite function for $g(f(x))$.
$$g(f(x)) = g(x^2) = (x^2) + 1 = x^2 + 1$$

3. So $f(g(x))$ is not equal to $g(f(x))$.

Powers and calculations

Higher powers and estimating powers

When we multiply a number by itself, we say it has been raised to a power (see page 22). Powers are also called exponents or indices. We've already covered numbers being raised to a power of 2 (squared) and raised to a power of 3 (cubed), but numbers can be raised to any power. Powers with an exponent number higher than 3 are called higher powers.

> **Key facts**
>
> ✓ Powers are also called exponents or indices.
> ✓ Numbers can be raised to any power.
> ✓ The value of decimals raised to a power can be estimated using a number line.

Powers of 10

Just as numbers are infinite, the number of powers to which a number can be raised is infinite, too. Raising 10 to different powers creates the sequence shown below.

Ten	10^1	10	10
Hundred	10^2	100	10×10
Thousand	10^3	1000	$10 \times 10 \times 10$
Ten thousand	10^4	10 000	$10 \times 10 \times 10 \times 10$
Hundred thousand	10^5	100 000	$10 \times 10 \times 10 \times 10 \times 10$
Million	10^6	1 000 000	$10 \times 10 \times 10 \times 10 \times 10 \times 10$
Billion	10^9	1 000 000 000	$10 \times 10 \times 10 \times 10 \times 10 \times 10 \times 10 \times 10 \times 10$
Trillion	10^{12}	1 000 000 000 000	$10 \times 10 \times 10 \times 10 \times 10 \times 10 \times 10 \times 10 \times 10 \times 10 \times 10 \times 10$

The exponent number tells you the number of zeros in the number.

Estimating powers

Calculating an exact answer for a decimal raised to a power can be complicated without a calculator, but using a number line can make it easy to estimate the answer. Here, we're estimating the value of 2.8^2.

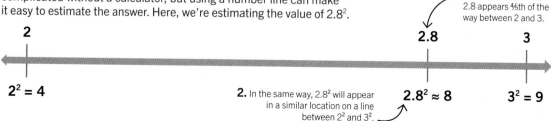

1. On a number line, 2.8 appears ⅘th of the way between 2 and 3.

2. In the same way, 2.8^2 will appear in a similar location on a line between 2^2 and 3^2.

2   2.8   3

$2^2 = 4$ $2.8^2 \approx 8$ $3^2 = 9$

Roots

Just as a number can be squared or cubed, there is an inverse or opposite process. This is called finding the square or cube root. Roots are represented with the symbol $\sqrt{\ }$.

Square roots
The square root of a number is a number that, when squared, equals the original number. For example, the square root of 9 is 3, because $3 \times 3 = 9$.

Square root symbol

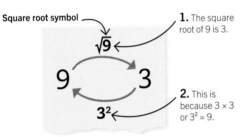

1. The square root of 9 is 3.

2. This is because 3×3 or $3^2 = 9$.

Cube roots
The cube root of a number is a number that, when cubed, equals the original number. For example, 3 is the cube root of 27, because $3 \times 3 \times 3 = 27$.

Cube root symbol

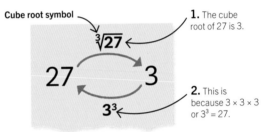

1. The cube root of 27 is 3.

2. This is because $3 \times 3 \times 3$ or $3^3 = 27$.

Estimating roots
Most roots are complicated decimals and are hard to estimate without a calculator. You can estimate the square root of a number by picking numbers above and below it that have whole number square roots and squaring the square roots of those numbers. Then refine your estimate with decimal values.

1. $\sqrt{21}$ will be between $\sqrt{16} = 4$ and $\sqrt{25} = 5$.

2. Start by squaring the number midway between the two square roots: 4.5^2. Then continue to refine your estimate.

3. This can be rounded up to 21.

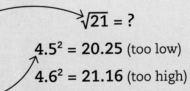

$\sqrt{21} = ?$

$4.5^2 = 20.25$ (too low)

$4.6^2 = 21.16$ (too high)

$4.55^2 = 20.7025$ (too low)

$4.58^2 = 20.9764$

🔍 Using a calculator to find roots

Scientific calculators have buttons you can use to find square roots, cube roots, and higher roots.

Square and cube roots
Enter the number you need to find the square or cube root for, then press the dedicated button.

$\sqrt{16} =$ | 16 | $\sqrt[2]{x}$ | = 4

$\sqrt[3]{216} =$ | 216 | $\sqrt[3]{x}$ | = 6

Higher roots
For higher powers, you use the root button. Enter the number, tap the root button, then enter the root.

$\sqrt[4]{81} =$ | 81 | $\sqrt[y]{x}$ | 4 | = 3

Negative powers

A power can be negative. Just as raising a number to a positive power is a way of expressing repeated multiplication, raising a number to a negative power is a way of expressing repeated division.

Inverting the number

There is a simple way to understand raising a number to a negative power. You turn the number upside down, writing it as the reciprocal, and change the power to a positive.

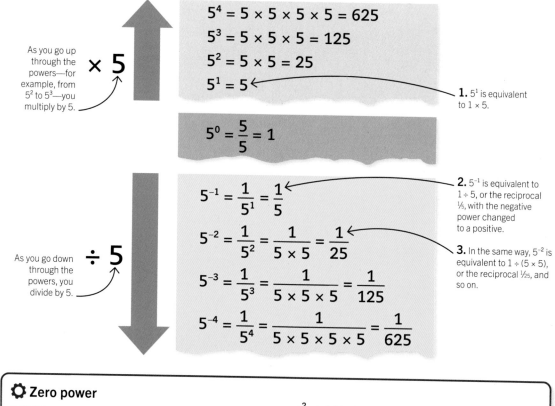

As you go up through the powers—for example, from 5^2 to 5^3—you multiply by 5.

$\times 5$

$$5^4 = 5 \times 5 \times 5 \times 5 = 625$$
$$5^3 = 5 \times 5 \times 5 = 125$$
$$5^2 = 5 \times 5 = 25$$
$$5^1 = 5$$

1. 5^1 is equivalent to 1×5.

$$5^0 = \frac{5}{5} = 1$$

$$5^{-1} = \frac{1}{5^1} = \frac{1}{5}$$

2. 5^{-1} is equivalent to $1 \div 5$, or the reciprocal $\frac{1}{5}$, with the negative power changed to a positive.

$$5^{-2} = \frac{1}{5^2} = \frac{1}{5 \times 5} = \frac{1}{25}$$

3. In the same way, 5^{-2} is equivalent to $1 \div (5 \times 5)$, or the reciprocal $\frac{1}{25}$, and so on.

As you go down through the powers, you divide by 5.

$\div 5$

$$5^{-3} = \frac{1}{5^3} = \frac{1}{5 \times 5 \times 5} = \frac{1}{125}$$

$$5^{-4} = \frac{1}{5^4} = \frac{1}{5 \times 5 \times 5 \times 5} = \frac{1}{625}$$

⚙ Zero power

You can see above that $5^0 = 5 \div 5 = 1$. Raising any number (other than 0) to the power 0 will always result in 1, because the result of dividing a number by itself is always 1. We can show this using algebra:

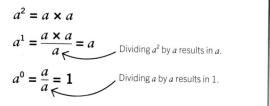

$$a^2 = a \times a$$

$$a^1 = \frac{a \times a}{a} = a$$

Dividing a^2 by a results in a.

$$a^0 = \frac{a}{a} = 1$$

Dividing a by a results in 1.

Multiplying and dividing with powers

There are some rules that make it easier to perform calculations with powers. These rules are called the exponent laws (or the laws of indices or index laws). Using these laws often means you can avoid writing out calculations involving powers in full.

Key facts

✓ Calculating with powers can be simplified using a series of rules called the exponent laws.

✓ When multiplying numbers raised to powers, add the powers together.

✓ When dividing numbers raised to powers, subtract one power from the other.

Multiplying powers
When multiplying numbers that have been raised by powers, the answer can be arrived at by simply adding the powers together. This general rule can be expressed using an algebraic formula. Note that this rule only works when the numbers being raised to a power in the calculation are the same.

The calculation becomes $4 \times 8 = 32$.

$2^5 = 32$

$$2^2 \times 2^3 = (2 \times 2) \times (2 \times 2 \times 2) = 2^5$$

$$2^2 \times 2^3 = 2^{2+3} = 2^5$$

The power of the answer is the sum of the powers being multiplied.

$$a^n \times a^m = a^{n+m}$$

Dividing powers
The rule of multiplying powers is reversed when dividing. Instead of adding the powers, one is subtracted from the other. Again, the law can be expressed using an algebraic formula. The law only works when the numbers being raised to a power in the calculation are the same.

The calculation becomes $81 \div 9 = 9$.

$3^2 = 9$

$$3^4 \div 3^2 = \frac{3 \times 3 \times 3 \times 3}{3 \times 3} = 3 \times 3 = 3^2$$

The fraction can be simplified.

$$3^4 \div 3^2 = 3^{4-2} = 3^2$$

Subtract the second power from the first power.

$$a^n \div a^m = a^{n-m}$$

Raising a power to a power

Another exponent law (see opposite) when calculating with powers concerns raising one power to another power. For example, what is $(3^3)^2$, or in other words, 3^3 multiplied by 3^3? This complex calculation can be simplified using the following exponent law.

Key facts

✓ Calculating with powers can be simplified using a series of rules called the exponent laws.

✓ When raising one power to another, multiply the powers together.

Raising one power to another

When a number that is already raised to a power is then raised to a further power, the resulting value can be found by multiplying the powers together. This rule can be expressed using an algebraic formula. The rule also works for negative powers—the normal rules of calculating with signs apply. More than two powers can be involved in the calculation.

The calculation becomes $27 \times 27 = 729$.

$3^6 = 729$

$$(3^3)^2 = 3^3 \times 3^3 = (3 \times 3 \times 3) \times (3 \times 3 \times 3) = 3^6$$

$$(3^3)^2 = 3^{3 \times 2} = 3^6$$

Multiply the powers together to find the new, higher power.

$$(a^n)^m = a^{nm}$$

Using the exponent laws

Question

Use the three exponent laws to find the value of $(2 \times 2^4 \times 2^{-3})^2 \div 2^2$.

Answer

1. First, evaluate the parentheses $(2 \times 2^4 \times 2^{-3})$ using the law of multiplying powers.

$$(2 \times 2^4 \times 2^{-3}) = 2^{1+4-3} = 2^2$$

2. Evaluate $(2^2)^2$ by multiplying the powers together.

$$(2^2)^2 = 2^{2 \times 2} = 2^4$$

3. Finally, evaluate $2^4 \div 2^2$ using the law of dividing powers.

$$2^4 \div 2^2 = 2^{4-2} = 2^2 = 4$$

Fractional powers and roots

Powers do not need to be whole numbers. They can also be fractions, written in the form $a^{1/2}$.

Powers as roots

Raising a number to a fractional power with a numerator of 1, such as $4^{1/2}$ or $4^{1/3}$, is equivalent to finding its root: $\sqrt{4}$ or $\sqrt[3]{4}$. We can prove this using the formula for multiplying powers: $a^n \times a^m = a^{n+m}$ (see page 118).

	Square roots	**Cube roots**

1. When multiplying two or more numbers raised to powers, add together the exponents to get the answer.

$$4^{1/2} \times 4^{1/2} = 4^{1/2 + 1/2} = 4^1 = 4$$

$$8^{1/3} \times 8^{1/3} \times 8^{1/3} = 8^{1/3 + 1/3 + 1/3} = 8^1 = 8$$

2. Roots multiplied together make the same number.

$$\sqrt{4} \times \sqrt{4} = 4$$

$$\sqrt[3]{8} \times \sqrt[3]{8} \times \sqrt[3]{8} = 8$$

3. Therefore, raising a number by a fractional power is the same as finding its root.

$$4^{1/2} = \sqrt{4} = 2$$

$$8^{1/3} = \sqrt[3]{8} = 2$$

4. This can be made into a general rule for any fractional power where the numerator is 1.

$$a^{1/n} = \sqrt[n]{a}$$

Mixed powers

Raising a number to a fractional power with a numerator greater than 1, such as $2/3$, is the equivalent of two actions: finding its root ($1/3$) and raising by a whole number power ($1/3 \times 2$). To calculate $1000^{2/3}$, split it into $(1000)^{1/3 \times 2}$.

1. Work out the root first.

$$1000^{1/3} = \sqrt[3]{1000} = 10$$

2. Then work out the power.

$$(\sqrt[3]{1000})^2 = 10^2 = 100$$

$$1000^{2/3} = 100$$

⚙ Negative fractional powers

A fractional power can be negative, and as with a negative whole number power (see page 117), this means applying the fractional power to the reciprocal. Therefore, to calculate $1000^{-2/3}$, we apply the root and the power to the reciprocal of 1000.

$$1000^{-2/3} = \frac{1}{(1000)^{1/3 \times 2}}$$

$$= \frac{1}{10^2} = \frac{1}{100} = 0.01$$

Practice questions
Calculating with powers

Using the exponent laws makes it much easier to calculate with powers. Here are a few practice questions to try out.

Question
Evaluate $(13^2)^4)^0$.

Answer
1. When raising a power to different powers, multiply the exponents together to get a single power.

$$(13^2)^4)^0 = 13^{(2 \times 4 \times 0)} = 13^0$$

2. A number raised to the power zero always equals 1.

$$(13^2)^4)^0 = 1$$

Question
Evaluate $(1\frac{1}{2})^3 + 5(8^2 \times 8^{-3}) - (16^{\frac{1}{4}})$.

Answer
1. Look at the first term of the expression. Apply the power to both the numerator and denominator of the mixed number.

$$\left(1\frac{1}{2}\right)^3 = \left(\frac{3}{2}\right)^3 = \frac{27}{8}$$

2. For the second term, multiply the numbers inside the parentheses by adding the exponents together.

$$5(8^2 \times 8^{-3}) = 5 \times 8^{(2 + -3)} = 5 \times 8^{-1}$$

3. Because the resulting power is negative, convert the number into a reciprocal fraction to make the power positive.

$$5 \times 8^{-1} = 5 \times \frac{1}{8} = \frac{5}{8}$$

4. Moving on to the third term, $16^{\frac{1}{4}}$ is the same as the fourth root of 16, or $\sqrt[4]{16}$.

$$\sqrt[4]{16} = 2$$

5. Add together the fractions derived from steps 1 and 3 to combine the first two terms.

$$\frac{27}{8} + \frac{5}{8} = \frac{32}{8} = 4$$

6. Complete the simplified expression by subtracting the result of step 4 from the result of step 5.

$$\left(1\frac{1}{2}\right)^3 + 5(8^2 \times 8^{-3}) - (16^{\frac{1}{4}}) = 4 - 2 = 2$$

Question
Evaluate $64^{-\frac{1}{3}} \div \left(\frac{1}{128}\right)^{\frac{3}{7}}$.

Answer
1. As the first term has a negative power, convert the number into a reciprocal fraction to make the power positive.

$$64^{-\frac{1}{3}} = \left(\frac{1}{64}\right)^{\frac{1}{3}}$$

2. Raising the fraction to the power of ⅓ is the same as finding its cube root.

$$\left(\frac{1}{64}\right)^{\frac{1}{3}} = \left(\frac{1}{\sqrt[3]{64}}\right) = \frac{1}{4}$$

3. The fractional power in the second term has a numerator above 1, so split it into its root and power.

$$\left(\frac{1}{128}\right)^{\frac{3}{7}} = \left(\frac{1}{128}\right)^{\frac{1}{7} \times 3}$$

4. Evaluate the root first, then the power.

$$\left(\frac{1}{128}\right)^{\frac{1}{7}} = \left(\frac{1}{\sqrt[7]{128}}\right) = \frac{1}{2}$$

$$\left(\frac{1}{\sqrt[7]{128}}\right)^3 = \frac{1}{8}$$

5. Complete the simplified expression.

$$64^{-\frac{1}{3}} \div \left(\frac{1}{128}\right)^{\frac{3}{7}} = \frac{1}{4} \div \frac{1}{8} = 2$$

Irrational square roots and irrational numbers

Only some whole numbers have a square root that is also a whole number. (These are called "square numbers"; see page 22). The square roots of all other whole numbers are irrational, which means they cannot be written as a fraction composed of integers or with a finite number of decimals.

Key facts

✓ An irrational number cannot be written as a fraction composed of integers and has an infinite number of nonrepeating decimals.

✓ An irrational square root is a square root that is an irrational number.

✓ The most accurate way to write the value of an irrational square root is as $\sqrt{a}$.

Irrational square roots

Irrational square roots are left in the form $\sqrt{a}$, because this is a totally accurate way of representing the number. Using decimals to express the number would be less accurate, because the decimals are infinite and therefore cannot be written out in full.

$\sqrt{4}$ is not irrational, because 2 is a whole number that can be written out in full.

$$\sqrt{4} = 2$$

$$\sqrt{5} = 2.2360679774997896964091 7366...$$

$\sqrt{5}$ has a never-ending string of nonrepeating decimals, so it is most accurately expressed in square root form.

Calculations with irrational square roots

It is impossible to write down an irrational square root in digits with total accuracy, but that does not mean it cannot be used in calculations. For example, for a square with an area of 3 m², the length of each of its sides has to be given in square root form.

1. To find the area of a square, you square the lengths of its sides.

$$\text{Length}^2 = \text{area of a square}$$

$$\text{Length} = \sqrt{\text{area}}$$

2. Therefore, to find the length of each side, you take the square root of the area.

3 m²

3. The area of the square is 3 m².

$\sqrt{3}$ m

4. The length of each side is therefore $\sqrt{3}$, which is the most accurate way of expressing the value.

Simplifying square root expressions

There are some basic rules we use to simplify expressions involving irrational square roots. These rules make it possible to reach an accurate answer without having to use approximate values for the irrational root.

Multiplying square roots

Multiplying two numbers and finding the square root of the result is the same as multiplying the square roots of the two numbers. When simplifying expressions involving square roots, look for pairs of factors, one of which is a perfect square. By finding the square root of each factor separately and multiplying them together using this rule, the result is simplified.

$$\sqrt{ab} = \sqrt{a} \times \sqrt{b}$$

$$\sqrt{45} = \sqrt{9 \times 5} = \sqrt{9} \times \sqrt{5} = 3\sqrt{5}$$

1. Simplify $\sqrt{45}$ by splitting it into factors of 9 and 5.

2. $\sqrt{9}$ is 3, so we can simplify further to $3 \times \sqrt{5}$.

3. $\sqrt{5}$ stays in square root form, because 5 can't be broken down further.

Squaring square roots

When a square root is squared, or multiplied by itself, it will give the number inside the square root sign. This is a result of applying the multiplying square roots rule to the same number.

$$\sqrt{a} \times \sqrt{a} = a$$

$$\sqrt{7} \times \sqrt{7} = 7$$

Dividing square roots

Dividing one number by another and finding the resulting square root is the same as dividing the square root of the numerator by the square root of the denominator.

$$\sqrt{\frac{a}{b}} = \frac{\sqrt{a}}{\sqrt{b}}$$

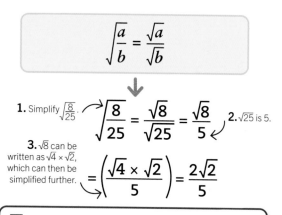

1. Simplify $\sqrt{\frac{8}{25}}$.

$$\sqrt{\frac{8}{25}} = \frac{\sqrt{8}}{\sqrt{25}} = \frac{\sqrt{8}}{5}$$

2. $\sqrt{25}$ is 5.

3. $\sqrt{8}$ can be written as $\sqrt{4} \times \sqrt{2}$, which can then be simplified further.

$$= \left(\frac{\sqrt{4} \times \sqrt{2}}{5}\right) = \frac{2\sqrt{2}}{5}$$

📄 **Writing expressions in the form $a\sqrt{b}$**

Question
Simplify $\sqrt{48}$ in the form $a\sqrt{b}$, where a and b are integers and b is prime.

Answer
1. Look for factors that are square numbers. 16 is a square number, and 16 and 3 are factors of 48.

$$\sqrt{48} = \sqrt{16 \times 3} = \sqrt{16} \times \sqrt{3}$$

2. As 3 is a prime, leave $\sqrt{3}$ in square root form but break down $\sqrt{16}$ further.

$$\sqrt{48} = 4\sqrt{3}$$

Irrational square roots in fractions

When a fraction is constructed using an irrational square root, there are a few rules to follow in order to complete a calculation correctly.

Key facts

✓ When a fraction has an irrational square root in its denominator, it should be "rationalized" so the square root is moved to the numerator.

✓ Rationalization involves multiplying the top and bottom of the fraction by the denominator.

✓ If the denominator is written in the form $a \pm \sqrt{b}$, change the sign in front of the root before rationalizing.

Rationalizing the denominator

A fraction with an irrational square root in the denominator is easier to work with in calculations if the square root is moved to the numerator. When the square root is the whole denominator, we do this by multiplying both the top and bottom of the fraction by the denominator. This process is called "rationalizing the denominator."

1. The denominator is an irrational square root.

3. The square root is now the numerator.

$$\frac{a}{\sqrt{b}} = \frac{a \times \sqrt{b}}{\sqrt{b} \times \sqrt{b}} = \frac{a\sqrt{b}}{b} \quad \rightarrow \quad \frac{1}{\sqrt{5}} = \frac{1 \times \sqrt{5}}{\sqrt{5} \times \sqrt{5}} = \frac{\sqrt{5}}{5}$$

2. Multiply the top and bottom by the square root in the denominator.

4. Multiplying a square root by itself produces the number under the root sign.

Rationalizing a more complex denominator

Things become more complicated where the denominator is made up of rational numbers and irrational square roots. The rationalization process is the same, but any sign in front of the square root should be changed for the multiplication. This is a neat trick designed to eliminate all irrational square roots in the denominator and is related to the difference of two squares (see page 105).

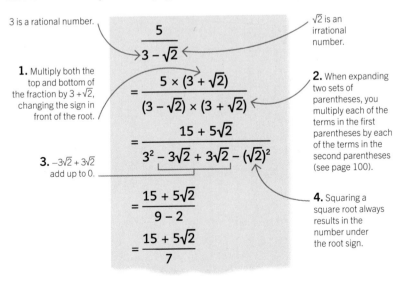

3 is a rational number.

$\sqrt{2}$ is an irrational number.

$$\frac{5}{3 - \sqrt{2}}$$

1. Multiply both the top and bottom of the fraction by $3 + \sqrt{2}$, changing the sign in front of the root.

$$= \frac{5 \times (3 + \sqrt{2})}{(3 - \sqrt{2}) \times (3 + \sqrt{2})}$$

2. When expanding two sets of parentheses, you multiply each of the terms in the first parentheses by each of the terms in the second parentheses (see page 100).

$$= \frac{15 + 5\sqrt{2}}{3^2 - 3\sqrt{2} + 3\sqrt{2} - (\sqrt{2})^2}$$

3. $-3\sqrt{2} + 3\sqrt{2}$ add up to 0.

4. Squaring a square root always results in the number under the root sign.

$$= \frac{15 + 5\sqrt{2}}{9 - 2}$$

$$= \frac{15 + 5\sqrt{2}}{7}$$

Irrational square root calculations

Question
Calculate the following and simplify your answer.

$$\frac{1}{\sqrt{2}} \times \frac{2}{\sqrt{6}} = ?$$

Answer
1. Multiply out the fractions.

$$\frac{1}{\sqrt{2}} \times \frac{2}{\sqrt{6}} = \frac{2}{\sqrt{12}}$$

2. Simplify your answer.

$$\frac{2}{\sqrt{12}} = \frac{2}{\sqrt{3} \times \sqrt{4}} = \frac{2}{2\sqrt{3}} = \frac{1}{\sqrt{3}}$$

3. Rationalize the denominator.

$$\frac{1}{\sqrt{3}} = \frac{1 \times \sqrt{3}}{\sqrt{3} \times \sqrt{3}} = \frac{\sqrt{3}}{3}$$

Exact calculations

Calculations that involve using an area, measured in square units, to find lengths often result in irrational values. The only way to express these resulting values exactly is to write the number in square root form.

Key facts

✓ Calculations that involve finding lengths from areas often give answers that involve irrational square roots.

✓ To represent the exact value of these resulting irrational square roots, we express the answer in square root form.

π with irrational square roots

If the area of this circle is 2 m², what is its radius (r)?
The result will require finding the square root of 2.
How do we write the answer as an exact value?

Area (A) = 2 m²

Radius (r) = ?

$$\text{Area of a circle } (A) = \pi r^2$$
$$\text{Radius of a circle } (r) = \sqrt{\frac{A}{\pi}}$$

$$\pi \times r^2 = 2$$

$$r^2 = \frac{2}{\pi}$$

π is also a type of irrational number and cannot be written out in full.

$$r = \sqrt{\frac{2}{\pi}} \text{ m}$$

This represents the exact value of the radius.

▤ Finding the exact value

Question

A cylinder has a cross-sectional area of 3 cm² and a height (h) that is 10 times the radius of the circular cross-section. What is the exact value of the volume of the cylinder in cm³?

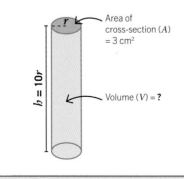

$h = 10r$

Area of cross-section (A) = 3 cm²

Volume (V) = ?

Answer

$$\text{Volume of a cylinder } (V) = \text{Area of cross-section} \times \text{height}$$
$$= \pi r^2 h$$

$$\text{Area } (A) = \pi r^2$$

$$\text{Radius } (r) = \sqrt{\frac{A}{\pi}}$$

1. First, work out the volume of the cylinder.

$V = 3h$, because $\pi r^2 = 3 \text{ cm}^2$
$= 3 \times 10r$ because $h = 10r$
$= 30r$

2. Then give the exact calculation.

$$r = \sqrt{\frac{3}{\pi}} \quad \text{so } V = 30\sqrt{\frac{3}{\pi}} \text{ cm}^3$$

Scientific notation

Very large and very small numbers can be cumbersome and time-consuming to write down. Scientific notation is a convenient shorthand way of writing these numbers using powers of 10.

Key facts

✓ Scientific notation is used to express very large and very small numbers using powers of 10.

✓ It is written in the form $a \times 10^n$.

✓ a must always be between 1 and 10 ($1 \leq a < 10$).

✓ The power is positive for numbers greater than 1 and negative for numbers less than 1.

Writing numbers in scientific notation
To convert a number into scientific notation, you must split it into two parts: a first number between 1 and 10, and a power of 10 (see page 115).

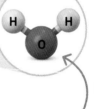

1 μm³ (cubic micrometer) is one trillionth of 1 cm³.

Volume of water on Earth (km³)

1,386,000,000

Volume of one water molecule (μm³)

0.00000000000282

1. Insert a decimal point (or find it if it's already there) and count how many places it needs to move to form a number between 1 and 10.

9 8 7 6 5 4 3 2 1
1 3 8 6 0 0 0 0 0 0 .

The decimal point moves 9 places to the left.

1 2 3 4 5 6 7 8 9 10 11 12
0 . 0 0 0 0 0 0 0 0 0 0 2 8 2

The decimal point moves 12 places to the right.

2. Multiply the number by a power of 10. The power is equal to the number of places the decimal point moved.

$$1.386 \times 10^9$$

The power is positive for numbers greater than 1.

$$2.82 \times 10^{-12}$$

The power is negative for numbers less than 1.

⚙ Formula for scientific notation

Numbers in scientific notation are always expressed in the same form.

a must be 1 or more and less than 10, which can be expressed as $1 \leq a < 10$.

n can be any positive or negative integer.

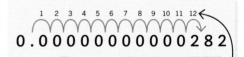

$$a \times 10^n$$

Multiplying and dividing with scientific notation

Calculating with very large or very small numbers is much simpler using scientific notation. Instead of working with long, unwieldy numbers, you convert each number to scientific notation to simplify the calculation, then present the answer in scientific notation to show the magnitude or size of the result.

Key facts

✓ Performing operations with scientific notation can simplify calculations.

✓ When calculating in scientific notation, calculate the first numbers separately from the powers of 10.

✓ Apply the laws of exponents to multiply or divide powers of 10.

Laws of exponents and scientific notation

To multiply or divide two or more numbers written in scientific notation, start by separating the first numbers from the powers of 10. Then perform the calculation on the first numbers and the powers of 10 separately, applying the laws of exponents for multiplying and dividing powers to the powers of 10 (see page 118). You may need to adjust your answer to express it in scientific notation. Here, you are calculating $3\,000\,000 \times 420\,000$.

$$3\,000\,000 \times 420\,000 = ?$$

1. First, convert each number into scientific notation (see opposite).

$$= (3 \times 10^6) \times (4.2 \times 10^5)$$

2. Separate the first numbers from the powers and multiply each separately. Add together the powers of 10.

$$= (3 \times 4.2) \times (10^6 \times 10^5)$$
$$= 12.6 \times 10^{6+5}$$
$$= 12.6 \times 10^{11}$$

3. The first number is not between 1 and 10, so your answer needs to be adjusted. Divide the first number by 10, and multiply the power of 10 by 10 to compensate.

$$12.6 \times 10^{11}$$
$$\div 10 \downarrow \qquad \downarrow \times 10$$
$$= 1.26 \times 10^{12}$$

The answer is now in scientific notation.

🗐 Calculating with scientific notation

Question
How many copies of Mars equal the mass of one Earth? Because the masses of both planets are huge, it's best to work this out using scientific notation. The masses below are rounded to four decimal places.

Mass of Earth (m_E) is 5.9742×10^{24} kg
Mass of Mars (m_M) is 6.4191×10^{23} kg

Answer
1. Divide the mass of Earth by the mass of Mars.

$$m_E \div m_M$$
$$5.9742 \times 10^{24} \div 6.4191 \times 10^{23}$$

2. Divide the front numbers first.
$$5.9742 \div 6.4191 = 0.9307$$

3. Then use the laws of exponents for dividing with powers. You need to subtract one power from the other.
$$0.9307 \times 10^{24-23}$$
$$= 0.9307 \times 10^1$$
$$= 9.307$$

You would need 9.307 copies of Mars to balance one Earth.

Adding and subtracting with scientific notation

When adding or subtracting long numbers in scientific notation, the first step is to make sure the powers of each number match.

Matching the powers
Before adding or subtracting numbers when one or more of the numbers is in scientific notation, you have to make sure they're raised to the same power of 10. Then calculate the first numbers separately. Calculate $(2.4 \times 10^7) - 170\,000$.

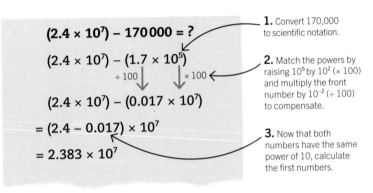

$(2.4 \times 10^7) - 170\,000 = ?$

$(2.4 \times 10^7) - (1.7 \times 10^5)$

$\div 100 \downarrow \qquad \downarrow \times 100$

$(2.4 \times 10^7) - (0.017 \times 10^7)$

$= (2.4 - 0.017) \times 10^7$

$= 2.383 \times 10^7$

1. Convert 170,000 to scientific notation.

2. Match the powers by raising 10^5 by 10^2 ($\times 100$) and multiply the front number by 10^{-2} ($\div 100$) to compensate.

3. Now that both numbers have the same power of 10, calculate the first numbers.

📄 Length of DNA

Question
A crime scene investigator has collected DNA from a burglary. They need at least 1 mm (1×10^{-3} m) to carry out a genetic fingerprint. The fragments are: 2×10^{-4} m, 9.6×10^{-5} m, 5.2×10^{-4} m, and 8.4×10^{-5} m. What is the total length of the collected DNA?

....

Answer
1. Convert all the lengths to the same power of 10. Because the goal is a 10^{-3} number, make all the lengths that order of magnitude.

$2 \times 10^{-4} \longrightarrow 0.2 \times 10^{-3}$ m
$9.6 \times 10^{-5} \longrightarrow 0.096 \times 10^{-3}$ m
$5.2 \times 10^{-4} \longrightarrow 0.52 \times 10^{-3}$ m
$8.4 \times 10^{-5} \longrightarrow 0.084 \times 10^{-3}$ m

2. Now add the first numbers together:
$(0.2 + 0.096 + 0.52 + 0.084) \times 10^{-3} = 0.9 \times 10^{-3}$

There is not enough DNA available to run the tests.

🔍 Using a calculator

Some scientific calculators have a dedicated button for scientific notation; on others, you'll need to use the exponent key. If the answer is too long to show on the calculator screen, it will be represented in scientific notation. Here, you are keying in 4×10^8.

....

Scientific notation button
The scientific notation key will automatically raise by a power of 10.

....

Exponent button
The exponent key can be used to raise by any power, so you need to specify the power of 10.

Equations
and graphs

Equations

An equation is a mathematical statement that joins two things, such as expressions, with an equals sign to show that they have the same value. An equation may contain one or more unknown values.

📌 **Key facts**

✓ The two sides of an equation are equal in value.

✓ Solving an equation means finding the value of an unknown in it.

✓ An identity is a type of equation linking two expressions that are always equal.

Solving equations
We can use the information in an equation to find the value of the unknown within it. This is called solving the equation. A solution might be a number or an expression.

There is a number that can be substituted for x that will keep the equation true. In this case, we can replace x with 2 and the equation will stay balanced, so 2 is the solution for x.

The two sides of the equation have the same value. In this case, $x + 4$ is equal to 6.

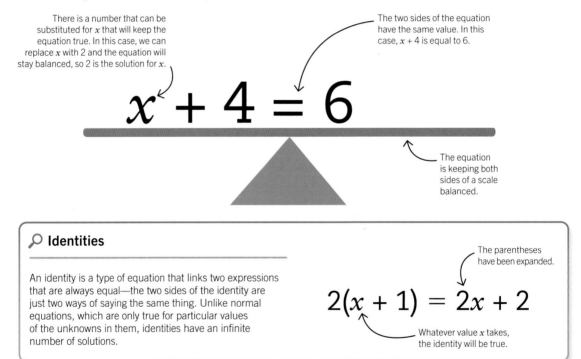

$$x + 4 = 6$$

The equation is keeping both sides of a scale balanced.

🔍 **Identities**

An identity is a type of equation that links two expressions that are always equal—the two sides of the identity are just two ways of saying the same thing. Unlike normal equations, which are only true for particular values of the unknowns in them, identities have an infinite number of solutions.

The parentheses have been expanded.

$$2(x + 1) = 2x + 2$$

Whatever value x takes, the identity will be true.

⚙️ **Functions and formulas**

Equations are just one of the things that can be made from the building blocks of algebra. We can also use terms and operations to create functions and formulas.

Function
This is a function (see page 111). The equals sign tells us the rule of the function. We don't solve the function, but use it to find the output for a particular value of x.

$$f(x) = 2x - 9$$

Formula
This is a formula (see page 109). It's a special kind of equation for describing a rule that links variables.

$$a^2 + b^2 = c^2$$

Solving simple equations

Solving an equation involves working out the value of an unknown within it. We do this by rearranging the equation until the solution is revealed.

Isolating the unknown

To solve an equation for an unknown, we manipulate the equation until the unknown value, such as x, is by itself on one side of it. We do this by performing inverse (opposite) operations on the unknown value and doing the same to the other side of the equation to keep it balanced.

Key facts

✓ We solve an equation by rearranging it until the unknown is isolated on one side.

✓ Isolating an unknown on one side of an equation gives a solution for that unknown.

✓ The equation remains true and balanced as long as the same operations are performed on both sides of the equation.

Reversing addition
To isolate the unknown, x, in this equation, we need to do the opposite of adding 7. So we subtract 7 from both sides to keep the equation balanced. The solution is 3.

$$x + 7 = 10$$
$$x + 7 - 7 = 10 - 7$$
$$x = 3$$

Reversing multiplication
To find x in this equation, we need to do the opposite of multiplying x by 2. So we divide both sides by 2. The solution is 2.

$$2x = 4$$
$$\frac{2x}{2} = \frac{4}{2}$$
$$x = 2$$

Reversing subtraction
To isolate x in this equation, we need to do the opposite of subtracting 6. So we add 6 to both sides. The solution is 9.

$$x - 6 = 3$$
$$x - 6 + 6 = 3 + 6$$
$$x = 9$$

Reversing division
To solve this equation, we need to do the opposite of dividing by 3. So we multiply both sides by 3. The solution is 6.

$$\frac{x}{3} = 2$$
$$\frac{x}{3} \times 3 = 2 \times 3$$
$$x = 6$$

⚙ Keeping the balance

If an operation is only performed on one side of an equation, the equation will be out of balance and no longer true. When you perform an operation on one side, you must also perform it on the other side.

$$x + 7 = 12$$

This equation is balanced.

$$x < 12$$

When you subtract 7 from the left-hand side only, the two sides are no longer equal.

$$x = 5$$

Subtracting 7 from the other side rebalances and solves the equation.

Solving harder equations

To solve complicated equations, it can be necessary to carry out more than one step to isolate the unknown. The order of these steps is important because of the order of operations.

Key facts

✓ You solve an equation by isolating the unknown value.

✓ When an unknown appears on both sides of the equation, it will need to be removed from one side.

Taking an equation apart

Sometimes an unknown value, such as x, will appear on both sides of an equation. To solve the equation, we still need to isolate the unknown. We do this by performing inverse operations on both sides of the equation, working our way backward through the order of operations (see page 28).

1. The unknown value x appears on both sides of this equation.

$$4x - 1 = x + 5$$

2. First, we subtract x from both sides so that x only appears on one side of the equation.

$$3x - 1 = 5$$

3. Next, reverse the subtraction by adding 1 to both sides.

$$3x = 6$$

4. Divide both sides by 3 to isolate x and solve the equation.

$$x = 2$$

The solution for x is 2.

📰 Equations in the real world

Problems from the real world can be translated into equations and then solved.

Question
A plant is 6 cm tall. It grows another 2 cm every week. After how many weeks will the plant be 20 cm tall?

Answer
1. The question can be written as an algebraic equation to help us work out the answer. The final height of the plant is 6 cm plus two times the number of weeks it's been growing.

x represents the number of weeks. $6 + 2x = 20$ This is the final height of the plant in cm.

2. Solve the equation by isolating x. First, subtract 6 from both sides, then divide both sides by 2.

$$2x = 14$$
$$x = 7$$

The plant will take 7 weeks to reach a height of 20 cm.

Equations with parentheses

Parentheses in an equation group terms together. When an unknown value is inside parentheses, it can be useful to eliminate the parentheses before solving the equation.

Expanding parentheses in equations

To solve an equation that contains one or more sets of parentheses, it can be helpful to expand the parentheses first (see page 99).

1. The parentheses in this equation need to be dealt with before it can be solved.

$$3\left(\frac{2x}{3} + 3\right) - 2(1 - x) = 2x + 11$$

2. Expand the parentheses by distributing the value outside the parentheses to each of the values inside, then combine the like terms.

Multiplying by 3 will cancel this denominator.

Multiplying by a negative number changes the signs of the numbers inside.

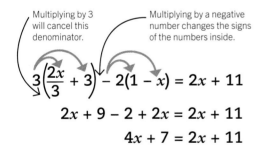

$$3\left(\frac{2x}{3} + 3\right) - 2(1 - x) = 2x + 11$$
$$2x + 9 - 2 + 2x = 2x + 11$$
$$4x + 7 = 2x + 11$$

3. Isolate x, working backward through the order of operations. First, subtract $2x$, then subtract 7 from each side. Lastly, divide both sides by 2.

$$4x + 7 = 2x + 11$$
$$2x + 7 = 11$$
$$2x = 4$$
$$x = 2$$

Eliminating common factors

Sometimes we can use a common factor to eliminate parentheses (see page 101) rather than expanding the parentheses.

1. The length of a parallelogram is $x + 2$ and its slanting height is $x - 3$. If we know its perimeter is 14 cm, we can find the value of x.

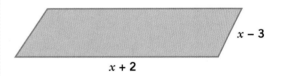

$x - 3$

$x + 2$

2. Arrange the given information into an equation. We know that the perimeter (the sum of the sides) is equal to twice the length plus twice the slant height.

$$2(x + 2) + 2(x - 3) = 14$$

3. Look for a common factor to divide both sides by. Both parentheses and the perimeter have a common factor of 2. So divide both sides by 2. This removes the parentheses without having to expand them.

$$x + 2 + x - 3 = 7$$

4. Combine the like terms and solve the equation.

$$2x - 1 = 7$$
$$2x = 8$$
$$x = 4$$

Simultaneous equations

An equation containing a single unknown variable provides enough information for us to solve it. When there are two unknowns, we need more information to solve it, in the form of a second equation. The two equations containing the same unknowns are called simultaneous equations.

> **Key facts**
>
> ✓ Simultaneous equations contain the same variables and are solved together.
>
> ✓ We can solve simultaneous equations by substituting one equation into the other or by eliminating a variable.

A system of simultaneous equations

The solution to a system, or pair, of simultaneous equations will give the value of both unknowns. There are two main ways of solving simultaneous equations: substitution and elimination.

$$3x - 5y = 4$$
$$4x + 5y = 17$$

These are simultaneous equations.

Both equations contain the same unknown x.

Both equations contain the same unknown y.

Solving by substitution

When one of a pair of simultaneous equations contains an unknown with a coefficient of 1, rearranging that equation and substituting it into the other equation will be enough to solve the system.

1. We can use the substitution method to solve this system of simultaneous equations, because x has a coefficient of 1 in the first equation.

The coefficient of this term is 1.

① $x + 2y = 10$

② $2x + 6y = 26$

It's a good idea to label the equations to keep track of them.

2. Isolate the x in the first equation.

① $x = 10 - 2y$

The expression for x from equation ① has been substituted for the x in equation ②.

3. Equation ① has given us an expression for x, which is $10 - 2y$. We can substitute this expression for the x in equation ② and rearrange it to reveal the solution for y.

② $2(10 - 2y) + 6y = 26$
$20 - 4y + 6y = 26$
$2y = 6$
$y = 3$

4. To find the value of x, substitute the value of y into one of the original equations and solve for the value of x.

The value of y is substituted into equation ①.

① $x + 2(3) = 10$
$x + 6 = 10$
$x = 4$

5. The values for x and y have now been revealed. These are the solutions for the pair of simultaneous equations.

$x = 4$
$y = 3$

Solving by elimination

For simultaneous equations that can't be easily rearranged to make one variable the subject, a method called elimination is used. Whole equations are multiplied to make the coefficients of one of the variables match and are then added or subtracted to produce an equation with only one variable.

1. This pair of simultaneous equations can be solved using elimination. This means we need to make either the x or the y coefficients match in both equations so that they can be eliminated.

① $3x + 2y = 19$

② $5x - 4y = 17$

2. Multiply the whole of equation ① by 2. The y values in equations ① and ② are now both $4y$. Number the new equation ③.

① $3x + 2y = 19$

$\downarrow \times 2$

③ $6x + 4y = 38$

3. Cancel out the y terms by adding the new equation ③ to equation ②.

③ $6x + 4y = 38$

$+$ ② $5x - 4y = 17$

$\downarrow$

$11x + 0y = 55$

Adding the two equations eliminates the y terms.

4. Solve for the variable x.

$11x = 55$

$x = 5$

5. The value for x can now be substituted into one of the original equations. Solve for y.

① $3(5) + 2y = 19$

$15 + 2y = 19$

$2y = 4$

$y = 2$

The value of x is substituted into equation ①.

6. The solutions of x and y have now been found. These are the solutions for the original pair of simultaneous equations.

$x = 5$

$y = 2$

⚙ Multiplying both equations

Sometimes both equations need to be multiplied before the elimination method can be used. We do this when multiplying only one equation won't make two coefficients the same.

1. In this system of simultaneous equations, none of the coefficients is a factor of another, so both equations need to be multiplied to make two coefficients match.

① $2x + 5y = 26$

② $3x + 2y = 17$

2. Multiply both equations to make the coefficients of y 10. Number the new equations ③ and ④.

① $2x + 5y = 26$

$\downarrow \times 2$

③ $4x + 10y = 52$

② $3x + 2y = 17$

$\downarrow \times 5$

④ $15x + 10y = 85$

3. Subtract equation ③ from equation ④ to cancel out the y and combine the like terms.

④ $15x + 10y = 85$

$-$ ③ $4x + 10y = 52$

$\downarrow$

$11x = 33$

$x = 3$

4. Substitute the value for x into equation ① to find the value for y.

$2(3) + 5y = 26$

$5y = 20$

$y = 4$

5. The solutions of x and y have been found.

$x = 3$

$y = 4$

Practice question
Real-world simultaneous equations

See also

97 Substitution

132 Solving harder equations

134–135 Simultaneous equations

Lots of situations in the real world involve more than one unknown quantity. In these cases, we can often use a system of simultaneous equations to represent the problem and solve it.

Question
In a café, one customer buys 2 cookies and 3 smoothies for $15.
A second customer buys 4 cookies and 5 smoothies, which costs $26.
What are the café's prices for cookies and smoothies?

Answer
1. Turn each customer's purchase into an equation to solve the problem. In these simultaneous equations, x represents the price of one cookie and y represents the price of one smoothie in dollars.

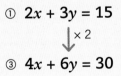

① $2x + 3y = 15$ — Purchase of customer 1
② $4x + 5y = 26$ — Purchase of customer 2

2. The coefficients of x and y are not 1, so use the elimination method to solve the equations. Multiply equation ① by 2 to make the coefficients of x the same. Label the new equation ③.

① $2x + 3y = 15$

$\downarrow \times 2$

③ $4x + 6y = 30$

3. Subtract equation ② from the new equation ③ to eliminate x.

③ $\quad 4x + 6y = 30$
$- ② \quad 4x + 5y = 26$

$\downarrow$

$0x + y = 4$
$y = 4$

4. Substitute the value for y into equation ① to find the value of x.

① $\quad 2x + 3y = 15$
$2x + 3(4) = 15$
$2x + 12 = 15$
$2x = 3$
$x = 1.5$

5. Substitute this value for x and the value for y into one of the equations to check whether these solutions are correct. The solutions must work in both equations to be correct.

② $\quad 4x + 5y = 26$
$4(1.5) + 5(4) = 26$
$6 + 20 = 26$

Because x is 1.5 and y is 4, the café charges $1.50 for a cookie and $4 for a smoothie.

Solving simple quadratic equations

A quadratic equation is an equation that contains a quadratic expression (see page 100). It will generally have two solutions.

(see page 100)

> **Key facts**
>
> ✓ A quadratic equation will usually have two solutions.
>
> ✓ Factoring can be used to solve some quadratic equations.

General form of a quadratic equation

When we want to solve quadratic equations, we write them in what's called their general form, with the x^2 term first, followed by the x term, and then the number (called the constant).

$$ax^2 + bx + c = 0$$

The coefficient of x^2 is represented by the letter a.

x represents the unknown value.

b is the coefficient of the x term.

c is a number called the constant term.

Solving by factoring

1. To solve this quadratic equation, we need to factor it.

$$x^2 + 3x + 2 = 0$$

2. Factoring the equation gives two sets of parentheses (see pages 102–103).

$$(x + 1)(x + 2) = 0$$

3. When the product of two factors is 0, then one of the factors must be 0. Our equation equals 0, so $(x + 1)$ or $(x + 2)$ must be equal to 0. Trying both these options gives us the two solutions to the equation.

(see pages 102–103)

Solution 1

$$(x + 1) = 0$$
$$x = -1$$

Solution 2

$$(x + 2) = 0$$
$$x = -2$$

4. Substitute the solutions into the original equation to check that they are correct.

Check solution 1

$$x^2 + 3x + 2 = 0$$
$$(-1)^2 + 3(-1) + 2 = 0$$
$$1 - 3 + 2 = 0$$
$$0 = 0$$

Check solution 2

$$x^2 + 3x + 2 = 0$$
$$(-2)^2 + 3(-2) + 2 = 0$$
$$4 - 6 + 2 = 0$$
$$0 = 0$$

When b is 0

In a quadratic equation, b and c can be equal to 0 (but a cannot). When b is 0, the equation can be solved by rearranging the equation to isolate x.

1. In this equation, b is 0, so there's no x term. Isolating x^2 and then x will solve the equation.

$$x^2 - 16 = 0$$

2. To isolate x^2, add 16 to both sides.

$$x^2 = 16$$

3. To solve, find the square root of both sides.

$$x = \pm\sqrt{16}$$

This symbol means "positive or negative."

4. The equation has two solutions, because the square root of 16 is either 4 or −4.

$$x = 4 \text{ or } -4$$

Solving harder quadratic equations

Sometimes we need to solve quadratic equations where a, the coefficient of x^2, isn't 1. There are techniques we can use to solve these harder equations.

> **Key facts**
>
> ✓ If you can factor a quadratic equation, you can find its solutions.
>
> ✓ A table of factors can help with factoring when a is not 1.
>
> ✓ A difference of two squares in the form $p^2 - q^2$ is factored as $(p + q)(p - q)$.

Factoring when a is not 1

It isn't always possible to factor a quadratic when a is not 1, but if there is, we can use a table to help us find the factors.

1. This equation is in the form $ax^2 + bx + c = 0$. To factor it, we first need to identify the factors of a and c. These will give us the possible values to go in the parentheses.

$$2x^2 + 7x + 6 = 0$$

a is 2. The only factor pair of 2 is 1, 2. b is 7. c is 6. The factor pairs of 6 are 6, 1 and 3, 2.

2. Use a table to try each of the factor pairs in parentheses. Expand out each set of parentheses to see which arrangement gives the original equation.

Possible factorization	Expanded expression	
$(x + 6)(2x + 1)$	$2x^2 + 13x + 6$	✗
$(2x + 6)(x + 1)$	$2x^2 + 8x + 6$	✗
$(x + 3)(x + 2)$	$2x^2 + 8x + 6$	✗
$(2x + 3)(x + 2)$	$2x^2 + 7x + 6$	✔

Swapping the order of the values in the parentheses will change the expansion.   This is the expanded expression we're looking for.

3. The table revealed that the correct factorization is $(2x + 3)(x + 2)$. If the correct expression had not appeared in the table, a method other than factoring would have been needed to solve the equation.

The factored equation → $(2x + 3)(x + 2) = 0$

4. Either of the parentheses can equal 0, so we can find two solutions to the equation.

$$(2x + 3) = 0 \qquad (x + 2) = 0$$
$$x = \frac{-3}{2} \qquad\quad x = -2$$

Solution 1   Solution 2

The difference of two squares

A quadratic expression that consists of one square value subtracted from another square value is known as the difference of two squares (see page 105). These quadratic expressions are in the form $p^2 - q^2$ and their factors will always be $(p + q)(p - q)$.

1. 9 and 25 are square numbers, so this quadratic expression is the difference of two squares. The equation is in the form $p^2 - q^2$.

$$9x^2 - 25 = 0$$

2. The difference of two squares can always be factored in the form $(p + q)(p - q)$, where p and q are the square roots of the values in the original equation.

$$(3x + 5)(3x - 5) = 0$$

5 is the square root of 25.

$3x$ is the square root of $9x^2$.

3. Now we can solve for the variable x. Either of the parentheses could equal 0, so we can find two possible solutions to the equation.

$$(3x + 5) = 0 \qquad (3x - 5) = 0$$
$$x = \frac{-5}{3} \qquad\qquad x = \frac{5}{3}$$

Solution 1   Solution 2

Completing the square

If a quadratic equation can't be factored into two parentheses, we can use an alternative technique called completing the square. This provides a version of the equation that can be solved by rearranging.

Key facts

✓ Completing the square is a way to solve quadratic equations that can't be factored into two parentheses.

✓ The equation is factored as a single squared parenthesis with a number subtracted to compensate.

Completing the area of a square

The quadratic equation $x^2 + 6x + 3 = 0$ can't be factored, because there's no pair of numbers whose product is 3 and sum is 6. Instead, we can use the method of completing the square to solve it. We work out what value can be added to the quadratic expression to make it a "complete square" that we can use to solve the equation.

1. Let's imagine each term in the equation represents the area of a rectangle. x^2 is a square x units tall and x units wide. $6x$ forms 6 rectangles 1 unit wide and x units tall. The number 3 becomes 3 squares, 1 unit by 1 unit.

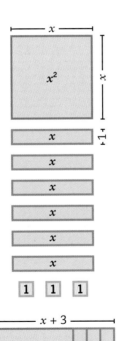

2. If we rearrange these rectangles, they almost form a perfect square. An expression for the whole square is $(x + 3)^2$, because the square we have made is $x + 3$ units tall and $x + 3$ units wide. But there's a bit missing.

3. The original equation represents the area of this whole square minus the missing part.

$$x^2 + 6x + 3 = (x + 3)^2 - ?$$

4. The missing part of the square we have made has an area of 6, because it is 3 units wide and 2 units tall. Subtracting this missing area from the expression for the whole square gives us an expression that is equivalent to the original expression.

$$x^2 + 6x + 3 = (x + 3)^2 - 6$$

The area of the small rectangle, 6, is subtracted from the area of the whole square, $(x + 3)^2$.

5. Now we can rearrange and solve the equation as usual, using the new expression that is equivalent to the original expression.

$$(x + 3)^2 - 6 = 0$$
$$(x + 3)^2 = 6$$
$$x + 3 = \pm\sqrt{6}$$
$$x = -3 \pm\sqrt{6}$$

This means the square root can be either positive or negative.

So the solutions to the equation $x^2 + 6x + 3 = 0$ are $x = -3 + \sqrt{6}$ and $x = -3 - \sqrt{6}$.

How to complete the square

It's not always practical to draw rectangles to work out how to solve a quadratic equation by completing the square, so there are a few set steps you can follow instead.

Six steps for completing the square

Completing the square involves working out a squared parentheses that is close to the quadratic equation you need to solve, then working out what needs to be added to or subtracted from that squared parentheses to make it equal to the original equation. This method can be used when a quadratic equation in the form $ax^2 + bx + c$ won't factor, but it is easiest to use it when a is 1 and b is even.

Key facts

✓ It is best to use this method when a is 1 and b is even.

✓ When a is 1, the parentheses will be in the form $(x + {}^b/_2)^2$.

✓ When a is 1, the value to subtract or add to the parentheses will be the difference between c and $({}^b/_2)^2$.

1. In this quadratic equation, a is not 1. So to use the method of completing the square, we divide the whole equation by 3 to make a 1. If a is 1, skip this step.

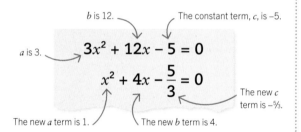

b is 12.

The constant term, c, is –5.

a is 3.

$$3x^2 + 12x - 5 = 0$$

$$x^2 + 4x - \frac{5}{3} = 0$$

The new c term is $-{}^5/_3$.

The new a term is 1.

The new b term is 4.

2. To begin constructing the completed square, divide the new b term by 2, add it to x, and put it inside squared parentheses. The parentheses will always be in this form, $(x + {}^b/_2)^2$.

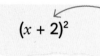

$$(x + 2)^2$$

The b term in our equation is 4, so we divide it by 2 to get 2 and write it in the parentheses.

3. Expand the parentheses and compare to the original equation. The squared parentheses we have created expand to give a c term of 4, while the c term of the original equation was $-{}^5/_3$.

Expanding the squared parentheses shows us that the c term is 4 instead of $-{}^5/_3$.

$$(x + 2)^2 = x^2 + 4x + 4$$

4. Find the value we need to add to or subtract from the squared parentheses to make it equal to the original equation. We must find the difference between c and $({}^b/_2)^2$.

$({}^b/_2)^2$ is 4.

c is $-{}^5/_3$.

$$-\frac{5}{3} - 4 = -\frac{17}{3}$$

This is the difference between the original equation and the squared parentheses.

5. Finally, we write this difference as a subtraction from the squared expression. This gives the completed square version of the original equation.

$$(x + 2)^2 - \frac{17}{3} = 0$$

6. We can now solve the equation by rearranging it.

$$(x + 2)^2 = \frac{17}{3}$$

$$x + 2 = \pm\sqrt{\frac{17}{3}}$$

$$x = -2 \pm\sqrt{\frac{17}{3}}$$

The possible solutions are:

$$x = -2 + \sqrt{\frac{17}{3}}$$ and $$x = -2 - \sqrt{\frac{17}{3}}$$

The quadratic formula

Sometimes the best way to solve a quadratic equation is by using the quadratic formula. It's very useful when it would be difficult or impossible to use other methods.

Using the quadratic formula
If you apply the completing the square method to the general quadratic equation $ax^2 + bx + c = 0$, you get what is called the quadratic formula. It is a useful alternative to completing the square, because you just substitute the numbers in and evaluate to get the solution.

Key facts

✓ We use the quadratic formula if solving a quadratic equation by factoring or completing the square would be difficult or impossible.

✓ The values of a, b, and c are substituted into the quadratic formula.

✓ Evaluate the discriminant part of the formula (the part in the square root) first.

General quadratic equation
To use the quadratic formula to solve a quadratic equation, the equation must be arranged in the general form, where the x^2 term is followed by the x term, then a number by itself. The letters a, b, and c represent numbers.

$$ax^2 + bx + c = 0$$

The quadratic formula
To use the quadratic formula to solve a quadratic equation for x, we simply substitute the values of a, b, and c from the quadratic equation into the formula, then evaluate it.

There are generally two solutions to a quadratic equation. Using both positive and negative square roots means no solutions are lost.

$$x = \frac{-b \pm \sqrt{b^2 - 4ac}}{2a}$$

📑 The formula in action

Using the quadratic formula is just a matter of substitution, but it makes sense to break it down into steps.

Question
Solve this equation to find the value of x.
$$3x^2 - 5x + 2 = 0$$

Answer
1. First, identify the value of a, b, and c in the quadratic equation.
$$a = 3$$
$$b = -5$$
$$c = 2$$

2. Next, calculate the part of the formula inside the square root (called the discriminant). Substitute a, b, and c into the discriminant and evaluate.

$$b^2 - 4ac$$
$$= -5^2 - 4 \times 3 \times 2$$
$$= 25 - 24$$
$$= 1$$

3. Substitute the remaining variables into the formula and evaluate it to find the solution. Take care when multiplying negative numbers.

So $x = 1, \frac{2}{3}$.

$$x = \frac{(-b \pm \sqrt{1})}{2a}$$
$$x = \frac{(5 \pm 1)}{6}$$
$$x = \frac{6}{6} = 1 \text{ or } x = \frac{4}{6} = \frac{2}{3}$$

Practice question
Choosing a method for quadratic problems

See also

137 Solving simple quadratic equations

138 Solving harder quadratic equations

140 How to complete the square

141 The quadratic formula

There are four main methods we can use for solving quadratic equations: the quadratic formula, factoring, completing the square, and the difference of two squares. When faced with an equation to solve, we must think carefully about which method is most appropriate.

$x + 4$

x

Question
A rectangular lawn is 4 m longer than it is wide. The area of the lawn is 11 m². What is the width of the lawn in meters? Give your answer to two decimal places.

Answer
1. The area of a rectangle is equal to its length multiplied by its width. Express the question as an equation using what you know about the lawn's length and width. Let x be the length in meters.

> **Area = length × width**

$$11 = (x + 4) \times x$$

2. This equation for the lawn is a quadratic. To solve it, rearrange it into the general form ($ax^2 + bx + c = 0$), then decide which method to use.

$$(x + 4) \times x = 11$$
$$x^2 + 4x = 11$$
$$x^2 + 4x - 11 = 0$$

3. There isn't a pair of numbers that will work for factoring, but for equations like this where a is 1 and b is even, completing the square is simple (see page 139).

$a = 1$ $\longrightarrow x^2 + 4x - 11 = 0$ b is even.

4. We put x and the value of $\frac{b}{2}$, which is 2, into a set of squared parentheses. The difference between c and $(\frac{b}{2})^2$ is −15, so write this as a subtraction from the squared parentheses. We now have a completed square version of the original equation.

$$(x + 2)^2 - 15 = 0$$

$c - (\frac{b}{2})^2$
$= -11 - 4$
$= -15$

5. Rearrange to solve for x.

$$(x + 2)^2 = 15$$
$$x + 2 = \pm\sqrt{15}$$
$$x = -2 \pm \sqrt{15}$$
$$x = -2 + \sqrt{15} \text{ or } x = -2 - \sqrt{15}$$

6. We are looking for a length measurement, so we take the positive solution from the two options.

$$x = -2 + \sqrt{15}$$
$$= 1.87$$

The lawn is 1.87 m wide.

Trial and error

Trial and error is typically used to solve problems involving powers and roots, where these keys aren't available on your calculator. It involves repeating (iterating) a calculation to move closer to the correct solution.

Converging on a solution

To solve a problem using trial and error, you try out different values, narrowing it down until you come to the solution. We can use trial and error to find $\sqrt{160}$ to one decimal place.

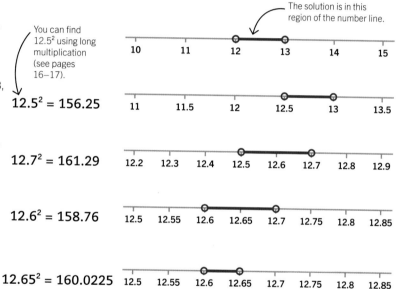

1. We know that 12^2 is 144 and 13^2 is 169, so $\sqrt{160}$ must be between 12 and 13.

You can find 12.5^2 using long multiplication (see pages 16–17).

The solution is in this region of the number line.

2. Try a number between 12 and 13, such as 12.5. The result is too low, so $\sqrt{160}$ is between 12.5 and 13.

$$12.5^2 = 156.25$$

3. Try a value between 12.5 and 13, such as 12.7. The result is too high, so $\sqrt{160}$ is between 12.5 and 12.7.

$$12.7^2 = 161.29$$

4. Now try 12.6. The result is too low, so $\sqrt{160}$ must be between 12.6 and 12.7.

$$12.6^2 = 158.76$$

5. Now try 12.65. The result is too high, so $\sqrt{160}$ lies between 12.6 and 12.65. This means that $\sqrt{160}$ to one decimal is 12.6.

$$12.65^2 = 160.0225$$

📑 Solving a cubic equation

A cubic equation can have up to 3 solutions, and trial and error is a good way to home in on these. One solution to the equation $x^3 - 2x^2 - x + 1 = 0$ is between 0 and 1. Trial and error can be used to find this solution to one decimal place.

The solution is between 0.55 and 0.6, so to one decimal place, the solution is 0.6.

x	$x^3 - 2x^2 - x + 1$	Accuracy
0	1	Too high
1	−1	Too low
0.5	0.125	Too high
0.7	−0.337	Too low
0.6	−0.104	Too low
0.55	0.011375	Too high

We try different possible solutions for x between 0 and 1 by substituting them into the expression.

The result of 1 is too high, so x must be a different value.

The accuracy of the previous attempt suggests what the next should be.

The coordinate grid

Sometimes it is useful to represent algebraic functions, equations, and inequalities on graphs so that we can understand more about them. Graphs are drawn on the coordinate grid.

Key facts

✓ The coordinate grid consists of the x axis, left to right, and the y axis, top to bottom. They intersect at the origin.

✓ Points on the grid are given by coordinates in the form (x, y).

Parts of the coordinate grid

The coordinate grid is made up of two lines, called the x axis and y axis, that intersect at a point called the origin. The axes create four areas, called quadrants. Points on the grid are given pairs of numbers, called coordinates, that describe their location along the x and y axes.

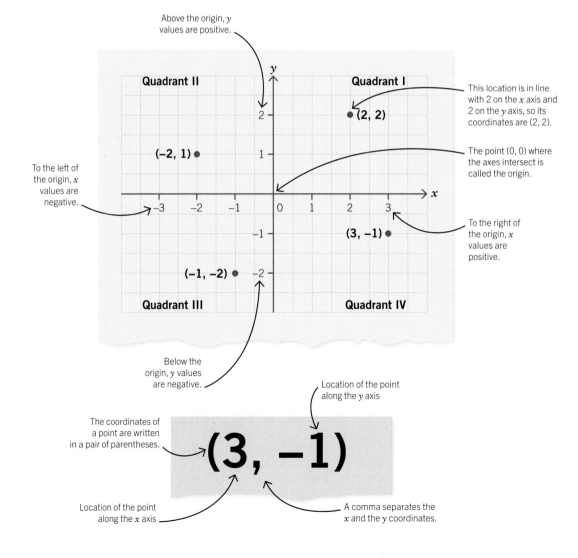

Linear graphs

A function (see page 111) can be plotted on the coordinate grid to produce its graph. The inputs of the function are plotted as the x coordinates, and the y coordinate represents the function's output.

Graphing a linear function
A linear function is one where all the variables are to the power of 1. The graph of a linear function will be a straight line. When drawing a linear function's graph, we can use a table to work out some coordinates.

Key facts

✓ A function can be plotted on the coordinate grid to produce a graph.

✓ A table of the outputs, y, for different values of x is made, and these values are used as coordinates.

✓ The points are joined together to form the graph of the function.

✓ If a function is linear, its graph will be a straight line.

1. A function defines the operations done on an input to produce an output. This function multiplies x by 2, then adds 1.

$$f(x) = 2x + 1$$

2. To find the coordinates to plot the function on a graph, rewrite the function as an equation, with y as the subject.

$$y = 2x + 1$$

3. Draw a table to identify some coordinate pairs with which to draw the graph. Values for x (inputs) are substituted into the formula to find the values of y (outputs).

The paired inputs (x) and outputs (y) give points on the function's graph.

Input, x	Output, y	Coordinates of point
−1	2(−1) + 1 = −1	(−1, −1)
0	1	(0, 1)
1	3	(1, 3)
2	5	(2, 5)

Choose four or five values for x around 0.

4. Plot the coordinates and use a ruler and pencil to join them. The points create a straight line.

This is the graph of the function $f(x) = 2x + 1$.

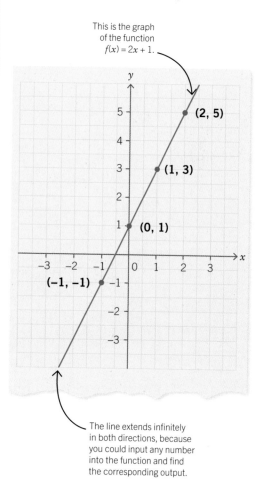

The line extends infinitely in both directions, because you could input any number into the function and find the corresponding output.

Equation of a line

The graph of a line will always have an equation based on the steepness of its slope, also known as the gradient, and the point where it crosses the y axis, called the y intercept.

Finding the equation of a line

The equation of a line on the coordinate grid has the general form $y = mx + b$. To identify a graph's equation, we substitute its slope (m) and its y intercept (b) into this equation.

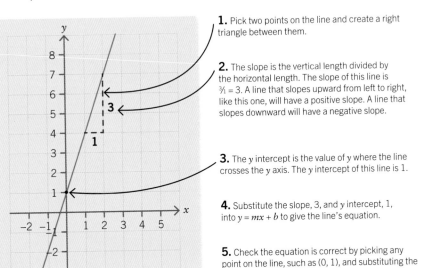

1. Pick two points on the line and create a right triangle between them.

2. The slope is the vertical length divided by the horizontal length. The slope of this line is $\frac{3}{1} = 3$. A line that slopes upward from left to right, like this one, will have a positive slope. A line that slopes downward will have a negative slope.

3. The y intercept is the value of y where the line crosses the y axis. The y intercept of this line is 1.

4. Substitute the slope, 3, and y intercept, 1, into $y = mx + b$ to give the line's equation.

$$y = 3x + 1$$

5. Check the equation is correct by picking any point on the line, such as (0, 1), and substituting the x and y coordinates of that point into the equation.

$$1 = 3 \times 0 + 1$$
$$1 = 1$$

🔍 **Slope formula**

You can also find the slope of a line by substituting the coordinates of any two points on the line into the formula for the slope.

$$\text{Slope} = \frac{\text{change in } y}{\text{change in } x} = \frac{(y_2 - y_1)}{(x_2 - x_1)}$$

Subtract each coordinate of the first point from the second point to find the change.

$$\text{Slope} = \frac{(4 - 1)}{(0 - 1)} = \frac{3}{-1} = -3$$

The line slopes downward, so it has a negative slope.

Parallel and perpendicular lines

If we know the equation of a line on the coordinate grid, we can use it to find the equation of a line parallel to it or to prove if a line is perpendicular to it.

Parallel lines

On the coordinate grid, parallel lines have the same slope (gradient). We can use this fact to work out the equation of a line that is parallel to another line.

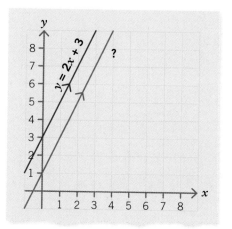

1. The equation of a line is $y = mx + b$, where m is the slope and b is the y intercept.

2. The equation of the blue line is $y = 2x + 3$. This means that its slope is 2 and it crosses the y axis at (0, 3).

3. The arrows on the two lines mean they are parallel, so we can work out the equation of the green line using the equation of the blue line.

4. Parallel lines have the same slope, so if the slope of the blue line is 2, then the slope (m) of the green line is also 2.

5. The green line crosses the y axis at (0, 1), so $b = 1$.

6. We can substitute these values into the equation for a line to give the equation of the green line:

$$y = 2x + 1$$

Perpendicular lines

Lines that form right angles when they intersect are called perpendicular lines. The product of the slopes of two perpendicular lines is −1. We can use this fact to prove that two lines are perpendicular.

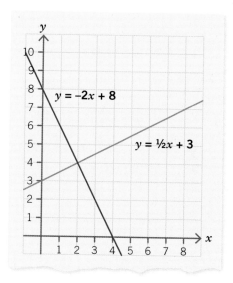

1. The equation of the purple line is $y = -2x + 8$.

2. The equation of the orange line is $y = \frac{1}{2}x + 3$.

3. We can prove these lines are perpendicular by multiplying their slopes together. If the product of their slopes is −1, they are perpendicular lines.

4. The slope of the purple line is −2 and the slope of the orange line is ½:

$$-2 \times \frac{1}{2} = -1$$

5. The product of the slopes is −1, so the lines are perpendicular.

Length and midpoint of a line segment

Not all straight line graphs continue on forever in each direction. A line segment is a line on a graph that has two endpoints. If you know the endpoints of a line segment, you can find its length and midpoint.

Length of a line segment

If you imagine a line segment as the hypotenuse of a right triangle, you can use the Pythagorean theorem (see page 196) to find its length. You can use the coordinates of the endpoints to work out the lengths of the triangle's other sides.

The length of this line can be found by rearranging the Pythagorean theorem:
$$a^2 + b^2 = c^2$$
$$c = \sqrt{(a^2 + b^2)}.$$

The length of this side of the triangle is the difference between the y coordinates of the line's endpoints: $y_2 - y_1$.

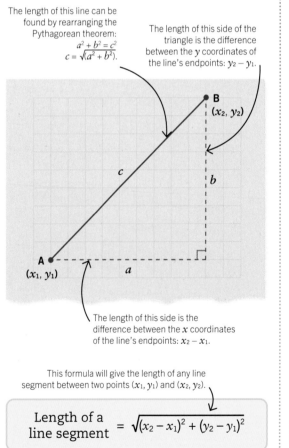

The length of this side is the difference between the x coordinates of the line's endpoints: $x_2 - x_1$.

This formula will give the length of any line segment between two points (x_1, y_1) and (x_2, y_2).

$$\text{Length of a line segment} = \sqrt{(x_2 - x_1)^2 + (y_2 - y_1)^2}$$

Midpoint of a line segment

The midpoint of a line segment is the point halfway between its two endpoints. You find the coordinates of the midpoint by adding together the coordinates of its two endpoints and dividing them by two to find their average (see page 231).

The x coordinate of M is the average of the x coordinates of points A and B. The y coordinate of M is the average of the y coordinates of points A and B.

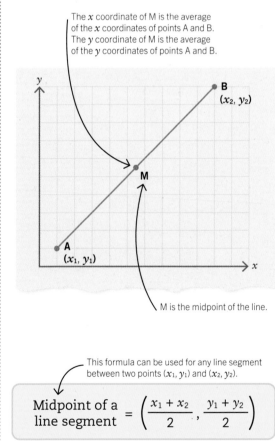

M is the midpoint of the line.

This formula can be used for any line segment between two points (x_1, y_1) and (x_2, y_2).

$$\text{Midpoint of a line segment} = \left(\frac{x_1 + x_2}{2}, \frac{y_1 + y_2}{2} \right)$$

Quadratic graphs

A quadratic function in the form $f(x) = ax^2 + bx + c$ will produce a quadratic graph. This type of graph is not a straight line, but a type of curve called a parabola.

Graphing a quadratic function
To graph a quadratic function, we substitute values into the function to identify coordinates that we can plot on the coordinate grid.

1. To graph the function $f(x) = x^2 + 2x - 3$, we first write it as an equation with y as the subject.

$$y = x^2 + 2x - 3$$

2. Draw a table to identify the coordinates needed to plot the graph. Choose some values for x around 0 and substitute them into the function to find the value of y (outputs). To draw a quadratic graph, you will need to identify at least five coordinates.

Substituting −3 into the function gives 0 as the output.

Input (x)	Output (y)	Coordinates of point
−3	$(-3)^2 + (2 \times -3) - 3 = 0$	(−3, 0)
−2	−3	(−2, −3)
−1	−4	(−1, −4)
0	−3	(0, −3)
1	0	(1, 0)
2	5	(2, 5)
3	12	(3, 12)

3. Plot the coordinates on the coordinate grid and join them with a smooth, symmetrical curve, called a parabola.

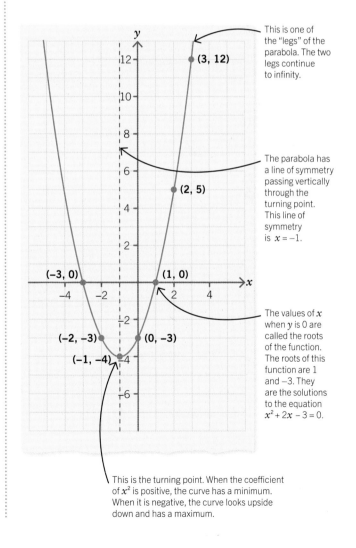

This is one of the "legs" of the parabola. The two legs continue to infinity.

The parabola has a line of symmetry passing vertically through the turning point. This line of symmetry is $x = -1$.

The values of x when y is 0 are called the roots of the function. The roots of this function are 1 and −3. They are the solutions to the equation $x^2 + 2x - 3 = 0$.

This is the turning point. When the coefficient of x^2 is positive, the curve has a minimum. When it is negative, the curve looks upside down and has a maximum.

Quadratics in the real world

Quadratic functions are often used to help describe physical situations in the real world, particularly ones involving gravity. Algebra and graphs are useful tools in understanding such situations.

Key facts

✓ Real-world situations can sometimes be expressed as a quadratic equation.

✓ To solve a real-world quadratic problem, first identify the roots of the given equation.

✓ Use the roots of the equation to sketch a simple graph and interpret the graph to solve the problem.

Throwing a ball

A ball is thrown vertically upward from a height of 2 m above the ground. Its starting velocity is 9 m/s. We can express the movement of this ball as a quadratic equation. If we then sketch this equation as a graph, we can use the graph to find out more about the movement of the ball. Let's work out the maximum height the ball reaches and the time taken for it to hit the ground.

An equation for the ball's movement

1. This is the quadratic equation for the movement of the ball. If we solve this equation and sketch its graph, we will be able to find out more about the movement.

$$y = -5t^2 + 9t + 2$$

y represents the height of the ball above ground.

t represents the time since the ball was thrown.

2. To sketch a graph of the equation, we need to know where the graph will cross the x axis (called the roots). Solving the equation for t when y is 0 will give the roots for the graph. So we replace y with 0 in the equation.

$$-5t^2 + 9t + 2 = 0$$

When the height is 0, the ball is on the ground.

3. Factor the equation as two sets of parentheses (see page 104).

$$(5t + 1)(-t + 2) = 0$$

4. Because the product of the two parentheses is 0, one of the two parentheses must equal 0. Solving each parentheses using this fact gives us the values for t, and therefore the roots for the graph.

$$(5t + 1) = 0 \qquad (-t + 2) = 0$$
$$5t = -1 \qquad 2 = t$$
$$t = -0.2 \qquad t = 2$$

The graph will cross the x axis at −0.2 and 2.

Sketching the graph

1. We can use the roots to sketch a simple graph of time against height that will help us find the ball's maximum height and the time taken for it to hit the ground.

2. We were told that the ball was thrown upward from a height of 2 m, so when time (shown along the *x* axis) was 0, the height (along the *y* axis) was 2. This gives us the *y* intercept (0, 2).

3. Solving the equation gave us the time (*t*) when the height (*y*) was 0. This gives us the coordinates (−0.2, 0) and (2, 0).

The curve shows the position of the ball over time.

Finding the turning point's coordinates will give us the maximum height of the ball.

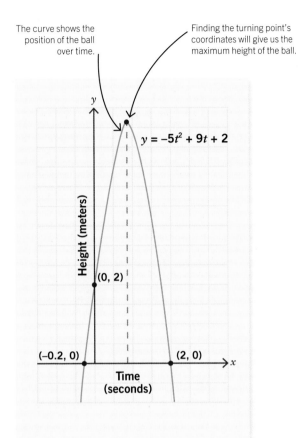

Reading the graph

1. Now we read the graph to find the time taken for the ball to hit the ground. The height is 0 m at −0.2 and 2. The time taken to hit the ground will be the positive of these two numbers, so the ball hits the ground after 2 seconds.

2. Next, we work out the maximum height represented by the turning point of the graph. To do this, we first find the *x* coordinate of the turning point.

3. Quadratic graphs have a line of symmetry running through their turning point. Therefore, the *x* coordinate of the turning point is exactly halfway between the two roots of the graph. We work out the *x* coordinate using the coordinates of the roots and the formula for the midpoint of a line segment (see page 148).

4. Substituting this *x* coordinate into the original equation gives the corresponding value for *y* and the maximum height of the ball. The maximum height is 6.05 m.

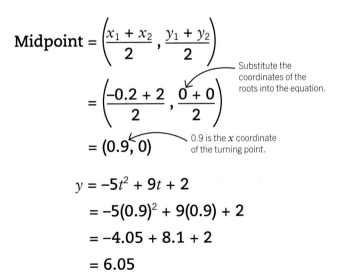

$$\text{Midpoint} = \left(\frac{x_1 + x_2}{2} , \frac{y_1 + y_2}{2} \right)$$

Substitute the coordinates of the roots into the equation.

$$= \left(\frac{-0.2 + 2}{2} , \frac{0 + 0}{2} \right)$$

$$= (0.9, 0)$$

0.9 is the *x* coordinate of the turning point.

$$y = -5t^2 + 9t + 2$$

$$= -5(0.9)^2 + 9(0.9) + 2$$

$$= -4.05 + 8.1 + 2$$

$$= 6.05$$

Solving simple equations using graphs

We can use graphs to solve equations, because all the points along the line of an equation's graph represent possible solutions of the equation.

Evaluating a function from a graph

The graph of a function $f(x)$ maps an input x to the output y. To evaluate a function from its graph, we simply read the y coordinate for a chosen value of x.

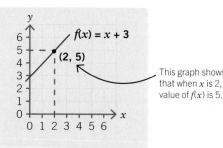

This graph shows us that when x is 2, the value of $f(x)$ is 5.

Solving simultaneous equations using a graph

Simultaneous equations can be solved quickly by plotting both of their graphs. The point at which the lines cross gives the solution that satisfies both equations, allowing us to solve the pair of simultaneous equations. Lines that are parallel will never cross, so they have no solution.

1. To solve these simultaneous equations using a graph, first rearrange them to make y the subject.

2. Use a table to work out some coordinates for each equation. Choose several values for x and substitute them into each equation to find values for y.

3. Plot the coordinates on the coordinate grid. The solution to this system of simultaneous equations is $x = 4$ and $y = 5$.

Equation ①
$$x + y = 9$$
$$y = -x + 9$$

Coordinates for Equation ①

x	y
1	$-1 + 9 = 8$
2	7
3	6

Equation ②
$$2x - y = 3$$
$$y = 2x - 3$$

Coordinates for Equation ②

x	y
1	$2 \times 1 - 3 = -1$
2	1
3	3

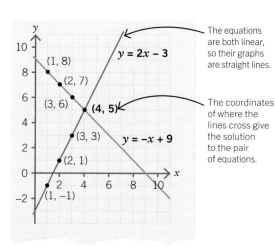

The equations are both linear, so their graphs are straight lines.

The coordinates of where the lines cross give the solution to the pair of equations.

Solving harder equations using graphs

For simultaneous equations where one of the equations is quadratic and the other is linear, the graphs may intersect twice, once, or not at all, revealing 2, 1, or 0 solution pairs respectively.

Simultaneous equations with quadratics

To solve a linear-quadratic pair of simultaneous equations, we can plot them both on the same coordinate grid. The coordinates of the points at which the lines cross are read as solutions for the two equations.

The lines intersect at two points, so there are two solution pairs:
$x = -2, y = -4$
and
$x = 1, y = 2$.

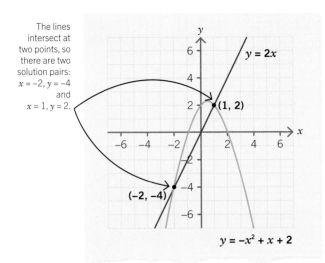

$y = 2x$

$\bullet (1, 2)$

$(-2, -4)$

$y = -x^2 + x + 2$

Checking the result

We can check the solutions are correct by substituting them into the original equations.

1. Check the first solution pair by substituting -2 for x and -4 for y in the two equations.

Solution 1

$$y = 2x \qquad\qquad y = -x^2 + x + 2$$
$$-4 = 2(-2) \qquad -4 = -(-2)^2 - 2 + 2$$
$$-4 = -4 \qquad\qquad -4 = -4$$

2. Check the second solution pair by substituting 1 for x and 2 for y in the two equations.

Solution 2

$$y = 2x \qquad\qquad y = -x^2 + x + 2$$
$$2 = 2(1) \qquad\quad 2 = -(1)^2 + 1 + 2$$
$$2 = 2 \qquad\qquad 2 = 2$$

⚙ The roots of a quadratic function

The points where a quadratic function crosses the x axis reveal its roots. The roots of a quadratic function are the values of x when $y = 0$. You can think of the process of finding these roots as solving a pair of simultaneous equations.

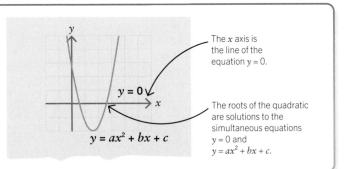

$y = 0$

$y = ax^2 + bx + c$

The x axis is the line of the equation $y = 0$.

The roots of the quadratic are solutions to the simultaneous equations $y = 0$ and $y = ax^2 + bx + c$.

Inequalities

Like an equation, an inequality shows a relationship between two expressions but uses different symbols to express facts about their values. An inequality has a set of possible solutions.

Inequality symbols

There are five symbols that can be used to express different types of inequality. The symbols work a little like an equals sign (=) but instead tell us that the expressions on either side may or may not be equal to each other.

$$x \neq y$$

This symbol means "not equal to" and tells us that the value of x is not equal to y. For example, $2 \neq 3$.

$$x > y$$

This symbol means "greater than" and tells us that x is greater in value than y. For example, $7 > 6$.

$$x \geq y$$

This symbol means "greater than or equal to" and tells us that x has a value greater than or equal to y.

$$x < y$$

This symbol means "less than" and tells us that x is lower in value than y. For example, $4 < 8$.

$$x \leq y$$

This symbol means "less than or equal to" and tells us that x has a value less than or equal to y.

Number lines

A number line can be used to represent an inequality. It helps us visualize the possible values of an expression.

The circle is filled in to show that 3 is a possible value of x.

$x \leq 3$

This green line tells us that x is a value greater than 5.

$x > 5$

This blue line tells us that x is any value less than or equal to 3.

This unfilled circle means that x could be any value more than 5 but cannot be 5.

Algebra with inequalities

We solve inequalities like equations—by isolating the variable. In the example below, we do the same operation to each side of the inequality to keep it true. But there is one important exception: when we multiply by a negative number, the direction of the inequality symbol must change.

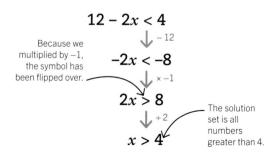

$$12 - 2x < 4$$

Because we multiplied by −1, the symbol has been flipped over.

$$-2x < -8$$

$$2x > 8$$

$$x > 4$$

The solution set is all numbers greater than 4.

Compound inequalities

Two inequality symbols can be used to show the highest or lowest value of an expression. The resulting compound inequality can be manipulated in much the same way as when there is just one inequality symbol.

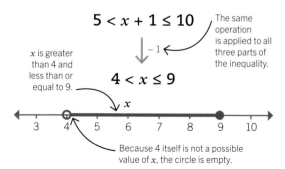

$$5 < x + 1 \leq 10$$

The same operation is applied to all three parts of the inequality.

$$4 < x \leq 9$$

x is greater than 4 and less than or equal to 9.

Because 4 itself is not a possible value of x, the circle is empty.

Graphing linear inequalities

Sometimes inequalities contain two variables and therefore they can be graphed on the coordinate grid. This allows the solutions to be visualized or for the solutions of combined inequalities to be shown.

Region of solutions

When an inequality contains two variables, the graph of its solution isn't a line but a region (area) on the coordinate grid. This region is on one side of the line you get by rephrasing the inequality as an equation.

1. We can graph this inequality to find its solution by turning the inequality into an equation that can be graphed.

$$4 + y > 3x$$

2. First, we replace the inequality sign with an equals sign to give the equation of the inequality's boundary.

$$4 + y = 3x$$

3. Next, we rearrange the equation into the form $y = mx + b$, which allows us to plot the graph as usual.

$$y = 3x - 4$$

Substitute the coordinates (2, 4) into the inequality.

4. The shaded region of the graph reveals the solution set of the inequality. The coordinates of any point, such as (2, 4), in the shaded region will satisfy the inequality.

$$y > 3x - 4$$
$$4 > (3 \times 2) - 4$$
$$4 > 2$$

The solution of the inequality $y > 3x - 4$ is anything that's above this line.

The line is dotted to show that values on the line are not included in the solution set.

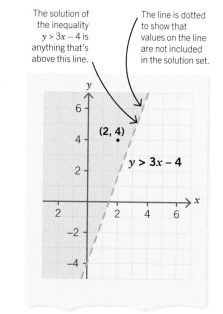

(2, 4)

$y > 3x - 4$

⚙ Graphs of multiple inequalities

Graphing systems of inequalities works similarly to graphing simultaneous equations, but the solution sets are represented by overlapping regions of the coordinate grid instead of by the intersection of the lines.

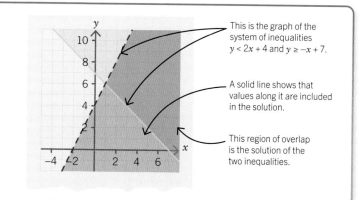

This is the graph of the system of inequalities $y < 2x + 4$ and $y \geq -x + 7$.

A solid line shows that values along it are included in the solution.

This region of overlap is the solution of the two inequalities.

Quadratic inequalities

Some inequalities contain a quadratic expression. These are not as straightforward to solve as linear inequalities, because a quadratic expression generally has two roots.

Graphing quadratic inequalities
Just as sketching the graph of a quadratic equation helps you find its solutions, sketching a graph can also help you work out the solution set of a quadratic inequality.

1. This inequality contains a quadratic expression.

$$-x^2 + 6x - 3 < 2$$

2. Rearrange the inequality to make one side 0, then convert it to an equation by replacing the inequality symbol with an equals sign.

$$-x^2 + 6x - 5 < 0$$
$$-x^2 + 6x - 5 = 0$$

3. Factor the quadratic equation (see page 102). Because the product of the two parentheses is 0, we know that either $(-x + 1)$ or $(x - 5)$ must be equal to 0. We use this fact to identify the two possible values of x.

$$(-x + 1)(x - 5) = 0$$
$$(-x + 1) = 0 \qquad (x - 5) = 0$$
$$x = 1 \qquad\qquad x = 5$$

4. Now use these values of x to sketch the graph of $-x^2 + 6x - 5 < 0$. We know that the curve equals zero when $x = 1$ or 5, so the curve needs to cross the x axis at $x = 1$ and $x = 5$.

The graph is hill shaped, because the coefficient of x^2 is negative.

The required inequality holds true when the curve goes below the x axis. This is at $x < 1$ and $x > 5$.

Use substitution to check if a point in the shaded region satisfies the original inequality:

$$-x^2 + 6x - 3 < 2$$
$$-6^2 + (6 \times 6) - 3 < 2$$
$$- 3 < 2$$

(1, 0) (6, 1) (5, 0)

$$-x^2 + 6x - 5 < 0$$

5. We can now solve the original inequality by plotting it on a number line. The number line is the same as the x axis of the graph above. It tells us that $x < 1$ or $x > 5$.

$$-x^2 + 6x - 3 < 2$$

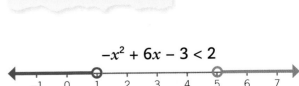

Ratio and proportion

Ratios

If a fruit bowl has twice as many apples as bananas, we say the ratio of apples to bananas is 2 : 1. Ratios are really useful for comparing two or more quantities. They show how much bigger one quantity is than another and are written in the form $a : b$.

Simplifying ratios
It is often possible to reduce a ratio to its simplest form. To reduce a ratio to its simplest form, you need to divide both sides of the ratio by the highest common factor. In this example, the highest common factor is 6.

12 apples   **6 bananas**

Simplify the ratio by dividing both numbers by 6.

$$12 : 6$$

÷ 6   ÷ 6

$$2 : 1$$

The ratio cannot be divided further, so it is now in its simplest form. This tells us that there are twice as many apples as bananas.

📑 **Ratios and units**

Ratios of quantities need to be in the same units. If the units are different, convert them into the same units before working out the ratio.

Question
Three sections of pipe have different lengths. Write the ratio between lengths in its simplest form.

120 cm $1\frac{2}{5}$ m   **1.6 m**

Answer
1. Change any fractions to their decimal equivalent (see page 55).

$$1\frac{2}{5} = 1.4$$

2. Change all the lengths to the same unit—cm in this case (see page 68).

1.4 m = 140 cm
1.6 m = 160 cm

3. Now that the lengths are all in the same unit, divide each by the highest common factor, which in this case is 20.

120 : 140 : 160
÷ 20 ÷ 20 ÷ 20
6 : 7 : 8

Dividing in a given ratio

Quantities, such as money, ingredients, and paint, can be divided into unequal shares by using a given ratio.

Key facts

✓ You can divide quantities into unequal amounts using ratios.

✓ To divide quantities in a given ratio, first find the value of one part.

Ratio diagrams

Three decorators share a total fee of $150 for painting a room. One of them spent 3 hours painting, another spent 1 hour, and the third spent 2 hours, so they decide to split the money in the ratio 3 : 1 : 2. How much money does each person get?

1. To divide a quantity in a given ratio, you need to find the value of one part. This is easier if you draw a simple diagram showing all the parts. In this case, there are 3 + 1 + 2 = 6 parts, so draw a rectangle with six sections. The $150 fee is split between 6 parts, so one part is $150 ÷ 6 = $25. Write this in each section.

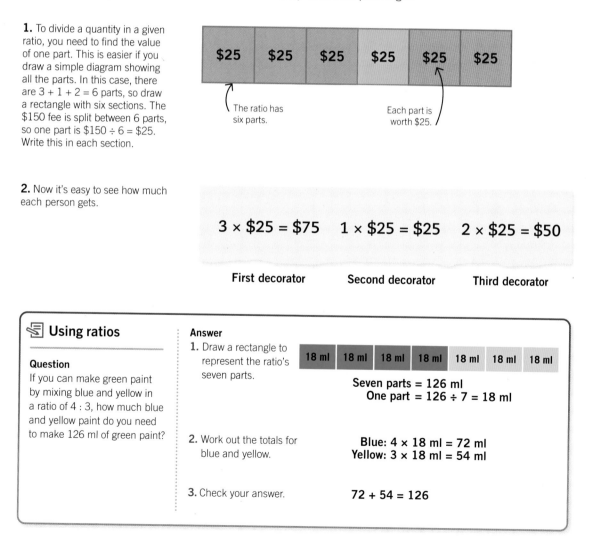

| $25 | $25 | $25 | $25 | $25 | $25 |

The ratio has six parts.

Each part is worth $25.

2. Now it's easy to see how much each person gets.

3 × $25 = $75   1 × $25 = $25   2 × $25 = $50

First decorator   Second decorator   Third decorator

📑 Using ratios

Question

If you can make green paint by mixing blue and yellow in a ratio of 4 : 3, how much blue and yellow paint do you need to make 126 ml of green paint?

Answer

1. Draw a rectangle to represent the ratio's seven parts.

| 18 ml | 18 ml | 18 ml | 18 ml | 18 ml | 18 ml | 18 ml |

Seven parts = 126 ml
One part = 126 ÷ 7 = 18 ml

2. Work out the totals for blue and yellow.

Blue: 4 × 18 ml = 72 ml
Yellow: 3 × 18 ml = 54 ml

3. Check your answer.

72 + 54 = 126

Direct proportion

When different quantities are increased or reduced by the same factor, their ratio to each other stays the same. We say they are directly proportional.

Staying in proportion

The cake on the left is only enough for four people. To make a cake for eight people, the quantities must be doubled. In both cakes, the ratio of different ingredients to each other stays the same. For example, there is three times as much flour as carrot in both cakes. The ratio of flour to carrot remains 3 : 1, so we say these quantities are directly proportional. We can write this using the symbol $\propto$, which means "is proportional to." If y is the quantity of flour and x is the quantity of carrot, $y \propto x$.

Key facts

✓ Two quantities are directly proportional if their ratio to each other remains constant when they change.

✓ To solve questions about proportion, divide to find the value of one of something.

✓ $y \propto x$ means y is directly proportional to x.

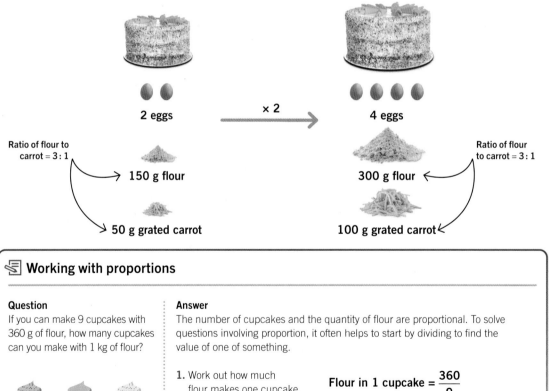

Ratio of flour to carrot = 3 : 1

2 eggs

× 2

4 eggs

150 g flour

300 g flour

Ratio of flour to carrot = 3 : 1

50 g grated carrot

100 g grated carrot

Working with proportions

Question

If you can make 9 cupcakes with 360 g of flour, how many cupcakes can you make with 1 kg of flour?

Answer

The number of cupcakes and the quantity of flour are proportional. To solve questions involving proportion, it often helps to start by dividing to find the value of one of something.

1. Work out how much flour makes one cupcake.

$$\text{Flour in 1 cupcake} = \frac{360}{9}$$
$$= 40$$

2. Now work out how many times 40 g goes into 1 kg (1,000 g).

$$\text{Number of cupcakes} = \frac{1000}{40}$$
$$= 25 \text{ cupcakes}$$

Inverse proportion

How long does it take to build a shed? It depends on how many people build it—the more builders there are, the shorter the time. When an increase in one quantity results in a corresponding decrease in another, we say the two quantities are inversely proportional.

Inverse proportion at work
Imagine it takes one person 60 minutes to build a shed. If two people share the work and work at the same rate, they can do it in half the time. If there are four people, they can do it in a quarter of the time. The number of people and the time taken are inversely proportional. When two quantities x and y are inversely proportional, their product is always the same, so $xy = k$, where k is a constant. In this case, the number of people multiplied by time taken equals 60 in each case.

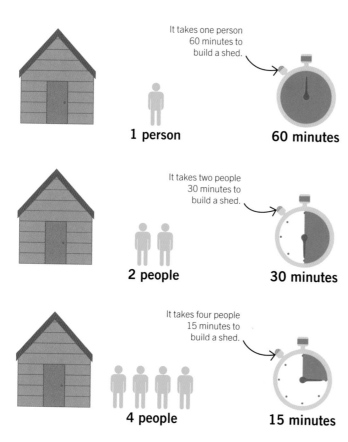

It takes one person 60 minutes to build a shed.

1 person   **60 minutes**

It takes two people 30 minutes to build a shed.

2 people   **30 minutes**

It takes four people 15 minutes to build a shed.

4 people   **15 minutes**

How many pizzas?

Question
If 3 pizza chefs can make 60 pizzas in 2 hours, how long will it take 6 pizza chefs to make 30 pizzas?

Answer
Be careful! The number of pizza chefs and the time taken are inversely proportional, which can make this question confusing.

1. Work out how long it will take for 1 pizza chef rather than 3 to make 60 pizzas. It will take three times as long.

   60 pizzas by 1 chef = 3 × 2 hours

   = 6 hours

2. Six pizza chefs will take a sixth of the time to make 60 pizzas, so divide the answer by 6.

   $$\text{6 pizzas by 6 chefs} = \frac{6 \text{ hours}}{6}$$

   = 1 hour

3. But they only need to make half as many pizzas, so divide 1 hour (60 minutes) by 2.

   $$\frac{60 \text{ minutes}}{2} = 30 \text{ minutes}$$

Unitary method

Understanding proportion helps solve problems that involve two related quantities, such as comparing prices. One way to compare prices is to find the value of a single unit, then multiply this value by the number of units you want to buy. This is called the unitary method.

Finding the value of a unit
Imagine that 5 m of carpet costs $30, and you want to work out how much 4 m will cost. You can use the unitary method, which involves finding out the value of a single unit.

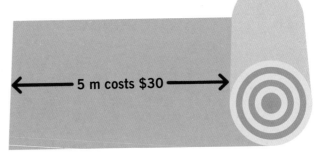

5 m costs $30

1. The cost of 5 m of carpet is $30.

2. The cost of 1 m of carpet will be:

$$\$30 \div 5 = \$6$$

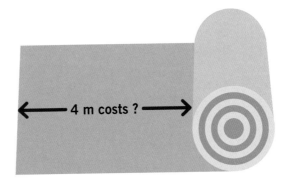

4 m costs ?

3. The cost of 4 m of carpet will be:

$$\$6 \times 4 = \$24$$

📑 **Best buy**

Question
Blackberry jam is sold in three sizes. Which size jar is the best value for money?

A 200 g jar costs $1.70

A 350 g jar costs $2.80

A 500 g jar costs $3.95

Answer
Convert the price of each jar to cents, and work out the price per gram.

$$170 \div 200 = 0.85 \text{ cents/gram}$$

$$280 \div 350 = 0.80 \text{ cents/gram}$$

$$395 \div 500 = 0.79 \text{ cents/gram}$$

The 500 g jar is best value for money, because it only costs 0.79 cents/gram.

Scaling method

The scaling method is similar to the unitary method but is often quicker. It is particularly useful when you need to scale amounts up or down, as in recipes.

Finding the scale factor

Consider the problem from the previous page: if 5 m of carpet costs $30, how much does 4 m cost? Instead of working out the unit price (price per meter) first, you simply scale down the price by the same factor used to scale down the length.

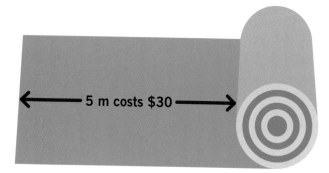

5 m costs $30

1. The cost of 5 m of carpet is $30.

2. The scaling factor for reducing 5 m to 4 m is:

$$4 \div 5 = 0.8$$

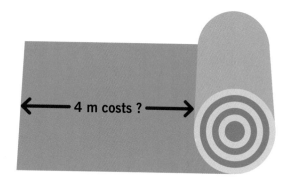

4 m costs ?

3. The cost of 4 m of carpet will be:

$$\$30 \times 0.8 = \$24$$

📑 **Price and weight**

Question

Gold is sold by weight. If a 1.25 kg gold bar costs $60,000, what is the value of a 50 g gold coin?

Answer

1. Use the same units (grams) to find the scale factor.

$$50 \div 1250 = 0.04$$

2. Multiply the price by the scale factor.

$$\$60,000 \times 0.04 = \$2,400$$

Proportion

Ratio is a way of describing proportion, just like fractions, decimals, and percentages. Proportion describes the relationship between two parts or between one part and the whole.

Key facts

✓ Proportion is the relationship of one part to another or to the whole.

✓ Proportions can be expressed as ratios, fractions, decimals, or percentages.

Ratios, fractions, decimals, and percentages

You can convert between ratios and other ways of expressing proportions—fractions, decimals, or percentages. The diagram shows how the relationship between two quantities in the ratio 3 : 5 can be expressed in these different forms.

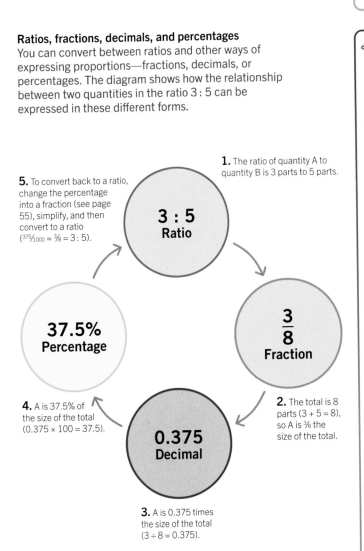

5. To convert back to a ratio, change the percentage into a fraction (see page 55), simplify, and then convert to a ratio ($^{375}/_{1000} = ^3/_8 = 3 : 5$).

1. The ratio of quantity A to quantity B is 3 parts to 5 parts.

3 : 5 Ratio

37.5% Percentage

3/8 Fraction

0.375 Decimal

4. A is 37.5% of the size of the total (0.375 × 100 = 37.5).

2. The total is 8 parts (3 + 5 = 8), so A is 3/8 the size of the total.

3. A is 0.375 times the size of the total (3 ÷ 8 = 0.375).

Calculating proportions

A pond contains two types of amphibian—frogs and toads—in the ratio 3 : 7.

Question 1
Write the proportion of frogs to the total number of amphibians as a decimal.

Answer 1
1. Add the parts of the ratio to find the total.
$$3 + 7 = 10$$

2. Divide the proportion of frogs by the total.
$$3 ÷ 10 = 0.3$$

The proportion of frogs is 0.3 of the total.

Question 2
The ratio of male to female toads is 2 : 1. There are 1,800 amphibians in total. How many female toads are there in the pond?

Answer 2
Of the total amphibians, 0.3 are frogs, which means that 0.7 are toads.
$$1800 × 0.7 = 1260 \text{ toads}$$

As the ratio of male to female toads is 2 : 1, ⅔ are male and ⅓ are female.
$$1260 × \frac{1}{3} = 420$$

There are 420 female toads.

Comparing proportions

When you need to compare the sizes of two or more proportions, it is helpful to convert them all into the same form. Comparing proportions is useful in a wide variety of everyday contexts.

Key facts

✓ You can compare proportions more easily if you convert them to the same form.

✓ Percentages are often the clearest way to compare proportions.

Comparing test results

To compare 18 out of 20 with 22 out of 25, write them out as fractions and then convert them to decimals or percentages.

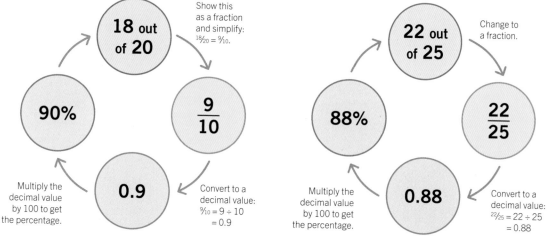

18 out of 20

Show this as a fraction and simplify: $^{18}/_{20} = ^{9}/_{10}$.

$\dfrac{9}{10}$

Convert to a decimal value: $^{9}/_{10} = 9 \div 10 = 0.9$

0.9

Multiply the decimal value by 100 to get the percentage.

90%

22 out of 25

Change to a fraction.

$\dfrac{22}{25}$

Convert to a decimal value: $^{22}/_{25} = 22 \div 25 = 0.88$

0.88

Multiply the decimal value by 100 to get the percentage.

88%

📧 Comparing proportions in different forms

Question

Each of a student's teachers for English, Science, and Math has a different way of marking her tests. Her English teacher gives her 87%, her Science teacher gives her $^{35}/_{40}$, and her Math teacher gives the ratio of correct to incorrect answers (17 : 3). On which test does the student get the best result?

Answer

Convert each test result to the same form. Percentages are easiest to compare.

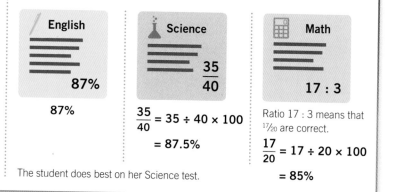

English

87%

87%

Science

$\dfrac{35}{40}$

$\dfrac{35}{40} = 35 \div 40 \times 100$

$= 87.5\%$

Math

17 : 3

Ratio 17 : 3 means that $^{17}/_{20}$ are correct.

$\dfrac{17}{20} = 17 \div 20 \times 100$

$= 85\%$

The student does best on her Science test.

Proportion equations

Statements about proportion, such as y is proportional to x, are easy to turn into equations. This is useful, because equations can be shown on graphs, which can help us solve problems involving algebra.

Key facts

✓ If the ratio of two quantities remains the same despite their values changing, they are directly proportional. Their equation is:
$$y = kx$$

✓ If the product of two quantities remains the same despite their values changing, they are inversely proportional and their equation is:
$$y = \frac{k}{x}$$

Direct proportion
We write y is directly proportional to x as $y \propto x$, where $\propto$ means "is directly proportional to." To turn this into an equation, replace $\propto$ with $= k$ (where k is a constant). Equations in the form $y = kx$ form a straight line that passes through the origin and has the slope k.

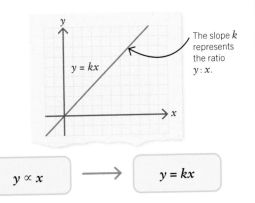

The slope k represents the ratio $y : x$.

$$y \propto x \longrightarrow y = kx$$

Inverse proportion
We write y is inversely proportional to x as $y \propto 1/x$. As with direct proportion, replace the $\propto$ with $= k$, so $y \propto 1/x$ becomes $y = k/x$. Equations showing an inversely proportional relationship form a curved line.

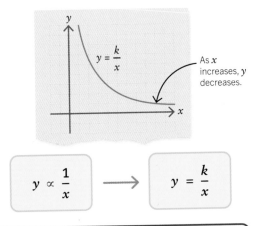

As x increases, y decreases.

$$y \propto \frac{1}{x} \longrightarrow y = \frac{k}{x}$$

Using proportion equations

Question
The graph here shows the values of euros (x axis) to dollars (y axis) on a certain date. Use the graph to work out the value of k in $y = kx$. Then use the equation to find out how much €250 is worth in dollars.

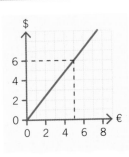

Answer
1. Select a point on the graph where x meets y. For instance, where $x = 5$, $y = 6$.

2. Substitute the values of x and y into $y = kx$ to find k.
$$6 = k \times 5$$
$$k = \frac{6}{5} = 1.2$$

So $y = 1.2x$.

3. Use k to work out y when $x = 250$.
$$y = 1.2 \times 250$$
$$= \$300$$

Practice questions
Ratio and proportion

To solve problems involving ratios and proportions, you usually need to scale up or down by multiplying or dividing. Here are some problems to try.

See also

159 Dividing in a given ratio
166 Proportion equations

Question
The ratio of male to female sheep in a field is 2 : 5. The farmer opens a gate and 17 male sheep enter the field, changing the male to female ratio to 3 : 5. How many female sheep are there?

Answer
1. If a question involves a changing ratio, drawing bar diagrams can help. Draw a diagram for the first ratio, which has 7 parts.

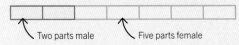

Two parts male   Five parts female

2. Draw a diagram for the second ratio, which has 8 parts.

The 17 new sheep form one extra part.

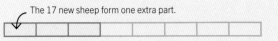

3. The diagram shows that each part consists of 17 sheep, so the total number of female sheep is:

$$5 \times 17 = 85$$

Question
A long-distance bike ride takes 6 hours to complete when cycling at 16 mph. How long would it take at 15 mph?

Answer
1. Journey time and speed are inversely proportional, so follow the formula $y = k/x$. Work out k by putting in the numbers.

$$\text{Journey time} = \frac{k}{\text{Speed}}$$

$$6 = \frac{k}{16}$$

$$k = 96$$

2. Use k to find the journey time when the speed is 15 mph.

$$\text{Journey time} = \frac{96}{15}$$

$$= 6.4 \text{ (6 hours 24 minutes)}$$

Question
Three rods A, B, and C have different lengths. A is 1¼ times the length of B. C is 2.4 times the length of A. C is 40 cm longer than B. How long is A?

Answer
1. Sketch a rough diagram of the rods. A is longer than B, and C is longer than A, so B is the shortest.

A
B
C

2. Write what you know as equations, then combine them to find the answer. Here's one way of doing it.

C is 40 cm longer than B, so:

$$C - B = 40$$

Call this equation 1.

A is 1¼ times B, so:

$$A = 1.25B$$

Call this equation 2.

C is 2.4 times longer than A, so:

$$C = 2.4A$$

Call this equation 3.

3. Substitute equation 2 into equation 3:

$$C = 2.4 \times 1.25B$$
$$= 3B$$

4. Substitute C = 3B into equation 1:

$$3B - B = 40$$
$$B = 20$$

5. Calculate A:

$$A = 1.25 \times 20$$
$$= 25$$

So A is 25 cm long. Check: A should be longer than B, which you can see on the sketch.

Geometry

Vectors

Most measurements are either what we call scalar quantities or vector quantities. Scalar quantities only have a size (magnitude), but vector quantities have a size and a direction.

Vector and scalar quantities

The purple arrow shows a jogger's journey as he runs around a park. How far has he traveled? One way to answer this is to measure the total distance of his winding path. This is a scalar quantity, as it has no particular direction. Another way is to measure his displacement—the distance and direction in a line between his start and end points. Displacement is a vector quantity, because it has direction, as well as magnitude.

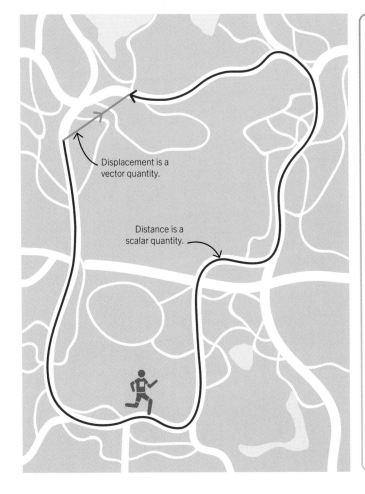

Displacement is a vector quantity.

Distance is a scalar quantity.

Writing vectors

Vectors are always shown as lines with arrowheads in diagrams, but there are several ways of writing them. A vector between points A and B can be written as $\overrightarrow{AB}$ or as a single letter that may be bold or underlined. You can also write a vector as a column vector like this:

$$\begin{pmatrix} 3 \\ 2 \end{pmatrix}$$

The top number shows distance moved along the x axis and the bottom number is distance moved on the y axis. Negative numbers mean the movement is from right to left along the x axis or from top to bottom on the y axis.

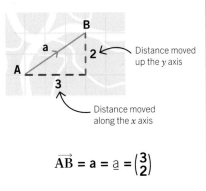

Distance moved up the y axis

Distance moved along the x axis

$$\overrightarrow{AB} = \mathbf{a} = \underline{a} = \begin{pmatrix} 3 \\ 2 \end{pmatrix}$$

Working with vectors

Vectors are easy to work with if you think of them as arrows on a grid, with positive or negative units telling you which way the vector points relative to the axes. A vector is specified by its size and its direction but not usually its position, so a vector can be equal to another vector in a different place on the grid.

Direction of vectors

The numbers in column vectors can be positive or negative, depending on which direction the vector points in. For example, the vector $\binom{2}{3}$ moves two units to the right along the x axis and moves 3 units up on the y axis. Similarly, the vector $\binom{-2}{-3}$ moves two units left on the x axis and 3 units down on the y axis.

A vector's horizontal and vertical units form a right triangle with it. As a result, you can use the Pythagorean theorem (see page 196) to calculate the vector's length.

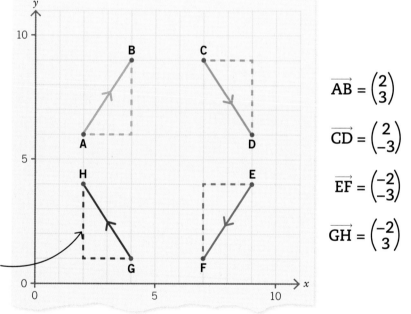

$$\overrightarrow{AB} = \binom{2}{3}$$

$$\overrightarrow{CD} = \binom{2}{-3}$$

$$\overrightarrow{EF} = \binom{-2}{-3}$$

$$\overrightarrow{GH} = \binom{-2}{3}$$

Equal vectors and opposite vectors

Two vectors are equal if they have the same horizontal and vertical units, even if they're in different positions on a coordinate grid. In this diagram, **a** and **b** are both $\binom{4}{6}$, so **a** = **b**. A minus sign switches a vector's direction, so it points the opposite way.

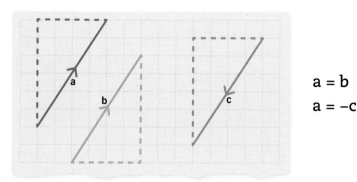

$$\mathbf{a} = \mathbf{b}$$

$$\mathbf{a} = -\mathbf{c}$$

Adding and subtracting vectors

Vectors can be added or subtracted just like any other type of quantity. You can do this in two ways: by drawing them on a grid or by writing them as column vectors.

Adding vectors

To add vectors by drawing, put the start of the second vector at the end of the first one to form a triangle. The third side of the triangle is the sum of the two vectors (called the resultant). To add using column vectors, add the top row of numbers (the horizontal units), then the bottom row (the vertical units). It doesn't matter which way around you add vectors, as the result is the same: **a** + **b** = **b** + **a**.

$$4 + 1 = 5$$

$$\begin{pmatrix} 4 \\ 3 \end{pmatrix} + \begin{pmatrix} 1 \\ -2 \end{pmatrix} = \begin{pmatrix} 5 \\ 1 \end{pmatrix}$$

a + **b** means go along **a**, then along **b**.

$$3 + -2 = 1$$

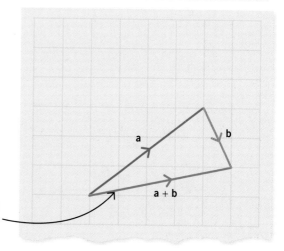

Subtracting vectors

To subtract one vector from another, you need to travel backward along the second vector (in the reverse direction). For example, **a** − **b** means go along **a**, then backward along **b**. You can think of it as **a** + −**b**. To subtract using column vectors, subtract the top row first, then do the same in the bottom row. Unlike adding vectors, it does matter which way around you put them: **a** − **b** does not equal **b** − **a**.

$$4 - 1 = 3$$

a − **b** means go along **a**, then backward along **b**.

$$\begin{pmatrix} 4 \\ 3 \end{pmatrix} - \begin{pmatrix} 1 \\ -2 \end{pmatrix} = \begin{pmatrix} 3 \\ 5 \end{pmatrix}$$

$$3 - -2 = 5$$

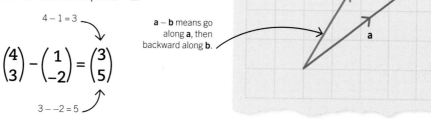

Multiplying vectors

You can multiply vectors by numbers to make them longer or shorter. If you multiply by a positive number, the vector's direction stays the same. If you multiply by a negative number, the direction reverses.

Scalar multiples

There are two methods you can use to multiply vectors: by drawing them and by writing them as column vectors. To multiply by drawing, draw a new vector parallel to the original one but longer or shorter, depending on the multiple used. For instance, to multiply by 2, double the length. We call the new vector a scalar multiple. Vectors that are scalar multiples are parallel to each other.

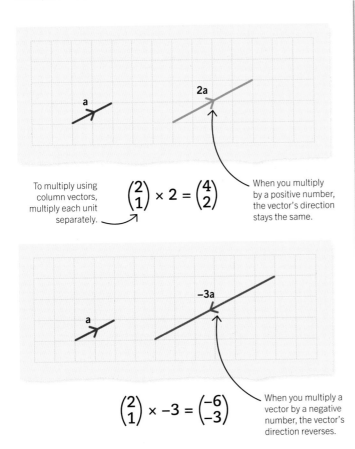

To multiply using column vectors, multiply each unit separately.

$$\begin{pmatrix} 2 \\ 1 \end{pmatrix} \times 2 = \begin{pmatrix} 4 \\ 2 \end{pmatrix}$$

When you multiply by a positive number, the vector's direction stays the same.

$$\begin{pmatrix} 2 \\ 1 \end{pmatrix} \times -3 = \begin{pmatrix} -6 \\ -3 \end{pmatrix}$$

When you multiply a vector by a negative number, the vector's direction reverses.

Points on a straight line

If vectors are joined and point in the same or opposite directions, they must be scalar multiples of each other. You can use this fact to prove that points are on a straight line (collinear).

Question

$\overrightarrow{AB}$ is the vector $\begin{pmatrix} 3 \\ 2 \end{pmatrix}$, and $\overrightarrow{AC}$ is the vector $\begin{pmatrix} -6 \\ -4 \end{pmatrix}$. Prove that the points A, B, and C lie on a straight line.

Answer

1. Try to find a multiple that turns one of the two vectors into the other.

$$\begin{pmatrix} -6 \\ -4 \end{pmatrix} = -2 \times \begin{pmatrix} 3 \\ 2 \end{pmatrix}$$

2. The two vectors are scalar multiples and have a point in common (A). Therefore, A, B, and C are collinear (they lie on a straight line).

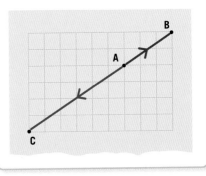

Practice question
Vectors and geometry

Geometry questions sometimes ask you to prove something is true by using vectors. To solve the question, think of each line in the shape as a vector.

See also

170 Working with vectors
171 Adding and subtracting vectors
172 Multiplying vectors

Question
The blue line ST in this triangle joins the midpoints of sides PQ and PR. Using vectors, prove that ST is parallel to the green line QR and half its length.

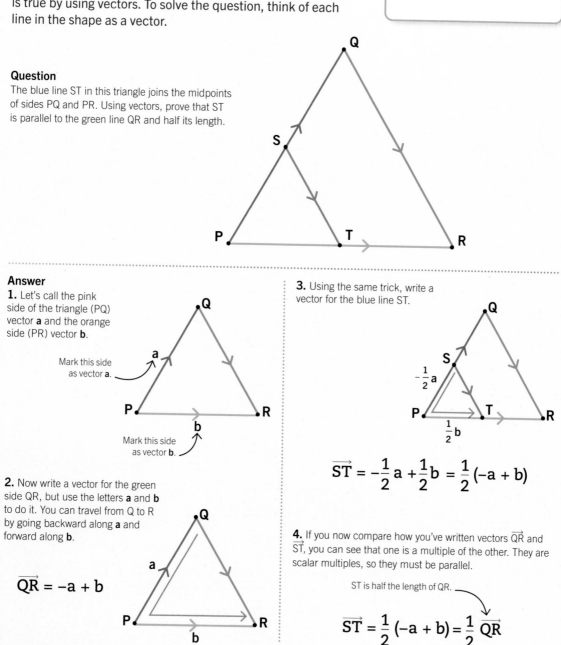

Answer
1. Let's call the pink side of the triangle (PQ) vector **a** and the orange side (PR) vector **b**.

Mark this side as vector **a**.

Mark this side as vector **b**.

2. Now write a vector for the green side QR, but use the letters **a** and **b** to do it. You can travel from Q to R by going backward along **a** and forward along **b**.

$$\overrightarrow{QR} = -a + b$$

3. Using the same trick, write a vector for the blue line ST.

$$-\frac{1}{2}a$$

$$\frac{1}{2}b$$

$$\overrightarrow{ST} = -\frac{1}{2}a + \frac{1}{2}b = \frac{1}{2}(-a + b)$$

4. If you now compare how you've written vectors $\overrightarrow{QR}$ and $\overrightarrow{ST}$, you can see that one is a multiple of the other. They are scalar multiples, so they must be parallel.

ST is half the length of QR.

$$\overrightarrow{ST} = \frac{1}{2}(-a + b) = \frac{1}{2}\overrightarrow{QR}$$

Translations

In geometry, a change in the size, position, or rotation of a shape is called a transformation. A translation is a type of transformation. It slides an object to a new position without changing its size, shape, or orientation. The translated object is called an image.

Key facts

✓ A translation is a transformation that slides an object to a new position without changing its size, shape, or orientation.

✓ Translations can be written in the form $(x + a, y + b)$

✓ The translated object is called an image.

Translation notation

Translations are written as vectors (see page 169). Here, a triangle is translated twice. The first translation moves it 9 units right and 4 units down, and the second moves it 8 units right and 1 unit up. We can write these translations as $(x + 9, y - 4)$ and $(x + 8, y + 1)$.

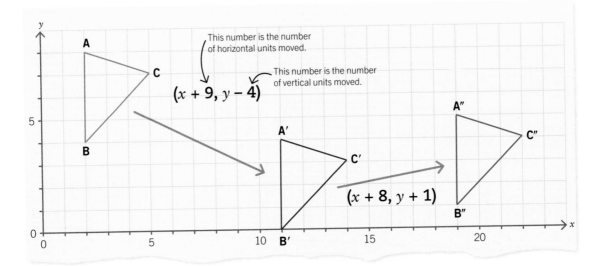

Describing translations

Question
Describe the transformation of rectangle ABCD to rectangle A′B′C′D′.

Answer
The transformation can be written as:

$$(x - 7, y - 3)$$

Reflections

A shape can be reflected across a mirror line to create an image. The original shape and its reflection are congruent, which means they are the same size and shape, though one is flipped relative to the other.

Mirror line
To define a reflection on a coordinate grid, state the equation of the mirror line. Here, the green shape is reflected twice to create two images. Reflection across the line $x = 0$ (the y axis) creates the blue shape. Reflection of the green shape across the line $y = x$ creates the orange shape.

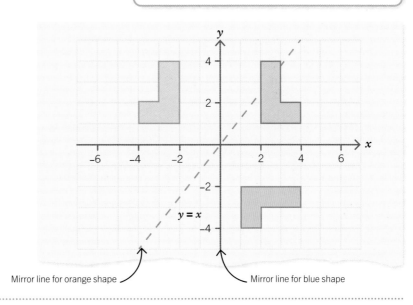

Mirror line for orange shape

Mirror line for blue shape

Constructing reflections
Each point on a reflected image is the same distance from the mirror line as the corresponding point on the original image. You can use this fact to construct a reflection.

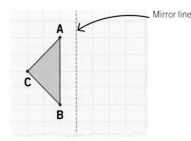

Mirror line

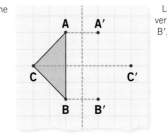

Label the vertices A', B', and C'.

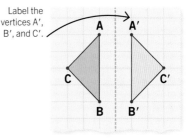

1. Start by drawing the mirror line. Label the vertices of the shape you want to reflect.

2. Draw a line from each vertex at right angles to the mirror line and beyond it. Measure how far each vertex is from the mirror line along the line. Mark the reflected points the same distance away on the other side.

3. Join the dots to complete the reflected image.

Rotations

An object can be rotated around a fixed point called the center of rotation. Objects are congruent after rotation, which means they don't change in size or shape.

Describing rotations
To describe a rotation, you need three things: the angle of rotation, the direction, and the precise location of the center of rotation. For example, the orange shape here has rotated 90° clockwise around the origin (0, 0). The pink shape has rotated 180° clockwise around the point (8, 3).

Key facts

✓ The fixed point around which an object rotates is called the center of rotation.

✓ Objects are congruent after rotation.

✓ To describe a rotation, you need three things: the angle, the direction, and the center of rotation.

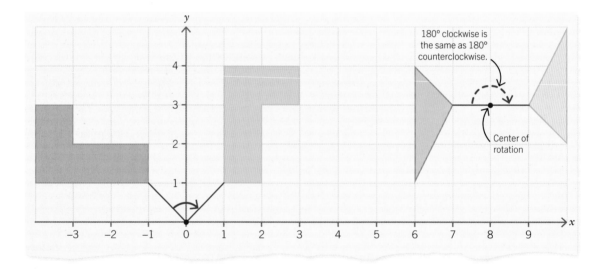

180° clockwise is the same as 180° counterclockwise.

Center of rotation

Finding the center and angle
Given an object and its rotated image, you can find the center and angle of rotation by following these steps.

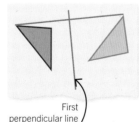

First perpendicular line

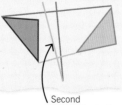

Second perpendicular line

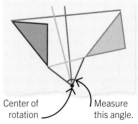

Center of rotation

Measure this angle.

1. Draw a line from a point in the shape to the equivalent point in the image. At the midpoint, draw another line at right angles. You can do this with a protractor or a compass (see page 184).

2. Do the same for another pair of points and draw another perpendicular line.

3. The center of rotation is where the two perpendicular lines meet. To find the angle, draw lines from the center of rotation to a point and its image and measure the angle between them with a protractor.

Constructing rotations

Constructing a rotation means rotating a shape around a center of rotation by a certain angle and drawing the new shape (the image). Follow the steps on this page to do it.

1. To rotate this triangle 90° counterclockwise around the origin (0, 0), start by placing your compass point on the origin. Draw an arc counterclockwise from each corner of the triangle.

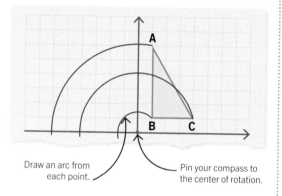

Draw an arc from each point.

Pin your compass to the center of rotation.

2. Place the center of a protractor over the center of rotation. Measure 90° counterclockwise from each point on the triangle and mark where the angle meets the arc.

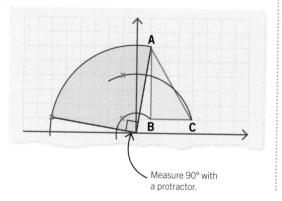

Measure 90° with a protractor.

3. Join the three crosses to draw the new triangle.

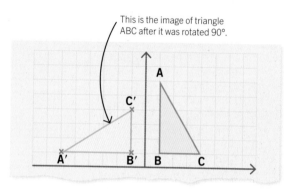

This is the image of triangle ABC after it was rotated 90°.

Using tracing paper

An easy way to check that you've constructed a rotation correctly is to trace the shape on a separate piece of paper, then rotate the copy while keeping the center of rotation pinned in place with the point of your pencil.

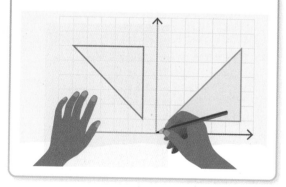

Dilations

Dilations change the position and size of a shape without affecting its angles or the ratios of its sides. Dilations are constructed using a fixed point called the center of dilation.

Describing dilations

To describe a dilation, you need two things: the location of the center of dilation and the scale factor. Here, the yellow triangle is dilated from a center of dilation at (1, 5) by a scale factor of 2 and 4 to create green and pink triangles. You can calculate the scale factor of a dilation by dividing the length of one side of the new shape by the old length. For example, A″B″ in the pink triangle is 12 and AB in the original triangle is 3, so the scale factor = $^{12}/_3$ = **4**.

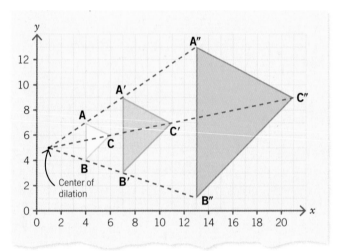

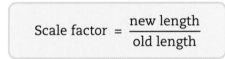

$$\text{Scale factor} = \frac{\text{new length}}{\text{old length}}$$

Constructing dilations

You can construct a dilation by drawing lines from the center of dilation through each vertex (corner) of a shape. For example, this is how to dilate the orange quadrilateral by a scale factor of 3 with a center of dilation (1, 4).

1. Draw lines from the center of dilation through each vertex of the shape.

2. Measure the distance from the center of dilation to each vertex of the original shape. Multiply this by 3 to find the distance to each new vertex.

3. Mark the new vertices and connect the marked points to draw the shape.

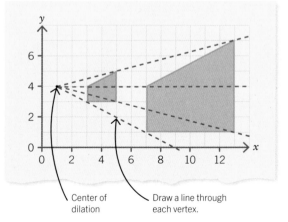

Fractional and negative dilations

Dilations can do more than simply make shapes larger. Fractional dilations can shrink shapes, and negative scale factors turn shapes upside down by projecting them through the center of dilation.

Fractional dilations

Scale factors between 0 and 1 make shapes smaller. Here, the pink triangle is dilated by a scale factor of ⅓, using a center of dilation at (20, 12). The new triangle is smaller, with each of its sides one-third of the original length. For example, A′B′ is 2 units, whereas AB is 6 units. If the dilation was done in reverse (from A′B′C′ to ABC), the scale factor would be 3 (the reciprocal of ⅓).

The image is smaller.

Center of dilation

The scale factor is ⅓.

Negative scale factors

If the scale factor is negative, a dilation projects the shape through the center of dilation, causing it to pop out on the other side, where it is upside down. The new shape may be smaller or larger than the original, unless the scale factor is −1, which has the same effect as a 180° rotation. Here, a green quadrilateral is dilated by a scale factor of −2.

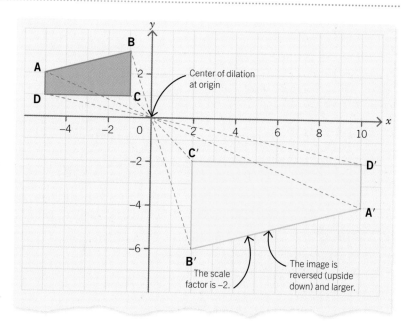

Center of dilation at origin

The scale factor is −2.

The image is reversed (upside down) and larger.

Scaling area and volume

If you dilate a shape by a scale factor of 2, its length and width double. However, surface area and volume increase by larger factors.

Key facts

✓ If the width or length of a shape increases by a scale factor of x, its area increases by a scale factor of x^2.

✓ If the width or length of a shape increases by a scale factor of x, its volume increases by a scale factor of x^3.

Scaling area
The red square is 1 cm wide. If it's dilated by a scale factor of 3, its length and width both increase by ×3, so its area increases by a scale factor of $3 \times 3 = 9$. If the width or length of a shape increases by a scale factor of x, its area increases by a factor of x^2.

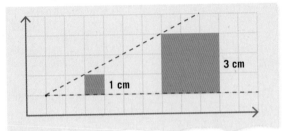

1 cm

3 cm

Scaling volume
The small cube is 1 cm wide and has a volume of 1 cm³. If it's dilated by a scale factor of 3, the new cube has a volume of 27 cm³, which is $3 \times 3 \times 3$ times greater. If the width or length of a shape increases by a scale factor of x, its volume increases by a factor of x^3.

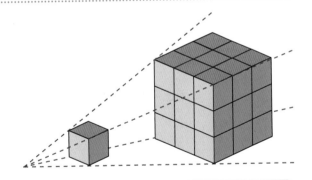

🗎 Scaling problem

Question
The pizza on the left is 15 cm wide, and the pizza on the right is 30 cm wide and costs twice the price. Which is better value for money and why?

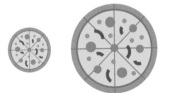

Answer
1. Calculate the width scale factor.

$$\text{Scale factor} = \frac{\text{Width of large pizza}}{\text{Width of small pizza}}$$

$$= \frac{30}{15} = 2$$

2. Now calculate the area scale factor.

Area scale factor = Square of the width scale factor

$$= 2^2 = 4$$

3. The large pizza contains four times as much food but is only twice the price, so it is much better value.

Practice questions
Combinations of transformations

See also

175 Reflections
176 Rotations
177 Constructing rotations

Transformations can be combined together in many different ways. Try the questions here to figure out which single transformation has the same result as a combination of steps.

Question

Shape A (right) is reflected in the line $x = -1$ to give shape B. Shape B is reflected in the line $y = 0$ to give shape C. Describe a single transformation that maps shape A onto shape C.

Answer

1. Draw the line $x = -1$ and create shape B by mapping each corner of the image the same distance from the mirror line as the original shape's corners.

2. Now do the same using $y = 0$ (the x axis) as the mirror line to create shape C.

3. You can now see that shape C can be created from shape A by a 180° clockwise or counterclockwise rotation around a center of rotation at $(-1, 0)$.

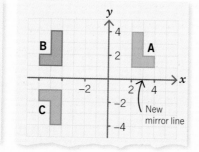

Question

Shape P (below) is rotated 90° clockwise around the origin $(0, 0)$ to give shape Q. Shape Q is reflected in the line $y = x$ to give shape R. Describe a single transformation that maps shape P onto shape R.

Answer

1. Trace P onto a piece of paper and, pinning the center of rotation in place with your pencil, rotate it 90° clockwise to find where shape Q is. Draw shape Q.

2. Draw the mirror line $y = x$. Construct a reflection of Q in the mirror line to create shape R. P can be mapped onto R with a reflection in the y axis (a reflection in the line $x = 0$).

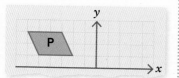

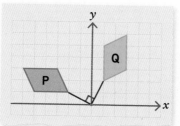

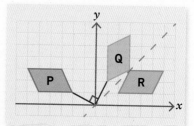

Scale drawings

A scale drawing shows an object or a location reduced in size by a fixed ratio, which is usually shown on the drawing. The ratio makes it possible to convert measurements taken from the drawing into distances or dimensions in the real world.

Key facts

✓ A scale drawing shows an object or location reduced in size by a ratio.

✓ The ratio allows distances in the real world to be calculated from measurements taken from the drawing.

Using scales
The bridge in this drawing measures 150 m long in real life, but the drawing is only 15 cm wide. The real bridge is 1,000 times larger, so the scale is shown on the drawing as 1 : 1000. To find the true size of any part of the bridge, measure the drawing and multiply by 1,000. Maps and scale drawings sometimes show the scale using units, such as 1 cm = 10 m. This makes it easier to calculate distances without having to convert from one unit to another.

One square of the grid represents 10 m.

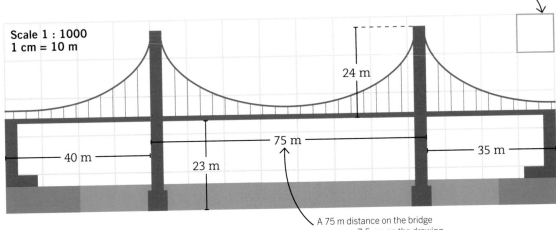

Scale 1 : 1000
1 cm = 10 m

24 m

75 m

35 m

40 m

23 m

A 75 m distance on the bridge measures 7.5 cm on the drawing.

📄 Calculating distance

Question
This map has a scale of 1 : 10 000. If the two villages A and B are 7.3 cm apart on the map, how far apart are they in reality?

• B

• A   Scale: 1:10 000

Answer
1. Calculate the real distance between the villages by multiplying the map measurement by the scale factor.

$$\text{Distance in cm} = \textbf{7.3 cm} \times \textbf{10 000}$$
$$= \textbf{73 000 cm}$$

2. To convert from cm to m, divide by 100 (the number of centimeters in a meter).

$$\textbf{Distance in m} = \frac{73\,000}{100}$$
$$= \textbf{730 m}$$

Bearings

A bearing is an angle measured clockwise from north. Bearings are used by hikers and pilots of boats and planes to plot the direction of a journey between two points.

Bearing diagrams

Diagrams of bearings always have two straight lines: a north line placed at the start of a journey and a line showing the journey. A bearing is the clockwise angle between these two lines. Be careful not to simply measure the small angle between the two lines, as bearings are often greater than a half-turn (180°). Bearings always have three digits, so some angles need a zero at the start, such as 060°.

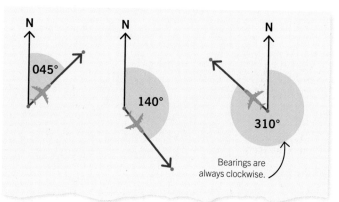

Bearings are always clockwise.

Calculating distance using bearings

Question

A plane flies on a bearing of 290° for 300 km, then flies at 045° for 200 km, then returns home. Plot its journey using a scale of 1 cm = 100 km. Use your diagram to measure the bearing and length of the final leg of the journey.

Answer

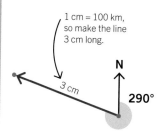

1 cm = 100 km, so make the line 3 cm long.

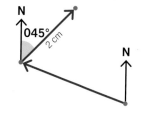

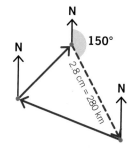

1. Draw a start point and north line and use a protractor centered on the start point to mark a 290° bearing. Draw a line to represent the first part of the journey, which is 300 km.

2. Draw a new north line and use your protractor to mark a 045° bearing. Draw in a 2 cm line representing 200 km.

3. Complete the triangle. Measure the angle to find the final bearing. Measure the line and convert to km. The final leg of the journey is about 280 km.

Constructing perpendicular lines

Constructions are diagrams drawn with a ruler and compass. Using only these tools, you can create a range of accurate shapes and angles, including perpendicular lines—lines that intersect at 90° to form right angles. When drawing constructions, leave all your construction lines visible.

Using a point on the line

To draw a perpendicular line through a point on a line, follow these steps.

1. Place the point of the compass on the point on the line and draw two arcs at equal distances to the right and left.

2. Open the compass slightly, move its point to where each arc crosses the line, and draw two new arcs crossing each other above the line.

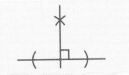

3. Use a ruler to draw a straight line between the cross and the point in the original line.

From a point to a line

Use a similar technique to construct a perpendicular line from a point above or below a line.

1. Place the point of the compass on the point and draw two arcs across the line at equal distances from the point.

2. Move the point of the compass to where each arc intersects the line and draw two new arcs crossing each other below the line.

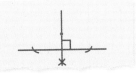

3. Use a ruler to draw a straight line from the cross and through the line to the point.

Perpendicular bisectors

A perpendicular bisector is a perpendicular line passing through the midpoint of another line.

1. Place the compass at one end of the line and draw an arc through the line beyond the midpoint.

2. Repeat from the other end.

3. Use a ruler to connect the crossing points between the two arcs.

Constructing angles

Use the techniques on this page to divide an angle into two equal parts and to draw an angle of 60° without using a protractor.

Bisecting an angle

Bisecting an angle means drawing a line through it to divide it into two equal parts. You need a ruler and compass for this.

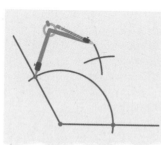

This line is called an angle bisector.

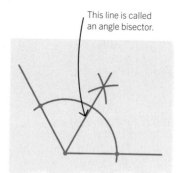

1. Place the point of the compass on the vertex and draw an arc across the lines.

2. Place the compass where the arc crosses each line and draw two new arcs crossing in the middle.

3. Use a ruler to draw a line from the cross to the vertex.

60° angle

Follow the steps below to draw a 60° angle. The angles inside an equilateral triangle are all 60°, so the technique can also be used to draw an equilateral triangle. Once your 60° angle is drawn, you can also bisect it (see above) to create a 30° angle.

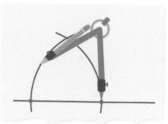

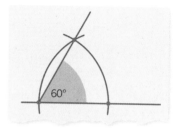

1. Draw a line, mark a point on it, and place the compass on the point to draw an arc through the line.

2. Keeping the compass set to the same width, draw a second arc centered on the point at which the first arc crosses the line.

3. Use a ruler to draw a line from the first point to the point where the arcs meet.

Loci

A locus (plural loci) is a set of points that obey a certain rule. For example, a circle is the locus of points that are a fixed distance from a point. Loci can be straight lines, curved lines, or more complicated shapes or even areas or volumes. Four examples are shown here.

Fixed distance from a point
A circle is the locus of points that are a fixed distance from a given point. A compass creates a circle, because it maintains a fixed distance from the center as it turns.

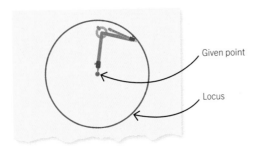

Given point

Locus

Fixed distance from a line
The locus of points that are a fixed distance from a line AB forms a sausage shape with semicircular ends. To construct this locus, draw the ends with a compass and the straight sides with a ruler.

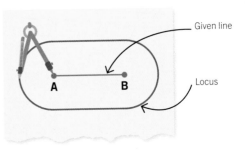

Given line

A   B

Locus

Equidistant from angled lines
The locus of points that are equidistant (the same distance) from two intersecting lines is an angle bisector (see page 185)—a line halfway between them.

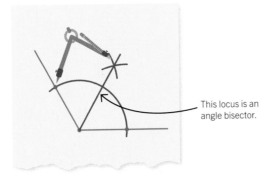

This locus is an angle bisector.

Equidistant from two points
The locus of points that are equidistant from two points A and B is a perpendicular bisector (see page 184)—a line midway between the points and at right angles to a line connecting the points.

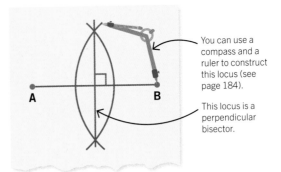

A   B

You can use a compass and a ruler to construct this locus (see page 184).

This locus is a perpendicular bisector.

Practice questions
Using loci

Loci can take many shapes, and different loci can be combined to create regions that meet several conditions at once. To solve the problems on this page, break down each answer into a series of simple steps.

See also

182 Scale drawings
184 Constructing perpendicular lines
185 Constructing angles
186 Loci

Question
A farmer decides to put up a second fence around a 20 m × 10 m rectangular chicken enclosure to keep out foxes. The new fence will be 2 m outside the old one all the way around. Draw a diagram of the fence at a scale of 1 cm = 1 m (see page 182).

Answer
1. Draw a 20 cm × 10 cm rectangle, then add straight lines parallel to the sides but 2 cm away from them.

2. Use a compass set to a width of 2 cm to draw quarter circles at each corner.

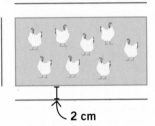

2 cm

Question
Two 200 m tall radio transmitters are 400 m apart, and each has a range of 250 m. Draw a scale diagram of the towers at a scale of 1 cm = 100 m and show the area where the ranges of both transmitters overlap.

Answer
1. Draw a diagram showing the towers 4 cm apart and 2 cm tall.

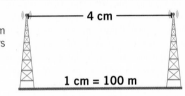

4 cm

1 cm = 100 m

2. Use a compass to draw circles showing the range of each tower. Each transmitter has a range of 250 m, so the radius of each circle should be 2.5 cm.

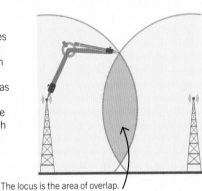

The locus is the area of overlap.

Question
The square ABCD is 4 cm wide. Accurately show the area within the square that is closer to C than B but more than 3 cm away from A.

A   B

C   D

Answer
1. Draw a diagonal line from A to D. Everywhere to the left of this is closer to C than B.

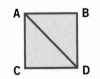

A   B

C   D

2. Set a compass to a width of 3 cm, place the point on A, and draw an arc across the square. Everything outside this arc is more than 3 cm away from A.

A   B

C   D

3. Shade the area that is both closer to C than B and farther than 3 cm from A.

A   B

C   D

Congruent and similar shapes

If two shapes are the same size and shape, they are described as congruent. However, shapes that look the same but differ in size are described as similar.

Congruent shapes

Congruent means the same shape and size. Congruent shapes have the same interior angles and the sides are of the same length, but they may be rotated differently or be mirror images (reflections) of each other or be in different positions. Here, the pink shapes are congruent, but the orange shapes are not.

Similar shapes

Similar means the same shape but not necessarily the same size. Similar shapes have the same interior angles and their sides are proportional, but they may be increased or reduced in size. Shapes remain similar after rotation, reflection, translation, or a change in size.

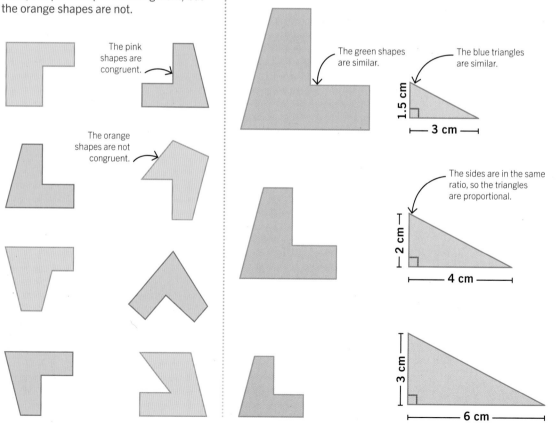

The pink shapes are congruent.

The orange shapes are not congruent.

The green shapes are similar.

The blue triangles are similar.

1.5 cm

3 cm

The sides are in the same ratio, so the triangles are proportional.

2 cm

4 cm

3 cm

6 cm

Congruent triangles

Triangles that are the same size and shape are described as congruent. Congruent triangles have the same angles as each other and corresponding sides of the same length, but they may be rotated differently or one may be a reflection of the other.

Proving congruence
You can prove that two triangles are congruent without knowing all their dimensions. If they meet any of the following five conditions, they are congruent.

1. Side, side, side (SSS)
When all three sides of a triangle are the same length as the corresponding three sides of another triangle, the two triangles are congruent.

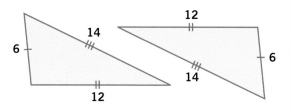

2. Angle, angle, side (AAS)
When two angles and a side that isn't between them are equal to two angles and the corresponding side of another triangle, the two triangles are congruent.

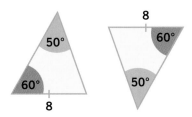

3. Side, angle, side (SAS)
When two sides and the angle between them (called the included angle) of a triangle are equal to two sides and the included angle of another triangle, the two triangles are congruent.

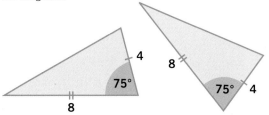

4. Angle, side, angle (ASA)
When two angles and the side between them are equal to the corresponding angles and corresponding side of another triangle, the two triangles are congruent.

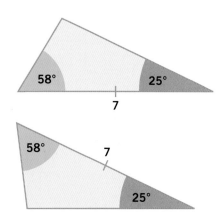

5. Hypotenuse leg (HL)
When the hypotenuse and leg of a right triangle are congruent to the hypotenuse and leg of another right triangle, the right triangles are congruent.

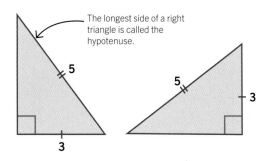

The longest side of a right triangle is called the hypotenuse.

Similar triangles

If triangles are described as similar, it means they are the same shape but not necessarily the same size. Similar triangles have identical angles, and the lengths of their sides are proportional.

Proving similarity
You can prove that two triangles are similar without knowing all their dimensions. If they meet any of the following four conditions, they are similar.

1. The same angles
If all the angles in two triangles match, the triangles are similar. This rule works even if you are only given two angles A and B, since the third angle must be 180° − (A + B).

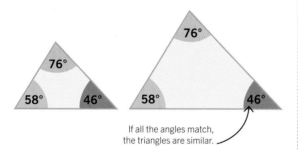

If all the angles match, the triangles are similar.

3. Two sides proportional and same angle between
If two sides of a triangle have the same ratio as corresponding sides in another triangle and the angle between them is the same, the triangles are similar.

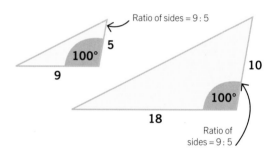

Ratio of sides = 9 : 5

Ratio of sides = 9 : 5

2. All three sides proportional
Both these triangles have sides in the ratio 3 : 4 : 5, which means their lengths are proportional to each other (see page 160). When all three sides of two triangles are proportional, the triangles are similar.

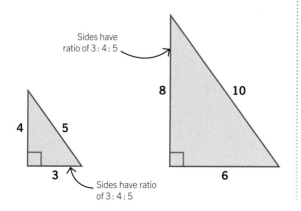

Sides have ratio of 3 : 4 : 5

Sides have ratio of 3 : 4 : 5

4. Two sides proportional in a right triangle
If the ratio between two sides of a right triangle is the same in another right triangle, the two triangles are similar.

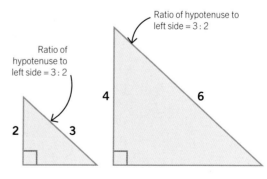

Ratio of hypotenuse to left side = 3 : 2

Ratio of hypotenuse to left side = 3 : 2

Practice questions
Similarity and congruence

See also

188 Congruent and similar shapes
189 Congruent triangles
190 Similar triangles

The rules about similar and congruent triangles are useful for comparing different shapes and finding missing dimensions. Use these three questions to test your understanding of the last three pages.

Question

You want to measure the height of a tall tree, but it's too tall for your tape measure. However, you know that its shadow is 7.5 m long, and a smaller tree measuring 3 m in height has a shadow 5 m long. Find h, the height of the tall tree in meters.

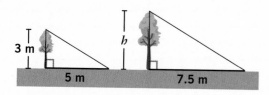

Answer

The trees and their shadows form two similar triangles. Similar triangles are proportional, so the ratio of shadow length to height is 5 : 3 for each tree. Therefore:

$$7.5 : h = 5 : 3$$
$$\frac{7.5}{h} = \frac{5}{3}$$
$$h = \frac{7.5 \times 3}{5}$$
$$= 4.5 \text{ m}$$

Question

Two of the angles in triangle A are 25° and 75°, and two of the angles in triangle B are 25° and 80°. Are the triangles congruent?

Answer

1. Work out the third angle in each triangle.

$$\text{Third angle in triangle A} = 180° - (25° + 75°)$$
$$= 80°$$

$$\text{Third angle in triangle B} = 180° - (25° + 80°)$$
$$= 75°$$

2. The two triangles have matching angles, so they must be similar triangles. However, they might be different sizes, so there isn't enough information to say whether they are congruent. To prove congruence, you need the length of at least one side of each triangle.

Question

In the triangle below, ED is parallel to CB. Find the value of x to three significant figures.

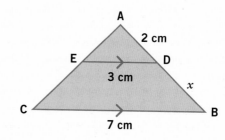

Answer

Triangle ADE is similar to triangle ABC, because they have the same angles, so the two triangles are proportional. Therefore:

$$\frac{2}{3} = \frac{2 + x}{7}$$
$$\frac{14}{3} = 2 + x$$
$$x = \frac{14}{3} - 2$$
$$x = 2.67 \text{ cm}$$

Constructing triangles

Constructing triangles means drawing them accurately with a ruler, a compass, and sometimes a protractor. Which tools you use to construct a triangle depend on what information you're given about the angles and lengths of the sides.

From three given sides (SSS)
You can construct any triangle with a ruler and compass if you're given the lengths of all three sides. For example, this is how to construct a triangle with sides of 6 cm, 7 cm, and 8 cm.

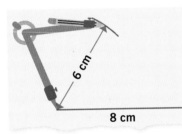

1. Choose any side to be the base and draw it with a ruler. Set the compass to the length of another side and draw an arc from one end of the base.

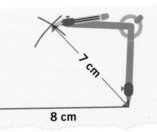

2. Set the compass to the length of the third side and draw an arc from the other end of the base so the two arcs cross.

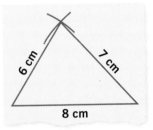

3. Use a ruler to draw the two remaining sides.

From sides and angles
If you're given an incomplete mixture of sides and angles, you need to use a protractor to mark each given angle. For example, this is how to construct triangle ABC given two sides (AB = 8 cm, AC = 5 cm) and the angle between them (∠CAB = 42°).

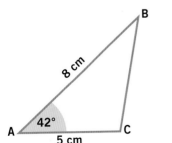

1. Draw a rough sketch of the triangle and write down what you know.

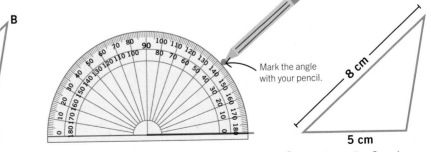

Mark the angle with your pencil.

2. Use a ruler to draw the base accurately. Use a protractor to mark the 42° angle.

3. Now draw a line 8 cm long through the point you marked and complete the triangle.

Circle theorems 1

Lines and shapes drawn in circles follow a set of rules called circle theorems. These rules are handy to know, as they make it easy to find angles and lengths without needing to measure or calculate them.

Key facts

✓ The angle formed by the diameter of a circle and any point on the circumference is 90°.

✓ The angle formed by an arc and the center of a circle is double the angle formed at the circumference.

✓ Opposite angles in a cyclic quadrilateral always add up to 180°.

✓ All the angles formed by a chord in the same segment of a circle are equal.

Angles in a semicircle

The angle formed between the diameter of a circle and a point on the circumference is always a right angle.

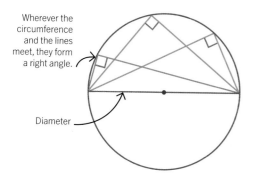

Wherever the circumference and the lines meet, they form a right angle.

Diameter

Angles at the center and circumference

The angle formed by an arc (a portion of a circle's circumference) and the center is double the angle formed by the same arc at the circumference.

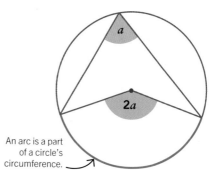

a

$2a$

An arc is a part of a circle's circumference.

Angles in a cyclic quadrilateral

A cyclic quadrilateral is a four-sided shape that fits exactly in a circle so that its corners meet the circumference. In such a shape, pairs of opposite angles always add up to 180°.

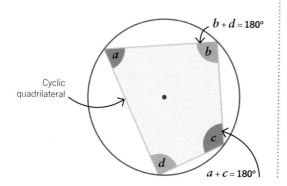

$b + d = 180°$

a

b

Cyclic quadrilateral

c

d

$a + c = 180°$

Angles in a segment

A straight line between two points on a circle's circumference is known as a chord, and the two parts it divides a circle into are called segments. All the angles formed by a chord in the same segment are equal.

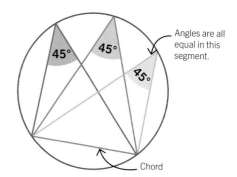

45°

45°

45°

Angles are all equal in this segment.

Chord

Circle theorems 2

Most of the circle theorems on this page involve tangents. A tangent is a line that touches a circle at a single point on the circumference.

Tangent and radius
A tangent is always perpendicular (at right angles) to the radius it meets at the circumference.

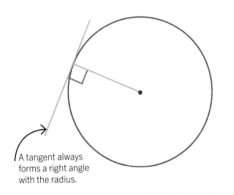

A tangent always forms a right angle with the radius.

Tangents from the same point
Two tangents from the same point outside a circle are always the same length.

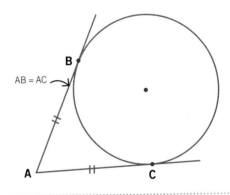

AB = AC

Alternate segment theorem
A chord is a straight line between two points on a circle's circumference. The angle formed by a chord and a tangent equals the angle formed by the chord in the opposite segment.

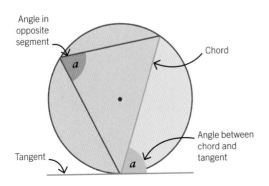

Angle in opposite segment

Chord

Angle between chord and tangent

Tangent

Bisector of chord
When a chord is bisected (divided equally in two) by a perpendicular line, the line (a perpendicular bisector) runs through the center of the circle.

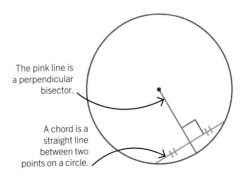

The pink line is a perpendicular bisector.

A chord is a straight line between two points on a circle.

Trigonometry

The Pythagorean theorem

Named after the philosopher Pythagoras, who lived in ancient Greece, the Pythagorean theorem explains the relationship between the lengths of the three sides of a right triangle. If two lengths are known, the third can be calculated using the theorem.

The sum of the squares
The Pythagorean theorem proves that if you square the lengths of the two short sides (legs) of any right triangle and add the results, the answer always equals the square of the long side (the hypotenuse). We can summarize this with a simple formula.

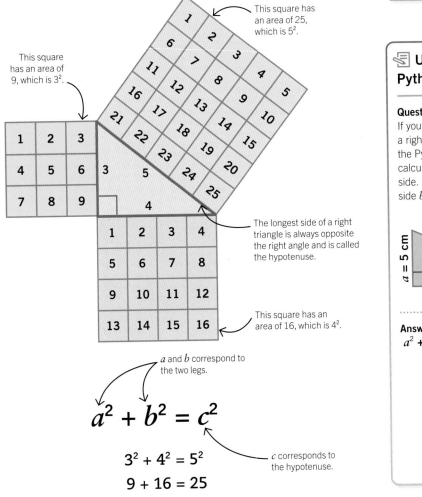

This square has an area of 25, which is 5^2.

This square has an area of 9, which is 3^2.

The longest side of a right triangle is always opposite the right angle and is called the hypotenuse.

This square has an area of 16, which is 4^2.

a and b correspond to the two legs.

$$a^2 + b^2 = c^2$$

$$3^2 + 4^2 = 5^2$$

$$9 + 16 = 25$$

c corresponds to the hypotenuse.

🖥 **Using the Pythagorean theorem**

Question
If you know how long two sides of a right triangle are, you can use the Pythagorean theorem to calculate the length of the third side. For example, how long is side b in this triangle?

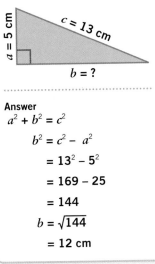

$a = 5$ cm

$c = 13$ cm

$b = ?$

Answer
$$a^2 + b^2 = c^2$$
$$b^2 = c^2 - a^2$$
$$= 13^2 - 5^2$$
$$= 169 - 25$$
$$= 144$$
$$b = \sqrt{144}$$
$$= 12 \text{ cm}$$

Trigonometry

Trigonometry is a branch of math that uses the ratios between the sides of right triangles to do calculations. For example, when a tree casts a shadow on a sunny day, the tree and its shadow form a right triangle that can be used to calculate the tree's height.

Key facts

✓ Trigonometry is a branch of math that uses the ratios between the sides of right triangles for calculations.

✓ Trigonometry can be used to find unknown dimensions, such as the side or angle of a triangle.

Finding an unknown height

Suppose you want to measure the height of a tree without climbing it. A much easier method is to measure the tree's shadow, then use the triangle this forms with the tree to calculate the height. The ratio between any two sides of a right triangle depends on the angle under the sloping side (the hypotenuse). For example, if the angle is 37°, the triangle's height is about three-quarters of the base. This ratio is known as the tangent of the angle, and you can find it on a calculator by pressing the tan button, then typing in the angle.

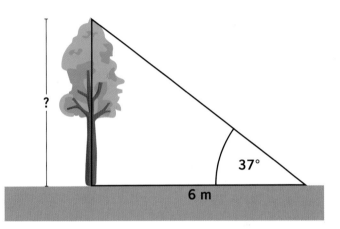

$$\frac{\text{Tree}}{\text{Shadow}} = \tan 37° = 0.753$$

$$\text{Tree} = 0.753 \times \text{Shadow}$$

$$= 4.5 \text{ m}$$

⚙ **Terms in trigonometry**

Trigonometry uses special terms for the sides of right triangles and the ratios between them. The triangle's longest side is known as the hypotenuse, and the side opposite the angle in question is known as the opposite. The side next to the angle is the adjacent. The ratios between the different pairs of sides are called sine (opposite/hypotenuse), cosine (adjacent/hypotenuse), and tangent (opposite/adjacent).

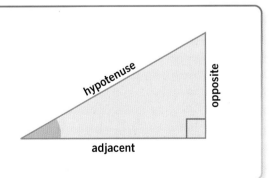

Sine, cosine, and tangent

Sine, cosine, and tangent are special names for the ratios between pairs of sides in right triangles. These ratios are very useful for trigonometry (see page 197)—calculations involving right triangles.

Trigonometry ratios
Each of the three main trigonometry ratios involves two sides of a right triangle and an angle that can vary, shown here by a. For example, the sine of an angle is the ratio between the side of the triangle opposite the angle and the longest side (the hypotenuse). The sine and cosine of an angle are always less than 1.

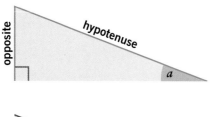

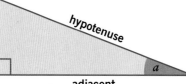

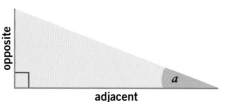

> **Key facts**
>
> ✓ Sine, cosine, and tangent are names for the ratios between pairs of sides in right triangles.
>
> ✓ The trigonometric ratios are:
>
> $$\sin a = \frac{\text{opposite}}{\text{hypotenuse}}$$
>
> $$\cos a = \frac{\text{adjacent}}{\text{hypotenuse}}$$
>
> $$\tan a = \frac{\text{opposite}}{\text{adjacent}}$$

Sine, cosine, and tangent are abbreviated to sin, cos, and tan.

$$\sin a = \frac{\text{opposite}}{\text{hypotenuse}}$$

$$\cos a = \frac{\text{adjacent}}{\text{hypotenuse}}$$

$$\tan a = \frac{\text{opposite}}{\text{adjacent}}$$

🔍 Trigonometry on calculators

Sine, cosine, and tangent are such useful functions that they have their own buttons on scientific calculators. To use them, press the relevant trigonometry button, key in the angle, and press equals.

cos 60° = 0.5

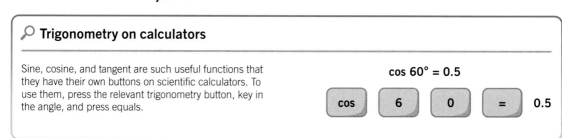

Finding lengths and angles

You can use the three trigonometry formulas to calculate an unknown length or an unknown angle in a right triangle. Be careful choosing the correct formula to match the pair of sides involved in the calculation.

Finding a length

To find a missing length, you need to know an angle and one other length. For example, in this triangle, you know the hypotenuse and the angle. How long is side p to three significant figures?

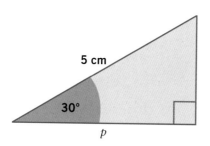

1. The calculation involves the adjacent (p) and the hypotenuse, so you need the cosine formula.

$$\cos a = \frac{\text{adjacent}}{\text{hypotenuse}}$$

2. Rearrange it to make the adjacent the subject.

adjacent = cos a × hypotenuse

3. Use a calculator to find cos a and substitute all the numbers into the equation.

$$p = \cos 30° \times 5$$
$$p = 4.33 \text{ cm}$$

Finding an angle

To find a missing angle, you need to know the lengths of any two sides. Use them to calculate the sine, cosine, or tangent of the angle, then use a calculator to convert this into the angle. For example, in the triangle below, what is the angle a to three significant figures?

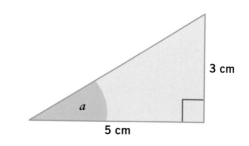

1. You know the opposite and the adjacent, so use the tangent formula:

$$\tan a = \frac{\text{opposite}}{\text{adjacent}}$$

$$\tan a = \frac{3}{5} = 0.6$$

2. To find the angle whose tangent is 0.6, you need to work in reverse and find the "inverse tangent" of 0.6. Use a calculator to do this. On most calculators, you'll see the inverse tangent written as tan^{-1} above the tan key. There should also be an inverse sine (sin^{-1}) and inverse cosine (cos^{-1}) above the sin and cos keys. Use the "shift" or "2nd" key to use these functions.

$$\tan^{-1} 0.6 = 31.0°$$

Special angles

The sines, cosines, and tangents of most angles are long decimals best handled using a calculator. However, a few special angles have trigonometric ratios that are whole numbers, simple fractions, or numbers involving square roots. You can work these out by drawing triangles.

Key facts

✓ A few special angles have trigonometric ratios that are whole numbers, simple fractions, or numbers involving square roots.

✓ You can work out the sines, cosines, and tangents of 30°, 45°, and 60° by drawing triangles.

30° and 60° angles
To find the sines, cosines, and tangents of 30° and 60°, draw an equilateral triangle with sides 2 cm long and divide it in two down the middle. Write in the dimensions and use the Pythagorean theorem (see page 196) to find the height. Then put the numbers into the trigonometry formulas to find the answers.

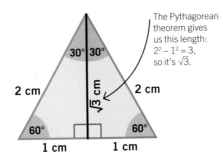

The Pythagorean theorem gives us this length: $2^2 - 1^2 = 3$, so it's $\sqrt{3}$.

Trigonometry formula		30°	60°
sine =	$\dfrac{\text{opposite}}{\text{hypotenuse}}$	$\dfrac{1}{2}$	$\dfrac{\sqrt{3}}{2}$
cosine =	$\dfrac{\text{adjacent}}{\text{hypotenuse}}$	$\dfrac{\sqrt{3}}{2}$	$\dfrac{1}{2}$
tangent =	$\dfrac{\text{opposite}}{\text{adjacent}}$	$\dfrac{1}{\sqrt{3}}$	$\sqrt{3}$

45° angles
To find the sine, cosine, and tangent of 45°, draw a right triangle 1 cm tall with 45° angles. Write in the dimensions and use the Pythagorean theorem to find the hypotenuse. Put the numbers into the trigonometry formulas to find the answers.

The Pythagorean theorem gives us the hypotenuse: $1^2 + 1^2 = 2$, so it's $\sqrt{2}$.

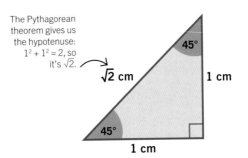

Trigonometry formula		45°
sine =	$\dfrac{\text{opposite}}{\text{hypotenuse}}$	$\dfrac{1}{\sqrt{2}}$
cosine =	$\dfrac{\text{adjacent}}{\text{hypotenuse}}$	$\dfrac{1}{\sqrt{2}}$
tangent =	$\dfrac{\text{opposite}}{\text{adjacent}}$	1

🔍 **0° and 90° angles**

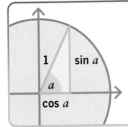

To find the sine, cosine, and tangent of the angles 0° and 90°, imagine a hypotenuse one unit long rotating in a circle as the angle changes. When the angle is 0°, the hypotenuse is flat, the opposite side is zero units long, and the hypotenuse and adjacent are both one unit. Therefore, sin 0° = 0, cos 0° = 1, and tan 0° = 0. Using similar logic, sin 90° = 1 and cos 90° = 0.

The law of sines

You can use trigonometry to do calculations with triangles that don't have right angles. The law of sines is a formula used to find missing values in a triangle if you know two angles and one side, or two sides and an angle that isn't between them.

The law of sines formula

The formula for the law of sines uses lowercase letters for the triangle's sides and uppercase letters for the angles opposite those sides. Take care to get these right. Although the formula has three parts, you only need to use two for calculations. Choose the parts with the dimensions you know and the dimensions you need to calculate.

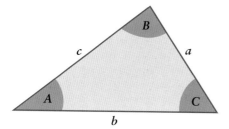

$$\frac{a}{\sin A} = \frac{b}{\sin B} = \frac{c}{\sin C}$$

📑 Finding an unknown side

If you know two angles in a triangle and any one side, use the law of sines to find an unknown side.

Question
Find the length of a to the nearest tenth.

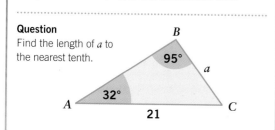

Answer
1. You know angle A, angle B, and side b, so use the first two parts of the formula.

$$\frac{a}{\sin A} = \frac{b}{\sin B}$$

2. Rearrange to find a.

$$a = \frac{b \times \sin A}{\sin B} = \frac{21 \times \sin 32°}{\sin 95°} = 11.2$$

📑 Finding an unknown angle

If you know two sides in a triangle and an angle that isn't between them, use the law of sines to find an unknown angle.

Question
Find the measure of angle C to the nearest tenth of a degree.

Answer
1. This time, you need the second and third parts of the sine formula.

$$\frac{b}{\sin B} = \frac{c}{\sin C}$$

2. Rearrange to find $\sin C$.

$$\sin C = \frac{c \times \sin B}{b} = \frac{4 \times \sin 95°}{5} = 0.797$$

$$C = 52.8°$$

The law of cosines

The law of cosines is a formula that can be used to find the unknown lengths of sides and angles in any triangle when certain lengths and angles are known.

The law of cosines for an unknown side
When the lengths of two sides of a triangle and the angle they create is known, the law of cosines can be used to find the length of the third side.

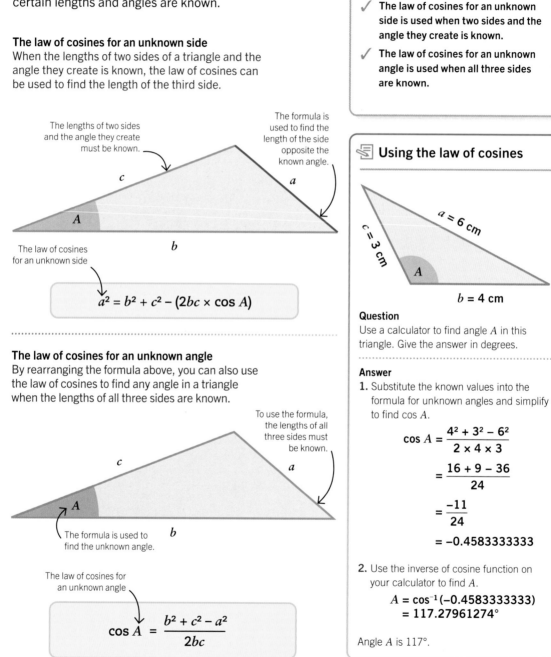

The lengths of two sides and the angle they create must be known.

The formula is used to find the length of the side opposite the known angle.

c

a

A

b

The law of cosines for an unknown side

$$a^2 = b^2 + c^2 - (2bc \times \cos A)$$

The law of cosines for an unknown angle
By rearranging the formula above, you can also use the law of cosines to find any angle in a triangle when the lengths of all three sides are known.

To use the formula, the lengths of all three sides must be known.

c

a

A

b

The formula is used to find the unknown angle.

The law of cosines for an unknown angle

$$\cos A = \frac{b^2 + c^2 - a^2}{2bc}$$

📌 **Key facts**

✓ The law of cosines can be used with any triangle.

✓ The law of cosines for an unknown side is used when two sides and the angle they create is known.

✓ The law of cosines for an unknown angle is used when all three sides are known.

🖹 **Using the law of cosines**

$a = 6$ cm

$c = 3$ cm

A

$b = 4$ cm

Question
Use a calculator to find angle A in this triangle. Give the answer in degrees.

Answer
1. Substitute the known values into the formula for unknown angles and simplify to find $\cos A$.

$$\cos A = \frac{4^2 + 3^2 - 6^2}{2 \times 4 \times 3}$$

$$= \frac{16 + 9 - 36}{24}$$

$$= \frac{-11}{24}$$

$$= -0.4583333333$$

2. Use the inverse of cosine function on your calculator to find A.

$$A = \cos^{-1}(-0.4583333333)$$
$$= 117.27961274°$$

Angle A is 117°.

Area of a triangle

The easiest way to find the area of a triangle is to multiply the base by the height and divide by two. However, if these measurements aren't available, trigonometry offers another way.

Key facts

✓ Trigonometry can be used to calculate the area of any triangle.

✓ Use the trigonometry formula when you know the lengths of any two sides and the angle between them.

Area formula
To calculate the area of a triangle using trigonometry, you need to know the lengths of two sides and the angle between them. Use the formula shown below left to do this. Note that the formula works for any pair of sides and the angle between them—not just a, b, and C.

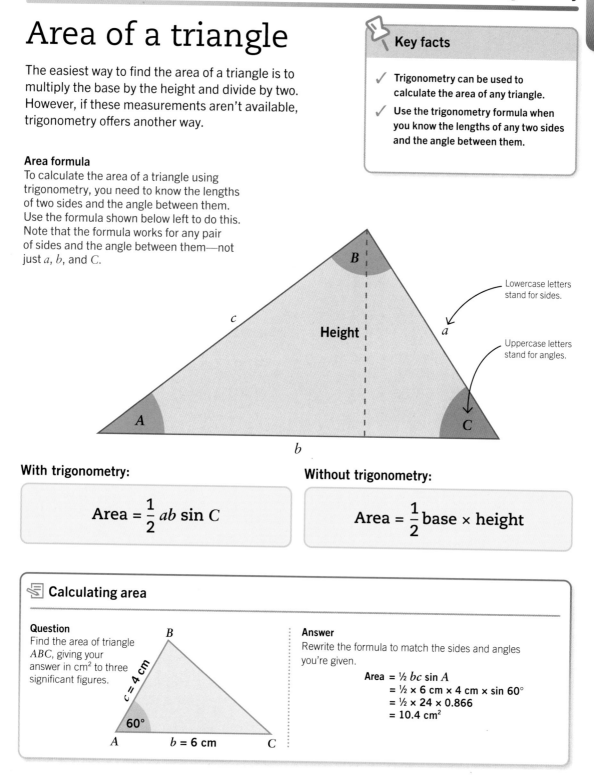

Lowercase letters stand for sides.

Uppercase letters stand for angles.

With trigonometry:

$$\text{Area} = \frac{1}{2}\, ab \sin C$$

Without trigonometry:

$$\text{Area} = \frac{1}{2}\, \text{base} \times \text{height}$$

📑 Calculating area

Question
Find the area of triangle ABC, giving your answer in cm² to three significant figures.

Answer
Rewrite the formula to match the sides and angles you're given.

$$\begin{aligned}\text{Area} &= \tfrac{1}{2}\, bc \sin A \\ &= \tfrac{1}{2} \times 6 \text{ cm} \times 4 \text{ cm} \times \sin 60° \\ &= \tfrac{1}{2} \times 24 \times 0.866 \\ &= 10.4 \text{ cm}^2\end{aligned}$$

Practice question
Using trigonometry

The Pythagorean theorem and the various trigonometry formulas can be put to use to calculate measurements in everyday life. To answer the question below, you'll need to choose two formulas from earlier in this chapter.

See also

196 The Pythagorean theorem

197 Trigonometry

198 Sine, cosine, and tangent

199 Finding lengths and angles

Question

You are designing a dry ski slope. You have been asked to make it 20 m tall and to give the ski slope an angle of 21°.

a) If there are five steps per meter of staircase and the base of the staircase is 21 m long, how many steps will there be to the top of the slope?

b) How long will the ski slope d be? Give your answer in meters to three significant figures.

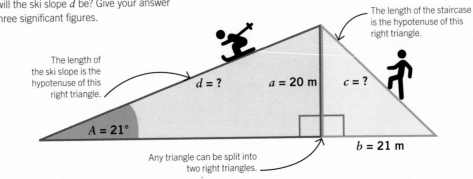

The length of the ski slope is the hypotenuse of this right triangle.

$d = ?$ $a = 20$ m $c = ?$

$A = 21°$

$b = 21$ m

The length of the staircase is the hypotenuse of this right triangle.

Any triangle can be split into two right triangles.

Answer

a) To calculate the number of steps, you need to know the length of the staircase c. Use the Pythagorean theorem (see page 196) to calculate the hypotenuse of the right triangle under the staircase.

$$a^2 + b^2 = c^2$$

$$20^2 + 21^2 = c^2$$

$$841 = c^2$$

$$c = 29 \text{ m}$$

Because there are five steps per meter, the staircase will need 29 × 5 steps, which equals 145 steps.

b) The ski slope forms a right triangle with an angle of 21° and an opposite side of 20 m. You need to find the hypotenuse d. To do this, use the sine formula (see page 198).

$$\sin A = \frac{\text{opposite}}{\text{hypotenuse}}$$

$$\sin 21° = \frac{20}{d}$$

$$d = \frac{20}{\sin 21°}$$

$$d = 55.8 \text{ m}$$

The ski slope will be 55.8 m long.

Angles of elevation and depression

The angle between someone's horizontal line of sight and an object above or below them is known as the angle of elevation or the angle of depression, respectively. We use these angles in trigonometry to find unknown distances.

Using an imagined triangle
Here, the angle of elevation is the angle between the observer's horizontal line of sight and the balloon above. The angle of depression is the angle between the observer's horizontal line of sight and the boat below. If we imagine each of these lines forms the hypotenuse of a right triangle, then we can use trigonometry formulas to find the distances between the observer and the objects.

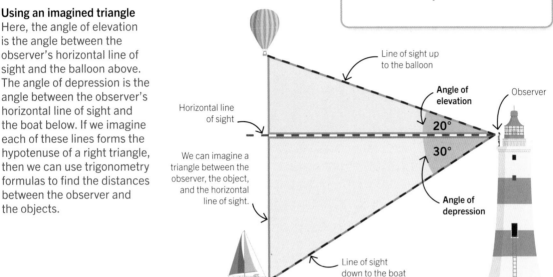

Line of sight up to the balloon

Angle of elevation

Observer

Horizontal line of sight

20°

30°

We can imagine a triangle between the observer, the object, and the horizontal line of sight.

Angle of depression

Line of sight down to the boat

🖩 Trigonometry and the angle of elevation

Question
How far is the balloon from the observer if the angle of elevation is 20° and the horizontal distance from the observer to a point directly beneath the balloon is 173 m? Give your answer in meters.

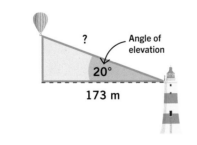

?   Angle of elevation

20°

173 m

Answer
1. The line between the observer and the balloon makes up the hypotenuse of the triangle. Because we know the angle of elevation and the adjacent side, the cos formula can be used to find the hypotenuse:

$$\cos A = \frac{\text{adjacent}}{\text{hypotenuse}}$$

2. Rearrange the formula to find the hypotenuse and work out the result.

$$\text{hypotenuse} = \frac{\text{adjacent}}{\cos A} = \frac{173}{\cos 20°} = 184 \text{ m}$$

The balloon is 184 m from the observer.

Pythagoras in 3D

The Pythagorean theorem (see page 196) allows you to calculate the length of any side of a right triangle if you know the other two sides. The theorem also works in 3D shapes, in which right triangles can be drawn.

Diagonal in a rectangular prism
A rectangular prism is a 3D shape with rectangular sides (a box). How long is the diagonal line d in this rectangular prism? To find the answer, we can draw right triangles inside the rectangular prism. Using two of these, we can calculate d.

1. First, use the Pythagorean theorem to work out e, the hypotenuse of the triangle in the base.

$$e^2 = a^2 + b^2$$
$$= 25 + 9$$
$$= 34$$
$$e = \sqrt{34}$$

2. Now work out d, the hypotenuse of the purple triangle.

$$d^2 = e^2 + c^2$$
$$= 34 + 4$$
$$= 38$$
$$d = \sqrt{38}$$

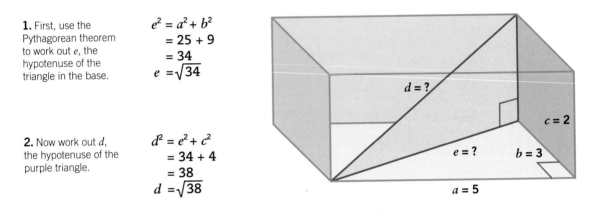

The Pythagorean theorem for rectangular prisms
We can combine steps 1 and 2 above by joining the two equations into one. This gives us the Pythagorean theorem for rectangular prisms, which is used to find the longest diagonal in a rectangular prism.

$$a^2 + b^2 + c^2 = d^2$$

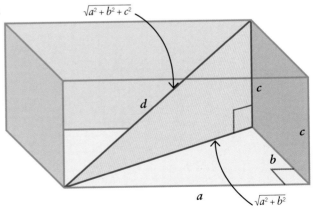

Practice question
3D trigonometry

Trigonometry works just as well in three dimensions as in two. Right triangles can often be created within 3D shapes, making it possible to calculate missing dimensions or angles.

See also

196 The Pythagorean theorem
197 Trigonometry
198 Sine, cosine, and tangent
199 Finding lengths and angles

Question
A pyramid has a square base 6 m wide and is 4 m tall, with its peak P directly above the center of its base Q. What is the measure of angle R to the nearest degree?

Answer
1. To find the measure of angle R, you need at least two sides of the purple triangle, but you only know the height PQ. You need to calculate the purple triangle's base QC, which is half of AC. Use the Pythagorean theorem to find AC.

$$(AC)^2 = (AD)^2 + (CD)^2$$

$$(AC)^2 = 6^2 + 6^2$$
$$(AC)^2 = 72$$
$$AC = \sqrt{72}$$

$$\text{So } QC = \frac{1}{2} \times \sqrt{72}$$

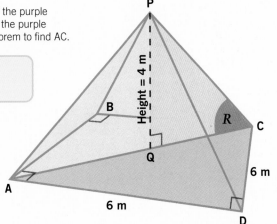

2. Now you know the length of the opposite and adjacent sides in the purple triangle. Use the tangent formula to find the angle.

$$\tan R = \frac{\text{opposite}}{\text{adjacent}}$$

$$\tan R = \frac{4}{\frac{1}{2} \times \sqrt{72}}$$

$$\tan R = 0.9428$$
$$R = \tan^{-1} 0.9428$$
$$R = 43°$$

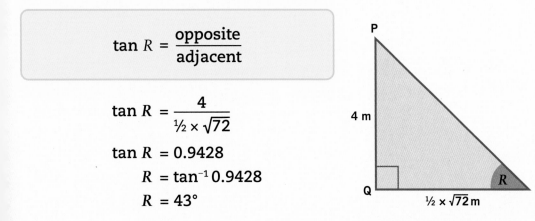

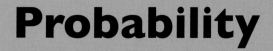

Probability

Probability scale

What's the chance of rain tomorrow? What's the chance of getting heads if you toss a coin? In math, chance is called probability, and it is always a number between zero and one.

Measuring probability
Probabilities can be written as fractions, decimals, or percentages. A probability of zero means something is impossible, and a probability of one means something is certain.

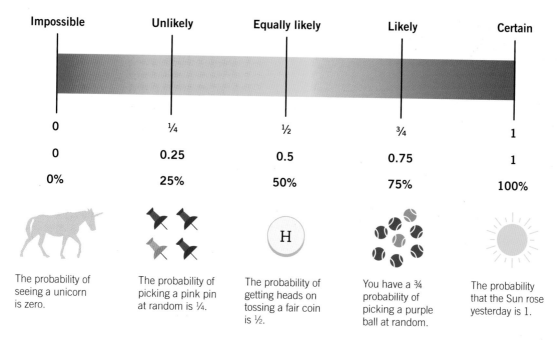

Impossible	Unlikely	Equally likely	Likely	Certain
0	¼	½	¾	1
0	0.25	0.5	0.75	1
0%	25%	50%	75%	100%

The probability of seeing a unicorn is zero.

The probability of picking a pink pin at random is ¼.

The probability of getting heads on tossing a fair coin is ½.

You have a ¾ probability of picking a purple ball at random.

The probability that the Sun rose yesterday is 1.

⚙ Theoretical and experimental probability

If you make a six-sided spinner like this and spin it, what's the chance of scoring a six? There are two ways of answering this question. One is to calculate the theoretical probability: there are six possible outcomes and only one six, so the chance is ⅙. Another approach is to work out the experimental probability. This involves spinning the spinner many times and recording the number of sixes as a fraction of the total. If the spinner is wonky, it might not be fair and might land more often on some numbers than on others. This is known as bias.

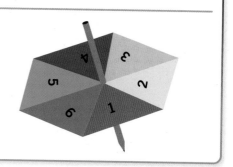

Calculating probability

The probability of rolling a six on a fair dice is $1/6$, but what is the probability of an even number? The answer is $1/2$, because three out of six numbers are even. To calculate probability, divide the number of ways an event can happen by the total number of outcomes.

Probability formula

A sock drawer contains 4 red socks, 4 blue, and 2 green. It's too dark to see the colors, so you pull out a sock at random. Random means that each possible outcome is equally likely to happen. What's the chance of picking a blue sock? To find the answer, use this formula.

In probability, an "event" means a particular outcome or combination of outcomes.

$$\text{Probability of an event} = \frac{\text{number of ways the event can happen}}{\text{number of possible outcomes}}$$

$$\text{Probability of blue sock} = \frac{\text{number of blue socks}}{\text{total number of socks}}$$

$$= \frac{4}{10}$$

$$= \frac{2}{5}$$

Simplify the fraction to find your final answer.

📑 The probability of either/or

Question
A bag of candy contains 3 green candies, 4 red, and 4 orange. What's the probability of picking either a green or a red candy if you choose one at random?

Answer
Fill in the formula with the numbers to find the answer.

$$\text{Probability of an event} = \frac{\text{number of ways the event can happen}}{\text{number of possible outcomes}}$$

$$= \frac{\text{green candy + red candy}}{\text{total number of candies}}$$

$$= \frac{3 + 4}{11}$$

$$= \frac{7}{11}$$

Mutually exclusive events

Tossing a coin once and getting both heads and tails is impossible. Two events that can't happen at the same time are called mutually exclusive. The probabilities of all possible mutually exclusive events add up to one.

Probabilities add up to one

If you pick one of the 10 socks below at random, it can only be one color. Picking blue, red, and green are all mutually exclusive events. If you take a sock, it's certain that it will be one of the three colors, so the separate probabilities for each color must add up to one. We can write the probabilities as shown below, where P (R) means the probability of picking red:

$$P (R) + P (B) + P (G) = \frac{4}{10} + \frac{4}{10} + \frac{2}{10}$$
$$= \frac{10}{10}$$
$$= 1$$

The probability of not

If you pick a random sock, what's the chance of not getting blue? Blue and not blue are mutually exclusive, so their probabilities must add up to one again. We can write this as shown below, where P (B′) means the probability of "the complement of blue"—all options besides blue.

$$P (B) + P (B') = 1$$

So to find the probability of "not blue," subtract the probability of blue from one:

$$P (B') = 1 - P (B)$$
$$P (B') = 1 - \frac{4}{10} = \frac{6}{10} = \frac{3}{5}$$

Calculating the probability of not

Question

A bag of candy contains 3 green, 4 red, and 4 orange candies. If you take one at random, what's the chance of not picking green?

Answer

1. First, work out the probability of picking green.

$$P (G) = \frac{\text{Number of green candies}}{\text{Total number of candies}}$$
$$= \frac{3}{11}$$

2. Subtract from one to find the probability of not picking green (the complement of picking green).

$$P (G') = 1 - \frac{3}{11} = \frac{8}{11}$$

Counting outcomes

To calculate the probability of something happening, such as scoring 12 when you roll two dice, you need to know the total number of possible outcomes. To do this, it helps to make a list or table of outcomes. This is called a sample space.

Sample space diagram
There's only one way of scoring 12 with two dice (two sixes), but there are lots of other possible outcomes. To count them, write down all possible outcomes in a list or a table. A list would be fine for one die, but a two-way table is better for two dice.

Key facts

✓ To calculate probability, you need to know the number of possible outcomes.

✓ A sample space is a list or table showing all possible outcomes.

✓ To find the number of outcomes from two activities, multiply the number of outcomes for each activity.

1. Write the results for one die down the side.

2. Write the results for the other die along the top.

	•	••	⚁	⚃	⚄	⚅
•	2	3	4	5	6	7
⚁	3	4	5	6	7	8
⚂	4	5	6	7	8	9
⚃	5	6	7	8	9	10
⚄	6	7	8	9	10	11
⚅	7	8	9	10	11	12

3. Fill in the outcomes by adding the scores of the two dice.

4. Count the number of outcomes. In this case, there are 36.

5. To find the probability of a particular score, such as 12, use the probability formula from page 210:

$$\text{Probability of an event} = \frac{\text{number of ways the event can happen}}{\text{total number of possible outcomes}}$$

$$\text{Probability of scoring 12} = \frac{1}{36}$$

▤ The product rule

When two or more activities are combined, you can use a shortcut to find the number of possible outcomes: multiply the number of outcomes for each activity together. This is called the product rule. For example, rolling one die has six possible outcomes, so rolling two dice has 6 × 6 = 36 outcomes.

Question
If a restaurant menu has 3 appetizers, 4 entrées, and 6 desserts, how many different three-course meals could you order?

Answer

Number of three-course meals = appetizers × entrées × desserts

= 3 × 4 × 6

= 72

Probability of two events

Sometimes you need to calculate the combined probability of two events—call them A and B. To find the probability of A and B taking place, use the AND rule, which tells you to multiply. To find the probability of A or B happening, use the OR rule, which tells you to add. Remember: multiply for AND, add for OR.

Key facts

✓ The AND rule means multiply to find the probability of two events both happening:
$$P(A \text{ and } B) = P(A) \times P(B)$$

✓ The OR rule means add to find the probability of either of two events happening:
$$P(A \text{ or } B) = P(A) + P(B)$$

✓ The AND rule applies to independent events.

✓ The OR rule applies to mutually exclusive events.

The AND rule

Suppose you spin two spinners—what's the probability of getting red on both? The result with the first spinner has no effect on the second spinner, so we call the two events independent. When events A and B are independent, multiply the probabilities to find the probability of both happening.

$$P(A \text{ and } B) = P(A) \times P(B)$$

$$P(\text{red and red}) = P(\text{red}) \times P(\text{red})$$

$$= \frac{1}{6} \times \frac{1}{6}$$

$$= \frac{1}{36}$$

The OR rule

What's the chance of getting either red or blue if you spin one spinner? These two events are mutually exclusive, which means they can't happen together. When events A and B are mutually exclusive, add the separate probabilities to find the probability of either A or B happening.

$$P(A \text{ or } B) = P(A) + P(B)$$

$$P(\text{red or blue}) = P(\text{red}) + P(\text{blue})$$

$$= \frac{1}{6} + \frac{1}{6}$$

$$= \frac{2}{6} = \frac{1}{3}$$

Working with probability

Question

You roll a blue die and a red die. What's the probability of getting an odd number on the blue die throw and a six on the red die throw?

Answer

Use the AND rule:

$$P(\text{odd number and six}) = P(\text{odd number}) \times P(\text{six})$$

$$= \frac{1}{2} \times \frac{1}{6}$$

$$= \frac{1}{12}$$

Tree diagrams

Probability questions can be tricky to answer, especially if there's a combination of two or three events. The easiest way to solve such questions is to draw a tree diagram.

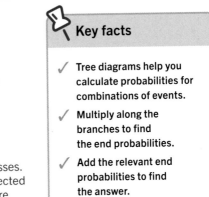

Key facts

✓ Tree diagrams help you calculate probabilities for combinations of events.

✓ Multiply along the branches to find the end probabilities.

✓ Add the relevant end probabilities to find the answer.

Independent events
You toss a coin twice. What's the chance of getting the same result each time? To find the answer, draw a tree diagram showing both tosses. In this example, the chance of heads (H) in the second toss is unaffected by the first toss. If one event is unaffected by another, we say they are independent. You can also use tree diagrams to calculate probabilities when the events are not independent (see opposite).

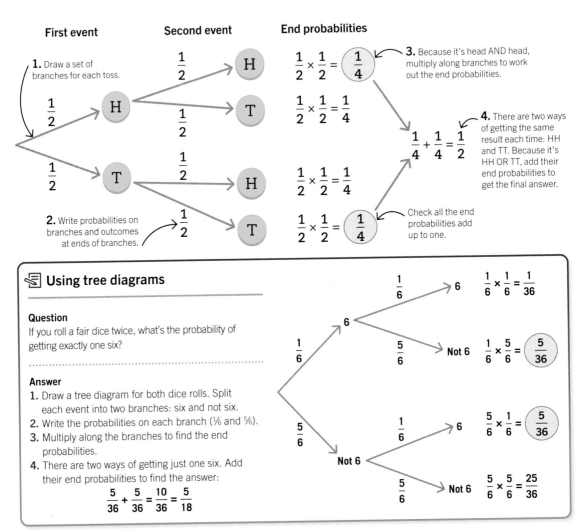

First event **Second event** **End probabilities**

1. Draw a set of branches for each toss.

$\frac{1}{2}$ → H

$\frac{1}{2}$ H $\frac{1}{2}$ → T

$\frac{1}{2}$ T $\frac{1}{2}$ → H

$\frac{1}{2}$ → T

2. Write probabilities on branches and outcomes at ends of branches.

$\frac{1}{2} \times \frac{1}{2} = \frac{1}{4}$

$\frac{1}{2} \times \frac{1}{2} = \frac{1}{4}$

$\frac{1}{2} \times \frac{1}{2} = \frac{1}{4}$

$\frac{1}{2} \times \frac{1}{2} = \frac{1}{4}$

3. Because it's head AND head, multiply along branches to work out the end probabilities.

4. There are two ways of getting the same result each time: HH and TT. Because it's HH OR TT, add their end probabilities to get the final answer.

$\frac{1}{4} + \frac{1}{4} = \frac{1}{2}$

Check all the end probabilities add up to one.

Using tree diagrams

Question
If you roll a fair dice twice, what's the probability of getting exactly one six?

Answer
1. Draw a tree diagram for both dice rolls. Split each event into two branches: six and not six.
2. Write the probabilities on each branch (⅙ and ⅚).
3. Multiply along the branches to find the end probabilities.
4. There are two ways of getting just one six. Add their end probabilities to find the answer:

$$\frac{5}{36} + \frac{5}{36} = \frac{10}{36} = \frac{5}{18}$$

$\frac{1}{6}$ 6 → $\frac{1}{6}$ 6 $\frac{1}{6} \times \frac{1}{6} = \frac{1}{36}$

$\frac{5}{6}$ → Not 6 $\frac{1}{6} \times \frac{5}{6} = \frac{5}{36}$

$\frac{5}{6}$ Not 6 → $\frac{1}{6}$ 6 $\frac{5}{6} \times \frac{1}{6} = \frac{5}{36}$

$\frac{5}{6}$ → Not 6 $\frac{5}{6} \times \frac{5}{6} = \frac{25}{36}$

Conditional probability

If you pick a random sock from a sock drawer and don't put it back, the probability of picking any particular kind of sock the second time depends on what you got the first time. When the probability of one event is affected by another event, we say the two events are dependent or conditional.

Tree diagram
There are five green socks and three red socks in a drawer. If you pick two at random, what's the probability of getting a matching pair? An easy way to solve questions about dependent events is to draw a tree diagram (see opposite). Note that the probabilities on the second part of the tree are different from the first part, because one sock has been removed.

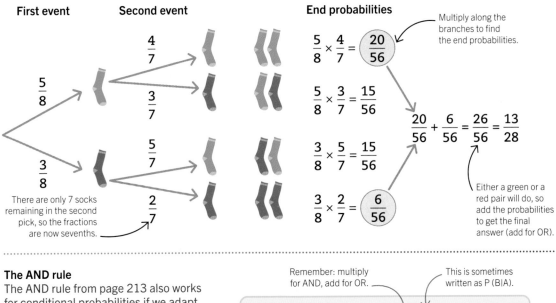

First event   **Second event**   **End probabilities**

$\dfrac{5}{8}$ $\dfrac{4}{7}$

$\dfrac{3}{7}$

$\dfrac{5}{7}$

$\dfrac{3}{8}$ $\dfrac{2}{7}$

Multiply along the branches to find the end probabilities.

$\dfrac{5}{8} \times \dfrac{4}{7} = \dfrac{20}{56}$

$\dfrac{5}{8} \times \dfrac{3}{7} = \dfrac{15}{56}$

$\dfrac{3}{8} \times \dfrac{5}{7} = \dfrac{15}{56}$

$\dfrac{3}{8} \times \dfrac{2}{7} = \dfrac{6}{56}$

$\dfrac{20}{56} + \dfrac{6}{56} = \dfrac{26}{56} = \dfrac{13}{28}$

There are only 7 socks remaining in the second pick, so the fractions are now sevenths.

Either a green or a red pair will do, so add the probabilities to get the final answer (add for OR).

The AND rule
The AND rule from page 213 also works for conditional probabilities if we adapt it slightly, as shown in the formula here. P (B given A) means the probability of event B happening given that A has happened. For example, the probability of picking a pair of green socks equals the probability of green multiplied by the probability of green given green.

Remember: multiply for AND, add for OR.

This is sometimes written as P (B|A).

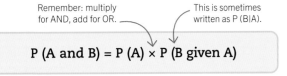

$$P \text{ (A and B)} = P \text{ (A)} \times P \text{ (B given A)}$$

$$P \text{ (green and green)} = P \text{ (green)} \times P \text{ (green given green)}$$

$$= \dfrac{5}{8} \times \dfrac{4}{7} = \dfrac{20}{56} = \dfrac{5}{14}$$

Conditional probability tables

A conditional probability is the probability of an event happening given that another event has happened. Using tables can help solve problems involving conditional probability.

Key facts

✓ When the probability of one event is affected by another event, we say the two events are dependent or conditional.

✓ Tables can help answer questions involving conditional probability.

Using tables

This table shows how many of 100 patients at a medical clinic are diagnosed with high blood pressure and whether or not they are smokers. What's the probability that any randomly chosen patient has high blood pressure? Given that a patient is a smoker, what's the probability they have high blood pressure?

	High blood pressure	Normal blood pressure	Total
Smoker	36	12	48
Nonsmoker	16	36	52
Total	52	48	100

1. To answer the first part of the question, use the totals in the bottom row.

$$\text{Probability of high blood pressure} = \frac{\text{Number of patients with high blood pressure}}{\text{Total number of patients}} = \frac{52}{100}$$

2. The word "given" tells you that the second part of the question involves conditional probability. You now need to look at the subset of people who smoke, so use the numbers in the smoker row to find the answer.

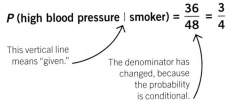

$$P\,(\text{high blood pressure} \mid \text{smoker}) = \frac{36}{48} = \frac{3}{4}$$

This vertical line means "given." — The denominator has changed, because the probability is conditional.

So given that a patient is a smoker, they have ¾ probability of having high blood pressure—a much higher probability than that for all patients.

📑 Finding conditional probability

Question
A survey of 150 guests at a mountain hotel revealed the following preferences for winter sports. What's the probability that a randomly chosen teenager preferred skiing?

Favorite winter sport	Sledding	Snow-boarding	Skiing	Total
Child	10	10	5	25
Teenager	5	30	10	45
Adult	0	25	55	80
Total	15	65	70	150

Answer
Find $P\,(\text{skiing} \mid \text{teenager})$ by using the numbers in the row for teenagers:

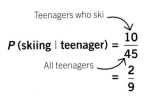

Teenagers who ski —

$$P\,(\text{skiing} \mid \text{teenager}) = \frac{10}{45}$$

All teenagers —

$$= \frac{2}{9}$$

Venn diagrams

Venn diagrams consist of overlapping circles that represent sets (collections of things). Each circle represents one set, and the rectangle around them represents everything of interest. Venn diagrams that show frequencies (number of things) can be useful for calculating probabilities.

Key facts

✓ Venn diagrams use overlapping circles to show sets.

✓ Venn diagrams showing frequencies can be used for calculating probabilities.

Using Venn diagrams

This Venn diagram shows which children in a class of 40 play tennis or football. The circles intersect, because some children play both sports. The numbers are frequencies—how many children in each category. You can use these numbers to calculate probabilities. For example, the probability that a child chosen randomly from the class plays only football is $^{16}/_{40} = ^2/_5$.

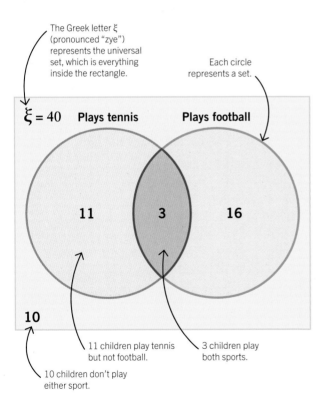

The Greek letter ξ (pronounced "zye") represents the universal set, which is everything inside the rectangle.

Each circle represents a set.

$ξ = 40$ Plays tennis   Plays football

11   3   16

10

11 children play tennis but not football.

3 children play both sports.

10 children don't play either sport.

Set notation

Special symbols are used for the math involving sets and Venn diagrams. Curly brackets are used when listing the elements (things) in a set. For example, if we call A the set of odd numbers less than 10, then A = {1, 3, 5, 7, 9}. The number of elements in set A is 5, which we can write like this: $n(A) = 5$. The pictures below show what some of the other symbols used in set notation mean.

A′ (the complement of set A) means everything in the universal set that is outside set A.

A ∩ B (intersection of A and B) means everything in the overlap between A and B.

A ∪ B (the union of A and B) means everything in both sets combined.

A ⊂ B means that A is a subset of B.

A ∩ B′ means the intersection between A and the complement of B (so everything in A but not B).

ξ means everything in the rectangle: the universal set.

Venn diagrams and probability

If you own a cat, what's the probability you also own a dog? Conditional probability questions like this one can often be answered by using a Venn diagram—a diagram made of overlapping circles that represent sets.

Conditional probability

A total of 100 people were asked in a survey whether they owned a cat or a dog. This Venn diagram shows the results. What's the probability that a randomly selected person is a dog owner, given that they own a cat?

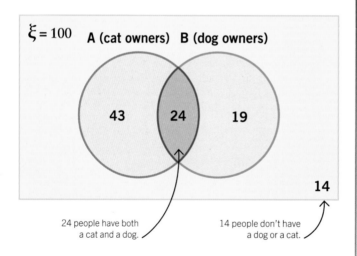

24 people have both a cat and a dog.

14 people don't have a dog or a cat.

1. The word "given" tells you this is a conditional probability question. First, find the number for the set of people that own a cat (A).

$$A = 43 + 24$$
$$= 67$$

2. Use this as the denominator in your probability fraction. The numerator is the number of people who have both a cat and a dog, so:

$$P(B \mid A) = \frac{24}{67}$$

The vertical line means "given."

🔖 **Find the probability**

Question
What's the probability that a person chosen randomly from the survey owns a dog, given that they don't own a cat?

....

Answer
1. First, find the number of people who don't own cats (A'):

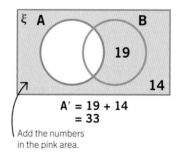

$$A' = 19 + 14$$
$$= 33$$

Add the numbers in the pink area.

2. Use this as the denominator in your probability fraction. The numerator is the number of people who own a dog but not a cat (19).

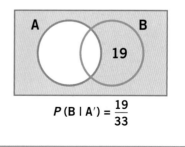

$$P(B \mid A') = \frac{19}{33}$$

Relative frequency

Suppose you make a six-sided spinner like the one below, but it's lopsided. The spinner may not be fair, which means the chance of landing on any particular color is not ⅙. You can estimate the true probability of each color by carrying out an experiment. This estimate is called relative frequency.

Probability experiment

To work out the relative frequencies for each color on your spinner, you would need to spin it many times in an experiment and count how often each color occurs. Each spin is called a trial. The more trials you carry out, the better your estimate. The count for each color is its frequency. Relative frequency is the fraction of the total. To calculate it, use the formula below.

$$\frac{\text{Relative}}{\text{frequency}} = \frac{\text{frequency}}{\text{number of trials}}$$

The table shows the results you might get if you spin the spinner 200 times. Blue occurs much more often than other colors, so the spinner is unlikely to be fair. We conclude that the spinner is probably biased. The greater the number of trials, the more confident our conclusion.

Outcome	Frequency	Relative frequency
Purple	46	46 ÷ 200 = 0.23
Orange	20	20 ÷ 200 = 0.10
Yellow	22	22 ÷ 200 = 0.11
Red	42	42 ÷ 200 = 0.21
Blue	60	60 ÷ 200 = 0.30
Green	10	10 ÷ 200 = 0.05
Total	200	1

Frequency means the number of times something happens.

The spinner lands on blue much more frequently than other colors.

📌 Key facts

✓ Relative frequency is an estimate of probability found by experiment.

✓ Relative frequency = frequency ÷ total number of trials

✓ The greater the number of trials, the more accurate the estimate.

✓ Expected frequency = probability × number of trials

Expected frequency

How many times would you expect your biased spinner to land on blue if you spin it 60 times? If you know the relative frequency, you can use it to estimate the result of a given number of trials. This is known as expected frequency:

$$\frac{\text{Expected}}{\text{frequency}} = \text{probability} \times \frac{\text{number}}{\text{of trials}}$$

If you spin the spinner 60 times:

Expected frequency = 0.30 × 60
= 18

If your spinner was fair rather than biased, the probability of blue would be ⅙ and the expected frequency would be lower:

$$\textbf{Expected frequency} = \frac{1}{6} \times 60 = 10$$

Remember, this is just an estimate—it doesn't mean you would get blue exactly 10 times.

Frequency trees

Frequency trees are useful for organizing data into clear categories. They look like probability tree diagrams (see page 214), but they show frequencies rather than probabilities. When all the numbers are filled in, they can be used to calculate probabilities.

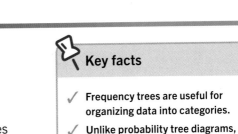

Key facts

✓ Frequency trees are useful for organizing data into categories.

✓ Unlike probability tree diagrams, they show frequencies rather than probabilities.

✓ Frequency trees can be used to calculate probabilities.

Filling a frequency tree
A school carried out a survey of 120 students to find out whether they had a laptop or a tablet (all students had one or the other), and how this varied by age. 70 students were under the age of 15. Of the students aged 15 or over, 11 had tablets. A total of 67 students had laptops. How many students under 15 had tablets?

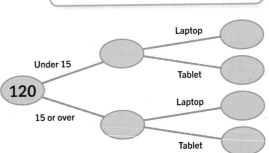

1. Start by filling in the frequencies for the two age groups.

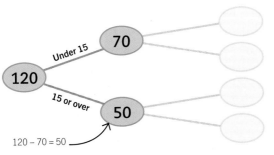

2. Then add the preferences for older students.

3. There are 67 laptops in total, so work out how many younger students have them.

4. Work out the last number by subtraction. 42 students under the age of 15 have tablets.

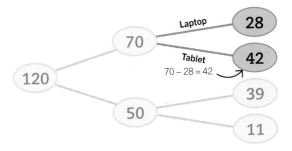

Probability distributions

A probability distribution is a mathematical function that tells you the probabilities of every possible outcome in an experiment, such as tossing a coin or rolling dice. Probability distributions are often shown on charts, graphs, or tables.

Uniform probability distribution

If you roll a fair die once, the probability of each number is the same: $\frac{1}{6}$. We can show these probabilities on a bar chart, with score on the x axis and probability on the y axis. Every outcome is equally likely, so the chart is rectangular. We call this a uniform probability distribution. The distribution is only uniform if the die is fair—a biased die would have a nonuniform probability distribution.

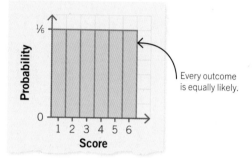

Every outcome is equally likely.

Symmetrical distribution

Suppose you roll two dice and add the numbers to get a total score. There's only one way of scoring 12 (two sixes), but there are six ways of scoring seven: $1 + 6$, $2 + 5$, $3 + 4$, $4 + 3$, $5 + 2$, $6 + 1$. So the probabilities of each score vary. If we put these probabilities on a chart, they form a nonuniform but symmetrical distribution.

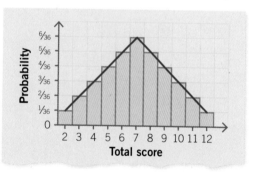

Binomial distribution

If you toss a coin 10 times, what's the chance of getting 10 heads? What's the chance of getting 5 heads? The number of heads follows a pattern called the binomial distribution, which curves up and then down. The binomial distribution applies to any activity that can have two mutually exclusive outcomes (outcomes that can't happen together) with fixed probabilities and is repeated a number of times (with each trial independent of the previous one).

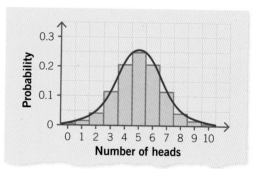

Statistics

Statistical inquiry

Statistics is the branch of mathematics that uses data to investigate questions about the world. We gather and analyze data—pieces of information—in order to test hypotheses (ideas). The process we use to pose and test hypotheses is called a statistical inquiry.

Key facts

✓ In a statistical inquiry, data is collected to test statistical hypotheses.

✓ We use different methods of collecting data to answer different kinds of questions.

✓ Data can be represented visually to make it easier to understand.

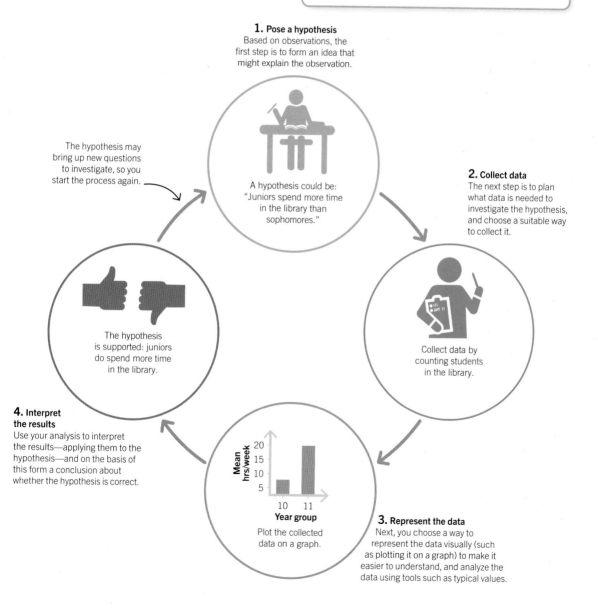

1. Pose a hypothesis
Based on observations, the first step is to form an idea that might explain the observation.

The hypothesis may bring up new questions to investigate, so you start the process again.

A hypothesis could be: "Juniors spend more time in the library than sophomores."

2. Collect data
The next step is to plan what data is needed to investigate the hypothesis, and choose a suitable way to collect it.

The hypothesis is supported: juniors do spend more time in the library.

Collect data by counting students in the library.

4. Interpret the results
Use your analysis to interpret the results—applying them to the hypothesis—and on the basis of this form a conclusion about whether the hypothesis is correct.

Plot the collected data on a graph.

3. Represent the data
Next, you choose a way to represent the data visually (such as plotting it on a graph) to make it easier to understand, and analyze the data using tools such as typical values.

Types of data

There are different types of data. The type of data you choose to collect will inform how the data is represented and interpreted. A collection of data about a particular subject is called a data set.

Primary data

Data gathered specifically for the purpose of answering the question that is posed in a hypothesis is called primary data.

A survey may be used to collect primary data.

Secondary data

Data originally collected for some other purpose but used to answer the new question asked in a hypothesis is called secondary data.

Historical census data is often used to answer new statistical questions.

Quantitative data

Data in the form of numbers is called quantitative data. It can be either continuous or discrete.

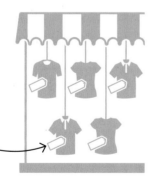

The prices of items in a store can form a quantitative data set.

Continuous data

Quantitative data that is continuous can take any value in a range.

A human's height can be any value (within the range of possible heights).

Discrete data

Quantitative data that is discrete can only have certain exact values.

The number of students in a classroom is an example of discrete data.

Qualitative data

Non-numerical data, usually in the form of words, is called qualitative data. It is also known as categorical data.

Different colors of bikes can form a qualitative data set.

Populations and samples

In statistics, a population is any set or group of things you want to collect data about. Sometimes it's not possible or practical to study the whole population, so instead we collect data about a sample. We then use this data to draw conclusions about the whole population.

Sampling methods

There are different methods of selecting individuals from a population to form a sample. Choosing a good sampling method helps answer the statistical question fairly.

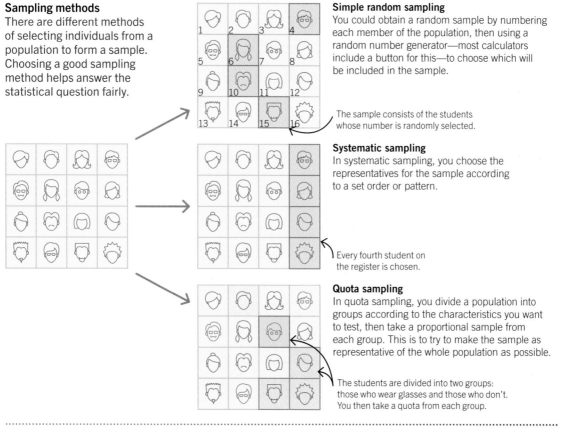

Simple random sampling

You could obtain a random sample by numbering each member of the population, then using a random number generator—most calculators include a button for this—to choose which will be included in the sample.

The sample consists of the students whose number is randomly selected.

Systematic sampling

In systematic sampling, you choose the representatives for the sample according to a set order or pattern.

Every fourth student on the register is chosen.

Quota sampling

In quota sampling, you divide a population into groups according to the characteristics you want to test, then take a proportional sample from each group. This is to try to make the sample as representative of the whole population as possible.

The students are divided into two groups: those who wear glasses and those who don't. You then take a quota from each group.

Limitations of sampling

When a certain group of a population is over- or underrepresented in a sample, we call the sample biased. Bias can happen even if the sample is chosen randomly—some members of the population may be more likely to be chosen than others. Having a small sample size can also lead to an unrepresentative sample.

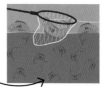

If you are taking a sample of fish in a pond, only collecting fish from near the surface might exclude smaller fish at the bottom from the data.

Frequency tables

Data is often organized into frequency tables. These show the frequency with which certain values appear in a set of data.

Tallying and tables

A company wants to make bike accessories to match the most popular bike colors, so it records the number of bikes in different colors that pass the office one day. Once the data has been collected, the first step in organizing it is to make a list of categories in a chart and make a tally mark for each answer. Then count the tally marks and enter the total for each category in a separate column to make a frequency table.

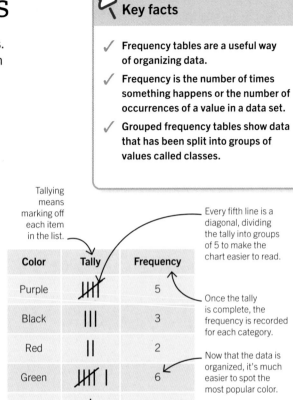

Tallying means marking off each item in the list.

Every fifth line is a diagonal, dividing the tally into groups of 5 to make the chart easier to read.

It's hard to spot any patterns from the raw data.

purple, black, red, green, purple, green, purple, purple, green, black, green, blue, red, black, purple, green, green

Color	Tally	Frequency
Purple	卌	5
Black	|||	3
Red	||	2
Green	卌		6
Blue			1

Once the tally is complete, the frequency is recorded for each category.

Now that the data is organized, it's much easier to spot the most popular color.

Grouped frequency tables

Sometimes it is useful to collect data into groups of values before making a frequency table. This is especially useful for continuous data, such as the times in a 100 m race for a school sports day. First, we need to decide on some categories to group the raw data into. These categories are called classes, and this type of table is called a grouped frequency table.

Using inequality symbols (see page 154) means that all the possible values in each class are covered.

One way of grouping the data is into 1 second intervals.

Each runner's time is sorted into one of the classes.

12.34, 14.29, 13.78, 14.06, 14.73, 15.08, 13.21, 13.46, 12.81, 11.25, 15.51, 13.1, 13.95

This raw data is a list of runners' times (in seconds).

Time, t, seconds	Tally	Frequency
$11 < t \leq 12$			1
$12 < t \leq 13$	||	2
$13 < t \leq 14$	卌	5
$14 < t \leq 15$	|||	3
$15 < t \leq 16$	||	2

Bar charts

Bar charts are a simple visual way of representing data. Bars of different lengths are drawn to represent the frequency of each group of data in the data set.

Key facts

✓ The frequencies of each group in a data set can be presented visually as a bar chart.

✓ Color and split bars can be used to represent different aspects of the data.

✓ The design of the bar chart should be chosen to suit the type of data being shown.

Visually representing frequency
In an ordinary bar chart, the frequency is usually shown on the y axis, while the x axis shows the data categories. The frequency table below shows the money earned in a week from the sale of different food and drink items in a coffee shop.

Items	Sales ($)
Hot drinks	1265
Cold drinks	399
Wraps	729
Cakes	682

Ordinary bar chart
In this bar chart, colors are used to split the data into subgroups of food and drink. The bars don't touch, because the categories are totally different.

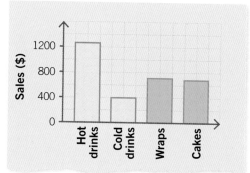

Different types of bar chart
Bar charts can be adapted to reveal more information about a data set. The frequency table below splits the same shop purchases into subgroups of cash and card payments.

Items	Cash ($)	Card ($)	Total ($)
Hot drinks	450	815	1265
Cold drinks	101	298	399
Wraps	242	487	729
Cakes	263	419	682

Composite bar chart
In a composite (or stacked) bar chart, two or more subgroups of data are shown as one bar, using color to differentiate them. A key is added so the colors can be interpreted.

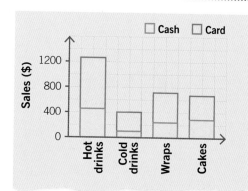

Dual bar chart
In a dual bar chart, the subgroups are placed next to each other. This allows you to compare the size of each subgroup.

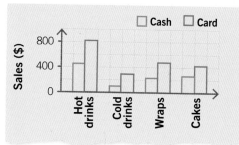

Pictograms

Pictograms are a bit like bar charts, but they represent frequency using pictures in place of the bars and don't usually include axes. They are typically used to represent qualitative (non-numerical) data.

Sunny days

A meteorologist records the number of days without rain in her hometown of Nowhereville for six months and summarizes the data in the frequency chart and pictogram below.

Month	Days without rain
January	13
February	6
March	10
April	20
May	13
June	10

The data for a pictogram is collected in a table first, just like for a bar chart.

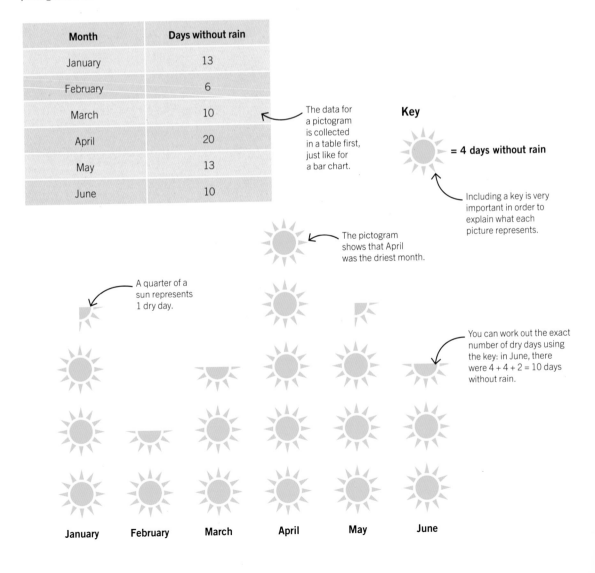

Key

= 4 days without rain

Including a key is very important in order to explain what each picture represents.

The pictogram shows that April was the driest month.

A quarter of a sun represents 1 dry day.

You can work out the exact number of dry days using the key: in June, there were 4 + 4 + 2 = 10 days without rain.

January   February   March   April   May   June

Line graphs

A line graph shows data plotted as points on a graph, which are then joined together by straight lines. Line graphs are particularly useful for showing data that changes over a period of time. They are therefore normally used to represent continuous data (see page 224).

(see page 224)

Key facts

✓ A line graph is useful for representing data that changes over time.

✓ Straight lines, not smooth curves, join the recorded data points.

✓ Two sets of data can be compared by drawing two lines on the same graph.

Interpreting line graphs

On a line graph, the data being analyzed is usually marked on the y axis—that way, we can interpret the relationship between the data from the height of the line. The line graph below represents the temperature at 6 A.M. each day for a week in Nowhereville.

The measurements are marked using crosses or dots as points on the grid.

The points are joined with straight lines, not curves, so we assume that the temperature changes steadily between points.

Day	Temp (°C)
Mon	−1
Tues	5
Wed	2
Thurs	−5
Fri	2
Sat	1
Sun	2

The temperature isn't measured continuously; instead, we take a daily snapshot.

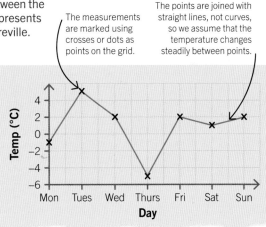

Double line graphs

Line graphs are especially useful for showing two related groups of data. The line graph below shows the differences in the patterns of growth between two siblings as they get older.

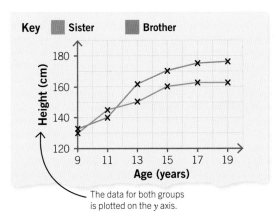

The data for both groups is plotted on the y axis.

⚙ When not to draw a line graph

Line graphs should generally not be used to present discrete data. For example, using a line graph to plot the different categories of sales in a coffee shop (see page 227) would be misleading, because the values in between the data points have no meaning.

(see page 227)

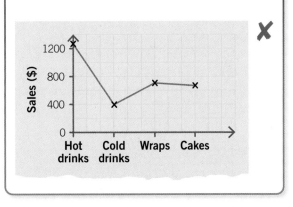

Pie charts

Pie charts show frequencies as a proportion of the whole. The size of the angles, and therefore the slices of the pie, represent the share of the total frequency in each category of the data set.

Drawing a pie chart
To get the information necessary to complete a pie chart, first gather all the data in a frequency table, then add columns for working out the sizes of the angles needed to draw each segment. The table below represents how many pieces of different types of cake were sold from a stall at a festival.

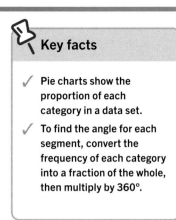

Key facts

✓ Pie charts show the proportion of each category in a data set.

✓ To find the angle for each segment, convert the frequency of each category into a fraction of the whole, then multiply by 360°.

2. Write each value in the frequency column as a fraction of the sum of the frequencies to indicate what proportion each cake sold represents of the total cake sales.

3. Because a whole circle is 360°, multiply each fraction by 360 to find the angle for each segment of the pie chart.

Type	Frequency	Fraction of whole	Degrees of circle
Sponge cake	9	$\frac{9}{30}$	$\frac{9}{30} \times 360 = \mathbf{108°}$
Carrot cake	3	$\frac{3}{30}$	$\frac{3}{30} \times 360 = \mathbf{36°}$
Red velvet cake	2	$\frac{2}{30}$	$\frac{2}{30} \times 360 = \mathbf{24°}$
Chocolate cake	11	$\frac{11}{30}$	$\frac{11}{30} \times 360 = \mathbf{132°}$
Fruit cake	5	$\frac{5}{30}$	$\frac{5}{30} \times 360 = \mathbf{60°}$
Total	30	1	**360°**

1. Add up the values in the frequency column to record the total number of cakes sold (30).

4. Check for mistakes by adding together all the angles—the total should be 360°.

5. Now draw the pie chart. Draw a circle and use the straight edge of the protractor to draw the first radius.

6. Using the first radius as 0°, draw the first segment at an angle of 108°.

7. Use the second radius to draw the second segment at 36°, and continue until all the segments are drawn.

8. Once you've drawn all the segments, color code the finished pie chart and add a title and key. If there's space on the chart, you could label the categories instead.

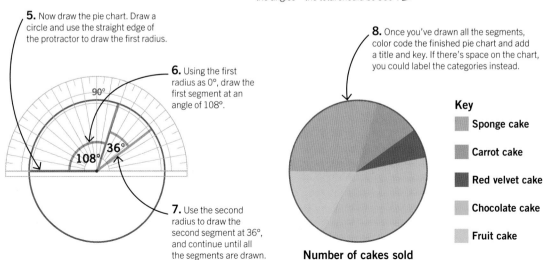

Key
- Sponge cake
- Carrot cake
- Red velvet cake
- Chocolate cake
- Fruit cake

Number of cakes sold

Mean, median, mode, and range

Summarizing data often involves working out a typical value that is useful for making comparisons. We call these typical values mean, median, and mode. The simplest measure of how spread out the data is— from the smallest value to largest—is called the range.

Key facts

✓ The mean is the sum of values in a data set divided by the total number of values.

✓ The median is the middle value of the set, arranged by size.

✓ If the frequency is even, the median is the mean of the two middle values.

✓ The mode is the most frequent value.

✓ The range is the difference between the largest and smallest values of a data set.

Different typical values
Eight students take a test, marked out of 50. You want to find the mean, median, and mode of their scores.

35, 43, 45, 38, 37, 45, 40, 29

Divide the total of the values by the total number of values to find the mean.

Mean
To find the mean, add up all the values, then divide by the total number of values. If a value in the data set is unusually large or small, the mean would not be the best method to calculate a typical value, because it would not represent a middle point.

$$\frac{35 + 43 + 45 + 38 + 37 + 45 + 40 + 29}{8} = \frac{312}{8} = 39$$

Median
The median is the middle value when all the values are listed in order. This can be useful if a very large or small value in the set skews the data. If there are two middle values, because there is an even number of total values, the median is the mean of these two middle values.

29, 35, 37, **38, 40**, 43, 45, 45

39

Rearrange the values in order.

In this case, the median is the mean of the two middle values:

$$\frac{38 + 40}{2} = 39$$

Mode
The mode is the value that appears most frequently in a data set. The mode can be useful when the data set is qualitative—for example, if an ice cream manufacturer created a survey to find out the most popular ice cream flavor—though it may not provide a middle point in a data set.

29, 35, 37, 38, 40, 43, **45, 45**

The mode doesn't provide a helpful typical value in this instance, because 45 is not a middle point in the data set.

Range
The range of the data is the difference between the largest and smallest values. To find it, you subtract the smallest value from the highest value.

Smallest value

→**29**, 35, 37, 38, 40, 43, 45, **45**

$$45 - 29 = 16$$

Highest values

This is the range.

Frequency tables and typical values

The mean, median, mode, and range of groups of data can all be found from frequency tables. When data is already summarized in a grouped frequency table (see page 226), we don't know the exact value of each data point, only its class, so any typical value we calculate is an estimate.

Range and mode

The frequency table to the right shows the total number of goals scored in each match in a small soccer competition. The range is the difference between the highest and lowest value. The mode is the most frequent value.

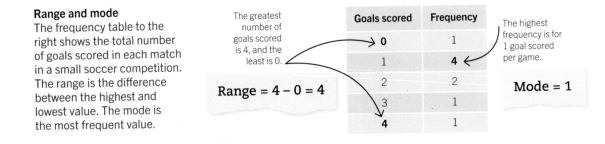

The greatest number of goals scored is 4, and the least is 0.

Range = 4 − 0 = 4

Goals scored	Frequency
0	1
1	4
2	2
3	1
4	1

The highest frequency is for 1 goal scored per game.

Mode = 1

Mean

To work out the mean number of goals per game, you need to add an extra column to the frequency table.

Goals scored	Frequency	Goals × Frequency
0	1	0
1	4	4
2	2	4
3	1	3
4	1	4
Total	9	15

1. Multiply each value (number of goals scored) by the frequency (number of games) and enter in the new column.

2. Add up this column to find the total number of goals scored in all games.

3. Divide the total number of goals by the total frequency to find the mean.

The mean isn't always a data value.

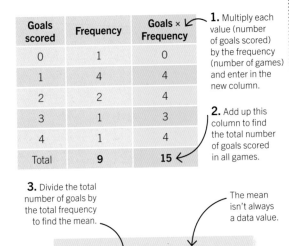

$$\text{Mean} = \frac{15}{9} = 1\frac{2}{3}$$

Median

The median value of the data is the number of goals scored in the middle game in the table. You can work this out by counting through the frequency column in the table until you get to the middle value.

Goals scored	Frequency
0	1
1	4
2	2
3	1
4	1
Total	9

1. Find the position of the median by adding 1 to the total frequency (9) and halving it, so $\frac{9+1}{2} = 5$.

2. Count down the frequency column until you reach the fifth value, or write the numbers out in a list (see below)

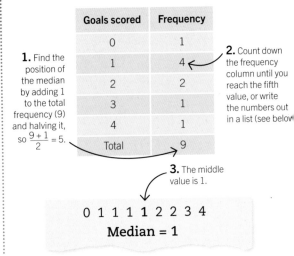

3. The middle value is 1.

0 1 1 1 1 2 2 3 4

Median = 1

Estimating typical values from a grouped frequency table

When data is collected in a grouped frequency table, we make estimates of the mode and median by giving the classes those values belong to. To calculate an estimate of the mean, we take the midpoints of each class. The frequency table below represents the heights of all the peaks in a mountain range above 900 m.

Range

The range is the maximum possible difference between the highest and lowest value.

$$\text{Range} = 1380 - 900 = 480 \text{ m}$$

Modal class

There's not enough information in the table to find the mode, so we use the class with the highest frequency (87). This is called the modal class.

$$\text{Modal class} = 900 \leq h < 960$$

Height (m)	Frequency	Midpoint	Frequency × Midpoint
$900 \leq h < 960$	87	930	80910
$960 \leq h < 1020$	86	990	85140
$1020 \leq h < 1080$	48	1050	50400
$1080 \leq h < 1140$	36	1110	39960
$1140 \leq h < 1200$	15	1170	17550
$1200 \leq h < 1260$	6	1230	7380
$1260 \leq h < 1320$	3	1290	3870
$1320 \leq h < 1380$	1	1350	1350
Total	**282**		**286560**

Median

The total number of mountains is 282, so the median height is at position $(282 + 1) \div 2 = 141.5$, or between the 141st and 142nd mountains. Count down the frequency column to find where these values appear: $87 + 86 = 173$, so 141.5 comes within the $960 \leq h < 1020$ class.

$$\text{Median} = 960 \leq h < 1020$$

Mean

There isn't enough information to calculate the exact mean height of the mountains. Therefore, we add a column and calculate the midpoint of each class as a representative value. Then add another column and multiply each frequency by each midpoint to find an estimate of all the heights.

1. Add together the upper and lower values in each class and divide by 2 to find each midpoint, so for example, $(900 + 960) \div 2 = 930$.

2. Multiply each midpoint by the frequency to find an estimate of the total heights in each class, so for example, $87 \times 930 = 80910$.

3. Add together all the estimated heights to find the total frequency × midpoint = 286560.

4. Divide the total frequency × midpoint by the total frequency to find the estimated mean to the nearest meter.

$$\text{Estimated mean} = \frac{286560}{282} = 1016 \text{ m}$$

Standard deviation

Standard deviation is a number that tells you how widely spread a set of measurements is. If standard deviation is low, most of the measurements are close to the mean. If standard deviation is high, the data is more widely spread.

> 📌 **Key facts**
>
> ✓ Standard deviation is a measure of how widely spread a set of data is.
>
> ✓ Low standard deviation means most measurements are near the mean. High standard deviation means fewer measurements are near the mean.

Comparing spreads of data

Suppose you survey the weights of hundreds of dogs of every breed and plot the results on a graph. Dog breeds vary, so the data would form a wide hill shape (called a normal distribution), with many measurements a long way from the central mean. However, data for a single breed would form a narrower distribution (below right), because the dogs would be less varied. Standard deviation is a measure of how widely dispersed the data is relative to the mean. It works as a kind of average distance from the mean.

All dog breeds (high standard deviation)

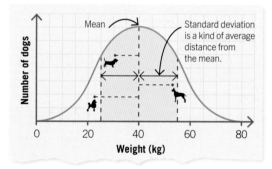

German shepherds (low standard deviation)

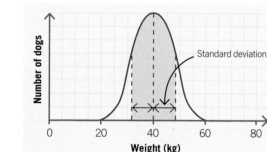

Calculating standard deviation

To calculate the standard deviation of a set of values, first find the mean of the data set, then use the formula to the right. To use the formula, we square the difference between each value and the mean, add the results together, divide by the number of values, and then square root the answer.

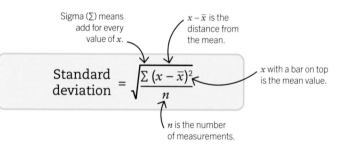

Sigma (Σ) means add for every value of x.

$x - \bar{x}$ is the distance from the mean.

$$\text{Standard deviation} = \sqrt{\frac{\Sigma\,(x - \bar{x})^2}{n}}$$

x with a bar on top is the mean value.

n is the number of measurements.

Practice question
Using standard deviation

See also

231 Mean, median, mode, and range

234 Standard deviation

Standard deviation is useful for comparing different sets of data to see which is more consistent (less widely spread).

Question
A sports coach has to select one of his two best javelin throwers, A and B, for an athletics team. The coach needs the person with the more consistent results, based on the table below. Who should the coach choose?

Throw	Player A	Player B
1	38	38
2	43	50
3	51	51
4	59	52
5	65	65

Answer
The more consistent thrower is the person with the lower standard deviation, so calculate the standard deviation for each athlete.

1. First, calculate the mean ($\bar{x}$) for player A and player B.

$$\bar{x} = \frac{\Sigma x}{n}$$

$$\bar{x}_A = \frac{38 + 43 + 51 + 59 + 65}{5} = 51.2$$

$$\bar{x}_B = \frac{38 + 50 + 51 + 52 + 65}{5} = 51.2$$

2. Calculate the squares of the distance from the mean $(x - \bar{x})^2$ for each throw of both the players. Add these together and write in the total $\Sigma(x - \bar{x})^2$.

Throw	Player A	$(x - \bar{x}_A)^2$
1	38	174.24
2	43	67.24
3	51	0.04
4	59	60.84
5	65	190.44
$\Sigma(x - \bar{x}_A)^2$		492.80

Throw	Player B	$(x - \bar{x}_B)^2$
1	38	174.24
2	50	1.44
3	51	0.04
4	52	0.64
5	65	190.44
$\Sigma(x - \bar{x}_B)^2$		366.80

3. Use the formula from page 234 to find the standard deviation for player A and player B.

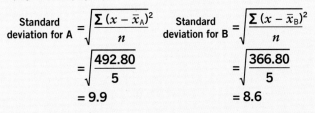

$$\text{Standard deviation for A} = \sqrt{\frac{\Sigma (x - \bar{x}_A)^2}{n}}$$

$$= \sqrt{\frac{492.80}{5}}$$

$$= 9.9$$

$$\text{Standard deviation for B} = \sqrt{\frac{\Sigma (x - \bar{x}_B)^2}{n}}$$

$$= \sqrt{\frac{366.80}{5}}$$

$$= 8.6$$

4. Player B has a smaller standard deviation and so is the best choice.

Cumulative frequency

Some frequency tables include an extra column showing a running total of total frequency so far. This is called cumulative frequency. Plotting the cumulative frequency on a graph makes it easier to make certain estimates from the data.

Cumulative frequency table

The owner of a pizzeria timed how long it took for pizzas to be made and delivered during a busy weekend. By adding a cumulative frequency column to the table, they could quickly see what proportion of pizzas were delivered in less than an hour.

The bottom and top of each class interval are called the lower and upper bounds.

Time (minutes)	Frequency	Cumulative frequency
$0 \leq t < 10$	5	5
$10 \leq t < 20$	6	11
$20 \leq t < 30$	14	25
$30 \leq t < 40$	21	46
$40 \leq t < 50$	16	62
$50 \leq t < 60$	12	74
$60 \leq t < 70$	3	77

Cumulative frequency is a running total of all the frequencies so far.

$5 + 6 = 11$

$5 + 6 + 14 = 25$

74 out of 77 pizzas were delivered in less than an hour.

Cumulative frequency graph

Plotting cumulative frequency on a graph makes it easy to estimate the median and other values. Make the y axis cumulative frequency, starting at 0. Plot each point using the highest value (upper bound) for each class as the x coordinate. Then join the points with straight lines or a smooth curve to form an S shape.

We can estimate that by 25 minutes, about 17 customers had received their pizza.

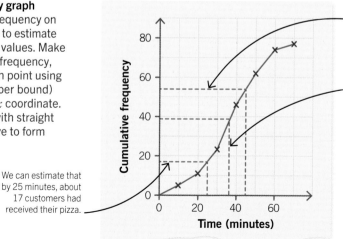

About 53 customers, or 69%, had their pizzas within 45 minutes.

To estimate the median, go halfway up the height of the curve and read off the x coordinate, which is approximately 36 minutes.

Quartiles

Quartiles work a bit like the median (see page 231), but instead of dividing a data set into halves, they divide it into quarters. You can measure how widely spread a data set is by calculating the interquartile range. This gives the spread of the middle 50 percent of values, so it is not affected by any extreme values.

Median and quartiles

These are the ages of 11 people at a birthday party, arranged in order. The median is the middle value. The lower quartile is in the middle of the bottom half of the numbers and the upper quartile is in the middle of the top half. To find the interquartile range, subtract the lower quartile from the upper quartile.

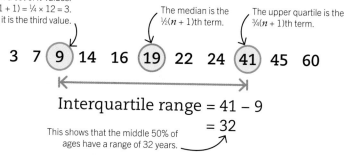

The lower quartile is the $\frac{1}{4}(n + 1)$th term in a set of n values:
$\frac{1}{4}(11 + 1) = \frac{1}{4} \times 12 = 3$.
Here, it is the third value.

The median is the $\frac{1}{2}(n + 1)$th term.

The upper quartile is the $\frac{3}{4}(n + 1)$th term.

3   7   ⑨   14   16   ⑲   22   24   ㊶   45   60

Interquartile range = 41 − 9
= 32

This shows that the middle 50% of ages have a range of 32 years.

Quartiles and graphs

You can estimate quartiles from a cumulative frequency graph (see opposite) even if the full set of data isn't known. For example, a candy factory counted the number of candies in a random sample of candy bags and recorded the results on a graph. The graph reveals that the median number of candies in a bag is about 59 and the interquartile range is about 6 candies.

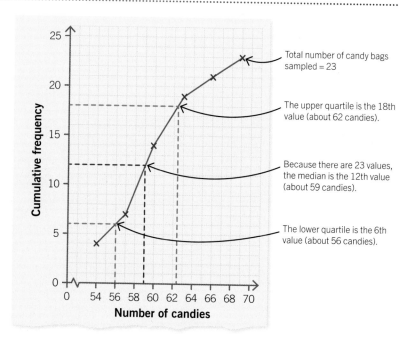

Total number of candy bags sampled = 23

The upper quartile is the 18th value (about 62 candies).

Because there are 23 values, the median is the 12th value (about 59 candies).

The lower quartile is the 6th value (about 56 candies).

Histograms

Histograms look like bar charts, but each bar represents a range of numbers within a continuous scale on the x axis. The area of each bar in a histogram usually represents the frequency of each class, but some simple histograms show frequency on the y axis instead.

Key facts

✓ Histograms resemble bar charts but are used for continuous data.

✓ If class intervals are equally wide, the heights of bars may be used to show frequency.

✓ If class intervals vary in width, the heights of the bars show frequency density and only the areas of bars show frequencies.

✓ Frequency density = frequency ÷ class width

A simple histogram

Histograms show "continuous" data, which means numerical data that varies throughout a range, such as measurements of time, distance, or weight. The continuous scale is put on the x axis and is divided into class intervals. In the simplest histograms, the vertical bars show the frequency for each class. For example, this histogram shows how long customers at a swimming pool spent swimming on a typical day.

The histogram reveals that 30–40 minute swims were most common.

Unlike a bar chart, there are no gaps between the bars, because the data is continuous.

When class intervals are equally wide, the heights of the bars may show frequencies.

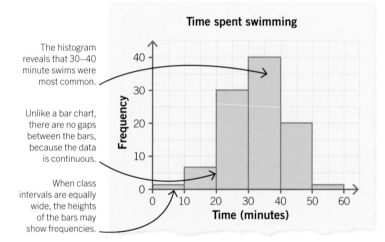

Unequal class intervals

Many histograms have class intervals of different widths. When class intervals vary, the y axis shows frequency density (frequency divided by class width) instead of frequency. This ensures that the area of each bar equals frequency, which stops the bars in the diagram from looking distorted and makes patterns in the data easier to spot. For instance, this histogram showing the number of pages in different books reveals that shorter books are more numerous than long books.

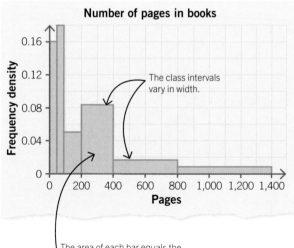

The class intervals vary in width.

The area of each bar equals the frequency for the class.

$$\text{Frequency density} = \frac{\text{frequency}}{\text{class width}}$$

Drawing histograms

To draw a histogram from a frequency table, follow the steps on this page. When interpreting a histogram, look for "skews" (asymmetrical shapes) in the chart.

Drawing a histogram

Histograms are based on tables of frequency data, such as this table showing weights of dogs. When drawing a histogram, check whether the class intervals are equal. If they aren't, add columns to the table to calculate class width and frequency density (see opposite).

1. Add columns for class width and frequency density to the table.

2. Calculate frequency densities (frequency density = frequency ÷ class width).

3. Put the continuous variable on the x axis.

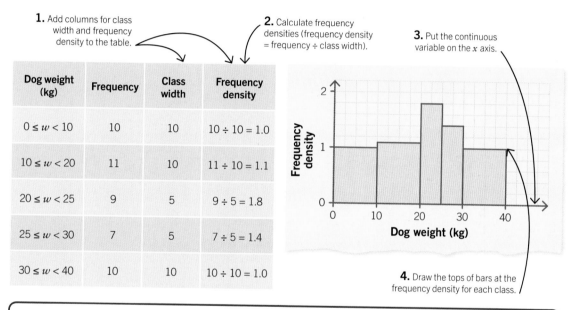

Dog weight (kg)	Frequency	Class width	Frequency density
$0 \le w < 10$	10	10	$10 \div 10 = 1.0$
$10 \le w < 20$	11	10	$11 \div 10 = 1.1$
$20 \le w < 25$	9	5	$9 \div 5 = 1.8$
$25 \le w < 30$	7	5	$7 \div 5 = 1.4$
$30 \le w < 40$	10	10	$10 \div 10 = 1.0$

4. Draw the tops of bars at the frequency density for each class.

🔍 Interpreting histograms

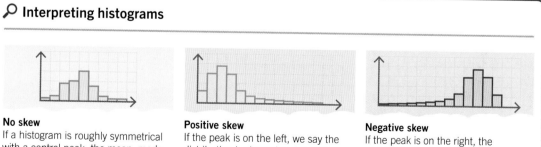

No skew
If a histogram is roughly symmetrical with a central peak, the mean, mode, and median are similar and all near the middle. A histogram showing people's heights forms this pattern.

Positive skew
If the peak is on the left, we say the distribution is skewed to the right (positive skew). The median value is higher than the peak (mode) value, and the mean is higher still. A histogram of people's incomes has this shape.

Negative skew
If the peak is on the right, the distribution is skewed to the left (negative skew) and the mean is lower than the median and mode. A histogram of people's age of death has this shape.

Time series

A series of measurements over a period of time is called a time series. Graphs of time series sometimes show a repeating pattern called seasonality. This can be smoothed out to reveal the underlying trend.

Key facts

✓ A time series is a series of measurements over a period of time.

✓ Seasonality is a repeating pattern in a time series.

✓ The underlying trend in a time series can be shown by using a moving average to smooth out seasonal variation.

Seasonality
The blue line on this graph shows the wholesale price of apples changing over several years. In winter, when apples are more scarce, the price is high. In summer, when apples are abundant, the price is low. When a variable shows a repeating pattern over time, we say it has seasonality (even if the pattern isn't directly related to the seasons). The time taken for the pattern to repeat is called a period.

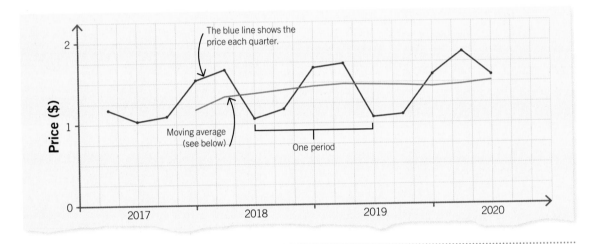

The blue line shows the price each quarter.

Moving average (see below)

One period

Moving average
A time series with a seasonal pattern can be smoothed out to reveal the underlying trend. In the graph above, the red line shows the average value of the previous four quarters (a four-point moving average). A moving average based on the length of one period removes the seasonal rise and fall from the numbers. This makes any long-term upward or downward trend easier to see. In this scenario, the price of apples is gradually increasing.

Date	Price ($)	Moving average	
Jan–Mar 2017	$1.23		There's no four-quarter average until four quarters have passed.
Apr–Jun 2017	$1.04		
Jul–Sept 2017	$1.12		
Oct–Dec 2017	$1.52	$1.23	Each average is the mean of the price in the previous four quarters.
Jan–Mar 2018	$1.71	$1.35	
Apr–Jun 2018	$1.16	$1.38	
Jul–Sept 2018	$1.21	$1.40	

Box plots

A box plot is a diagram that shows how a set of data is spread out within its range. Box plots allow you to see the range, quartiles, and median at a glance.

Box plot of ages

This box plot shows the ages of a sample of customers who visited a café. The central box shows the lower quartile (age 13), median (age 18), and upper quartile (age 21), while the "whiskers" to the left and right show the lower and upper ends of the range.

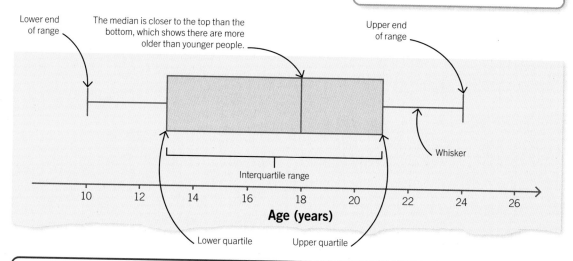

Lower end of range

The median is closer to the top than the bottom, which shows there are more older than younger people.

Upper end of range

Whisker

Interquartile range

Lower quartile

Upper quartile

📑 Interpreting box plots

If a whisker in a box plot is very long, there may be outliers—data points that don't fit the general pattern. If the median is not in the center, the data may be skewed (see page 239).

Question

This box plot shows heights of members of a football team. Describe the distribution of heights, referring to any skew or outliers.

Height (cm)

Answer

The median is in the center of the box, so the box plot indicates a symmetrical distribution of heights centered around approximately 169 cm. The upper end of the range is a long way from the upper quartile, so there may be an outlier, such as an unusually tall player.

Practice questions
Comparing distributions

See also

238 Histograms
239 Drawing histograms
241 Box plots

Sometimes we need to compare two different sets of data to see how the distributions differ. Comparing data sets is much easier if the data is shown in box plots or histograms.

Question

A biology teacher gave two different classes the same test and got the results shown below.

Class A:
20, 24, 31, 38, 39, 39, 40, 41, 45, 46, 50
Class B:
11, 23, 27, 32, 34, 36, 39, 41, 41, 45, 49

a) Which class did better in the test?
b) Which class got the most consistent results?

Answer

First, draw a scale representing the complete range of scores (from 11 to 50). Above the scale, draw box plots for each class showing the range, quartiles, and medians. There are 11 students in each class, so the median is the 6th value when scores are arranged in size order, and the quartiles are the 3rd and 9th values (see page 237).

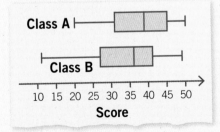

a) Class A has a higher median and so did better in the test.
b) Although both classes have the same interquartile range, class A has a smaller range and so had the most consistent results.

Question

Two films were shown at the same time in a movie theater. The ages of people in the audience are shown on these histograms. What does the distribution of ages in each histogram suggest about the kind of film being shown?

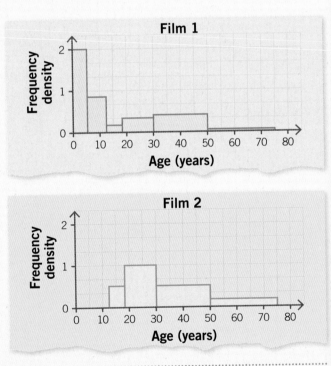

Answer

The most numerous visitors in film 1 are young children, followed by adults aged 30–50. There are very few teenagers. This film is probably aimed at young children, who tend to be accompanied by a parent. The most numerous visitors in film 2 are adults aged 18–30. Nobody in the audience was under 12, so film 2 may be age-restricted.

Scatter graphs

Scatter graphs are used to show the relationship between two different variables. If a change in one variable is associated with a change in another, we say the variables are correlated.

Key facts

✓ Scatter graphs show the relationship between two different variables.

✓ If a change in one variable is associated with a change in another, they are correlated.

Positive correlation

This scatter graph shows the relationship between the price of flights and distance traveled. As distance increases, so does the price. This is called a positive correlation. When variables are positively correlated, the points form a diagonal pattern running from bottom left to top right.

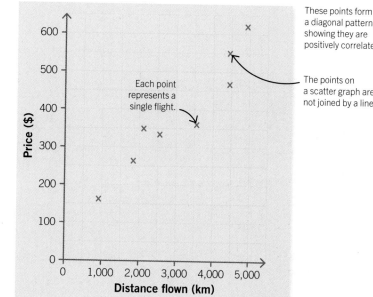

These points form a diagonal pattern, showing they are positively correlated.

Each point represents a single flight.

The points on a scatter graph are not joined by a line.

Types of correlation

Scatter graphs can show several different kinds of correlation or no correlation. A correlation between two variables does not necessarily show that one causes the other. For example, there may be a negative correlation between sales of ice cream and sales of umbrellas, but this is because both are related to a third factor: the weather.

Zero correlation
The data points are scattered randomly and show no pattern. There is no correlation between the variables.

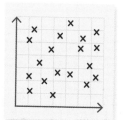

Negative correlation
The line formed by these points shows that one variable decreases as the other increases. This is a negative correlation.

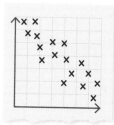

Strong positive correlation
The points form a roughly diagonal line, showing that one variable increases as the other one does.

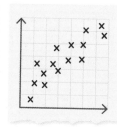

Weak positive correlation
The points look as if they might be grouped around a diagonal line. The large scatter means this is only a weak relationship.

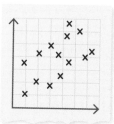

Lines of best fit

A line of best fit is a line drawn on a scatter graph to show how two variables are related. Draw a line of best fit when the variables appear to be correlated (see page 243).

(see page 243)

Key facts

✓ A line of best fit is drawn on a scatter graph to show correlation.

✓ A line of best fit should have the same number of points above and below it.

✓ Interpolation and extrapolation use a line of best fit to estimate unknown values.

Drawing a line of best fit

This scatter graph shows the length of a spring that stretched as increasing weights were hung from it. The two variables—weight and extension—form a strong positive correlation. When variables on a scatter graph are correlated, use a ruler and pencil to draw a line of best fit.

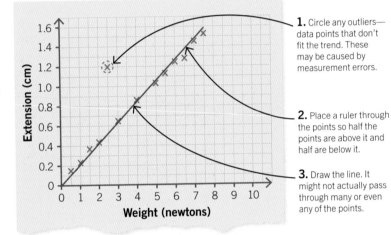

1. Circle any outliers—data points that don't fit the trend. These may be caused by measurement errors.

2. Place a ruler through the points so half the points are above it and half are below it.

3. Draw the line. It might not actually pass through many or even any of the points.

Interpolation and extrapolation

You can use a line of best fit to predict results that haven't been measured by an experiment. Estimating values within the range of the data is called interpolation. Estimating values outside the range of the data is called extrapolation.

Line of best fit

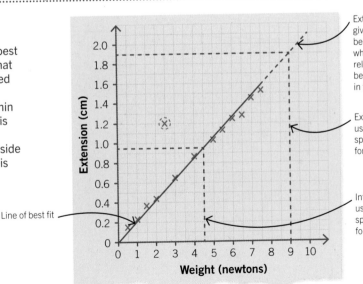

Extrapolation might not give a reliable estimate, because we don't know whether the linear relationship continues beyond the range tested in the experiment.

Extrapolation allows us to predict the spring's extension for a load of 9 N.

Interpolation allows us to predict the spring's extension for a load of 4.5 N.

Further graphs

Distance-time graphs

We can use graphs to show and analyze the relationship between two real-life variables, such as distance and time. Distance-time graphs are used to model the movement of an object over time.

Graphing a journey
Distance-time graphs plot the distance traveled from a point against the time that has passed. A journey may finish some distance from its starting point, or it may be a round trip, coming back to its starting point. Whatever is traveling will always move forward in time, represented on the x axis.

This graph shows a person's journey over 10 hours.

Finding the slope of a section of the graph tells us the person's speed for that section:

Speed $= \dfrac{4}{1} = 4$ **km/h**

Horizontal sections of the graph show that no distance is traveled over that period of time, so the person is stationary. The slope, and therefore the speed, is 0.

A downward slope shows the person is traveling back toward their starting point.

The y axis shows the person's distance from the start, called their displacement.

Time passed is shown on the x axis.

Distance from start (km) / **Time (hours)**

📑 Getting to school

Question
A student gets to school by walking to the bus stop, waiting for the bus, riding on the bus, then walking to school from the bus. The journey is shown in this distance-time graph. What's the speed of the bus in kilometers per hour?

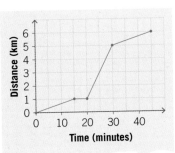

Distance (km) / **Time (minutes)**

Answer
The section of the graph where the slope is steepest (so the speed is highest) must represent the student's time on the bus. To find the speed, we work out the slope of this section, then convert it to the correct unit.

$$\dfrac{4}{10} = 0.4 \text{ km/min}$$

$$0.4 \times 60 = 24 \text{ km/hour}$$

Speed-time graphs

We can use graphs to analyze how a person or object's speed changes over time. These graphs, called speed-time graphs, can be used to find the acceleration and distance traveled.

Graphing movement
Speed-time graphs tell the story of an object's movement by plotting speed against time. This graph shows an object speeding up (accelerating) from rest, then traveling at a constant speed, before slowing down (decelerating) and coming to a stop.

The slope tells us the acceleration, which is measured in meters per second per second (m/s²).

Where the graph is flat, the object is moving at constant speed and not accelerating.

A negative slope represents deceleration. Here, it is −1 m/s².

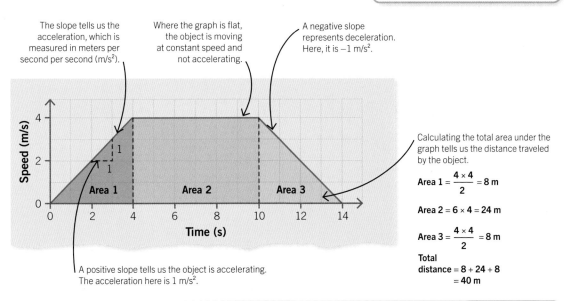

Calculating the total area under the graph tells us the distance traveled by the object.

$$\text{Area 1} = \frac{4 \times 4}{2} = 8 \text{ m}$$

$$\text{Area 2} = 6 \times 4 = 24 \text{ m}$$

$$\text{Area 3} = \frac{4 \times 4}{2} = 8 \text{ m}$$

Total distance = 8 + 24 + 8
= **40 m**

A positive slope tells us the object is accelerating. The acceleration here is 1 m/s².

Velocity-time graphs

Velocity is the measure of speed in a particular direction. While the area under a speed-time graph represents the distance traveled, the area under a velocity-time graph represents the displacement (its distance from its starting point). As with speed-time graphs, the slope on a velocity-time graph represents acceleration.

Question
The graph here shows the velocity of an athlete sprinting over 60 seconds. How far did they run at their maximum velocity?

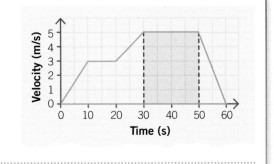

Answer
The athlete's fastest running occurs between the 30- and 50-second marks. The distance traveled can be found by calculating the area under this part of the graph.

$$5 \times 20 = 100 \text{ m}$$

Area under a curve

Finding the area under a graph can help us understand the relationship between the graph's variables. When the graph is a curve, we estimate its area by dividing it into parts.

Key facts

✓ The area under a speed-time curve is the distance traveled.

✓ The area under a curve is estimated by splitting it into triangles, rectangles, and trapezoids, calculating the area of each shape and adding the results together.

Estimating distance traveled
It's easy to accurately work out the area under a graph that is made up of lines, because we can split the area into neat triangles, rectangles, and trapezoids. When a graph is curved, we can estimate the area by roughly splitting it into these shapes. The more shapes you split it into, the more accurate your estimate will be.

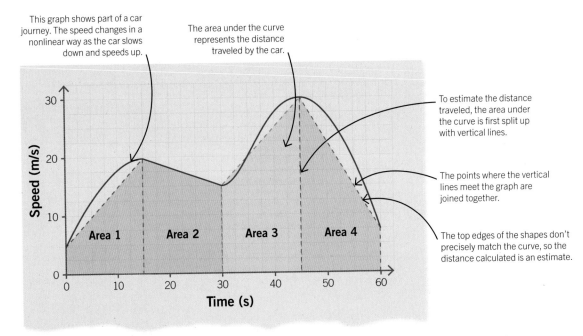

This graph shows part of a car journey. The speed changes in a nonlinear way as the car slows down and speeds up.

The area under the curve represents the distance traveled by the car.

To estimate the distance traveled, the area under the curve is first split up with vertical lines.

The points where the vertical lines meet the graph are joined together.

The top edges of the shapes don't precisely match the curve, so the distance calculated is an estimate.

Calculating the area
To estimate the total distance traveled, work out the area of each trapezoid using the formula Area = ½(a + b) × h, where a and b are the heights of the parallel sides and h is the distance between them. Then add the areas together.

$$\text{Area 1} = \frac{1}{2}(5 + 20) \times 15 = 187.5 \text{ m}$$

$$\text{Area 2} = \frac{1}{2}(20 + 15) \times 15 = 262.5 \text{ m}$$

$$\text{Area 3} = \frac{1}{2}(15 + 30) \times 15 = 337.5 \text{ m}$$

$$\text{Area 4} = \frac{1}{2}(30 + 7.5) \times 15 = 281.25 \text{ m}$$

Total distance traveled = 187.5 + 262.5 + 337.5 + 281.25 = 1068.75 m

Slope of a curve

Measuring the slope (or gradient) of a line is straightforward, because its slope is the same at all points. Finding the slope of a curve is trickier, because its slope varies depending on which part of the curve you measure.

Finding the slope

We find the slope at a particular point on a curve by drawing a line tangent to the curve at that point. The slope of this line can be found in the usual way, using the formula for the slope of a line (see page 146).

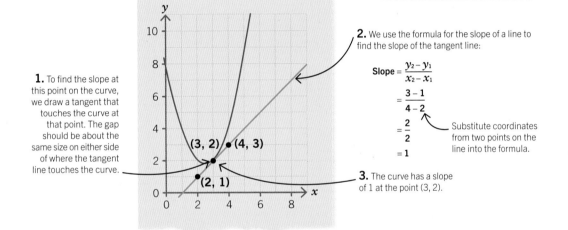

1. To find the slope at this point on the curve, we draw a tangent that touches the curve at that point. The gap should be about the same size on either side of where the tangent line touches the curve.

(3, 2) (4, 3)

(2, 1)

2. We use the formula for the slope of a line to find the slope of the tangent line:

$$\text{Slope} = \frac{y_2 - y_1}{x_2 - x_1}$$

$$= \frac{3 - 1}{4 - 2}$$

$$= \frac{2}{2}$$

$$= 1$$

Substitute coordinates from two points on the line into the formula.

3. The curve has a slope of 1 at the point (3, 2).

📌 Key facts

✓ **The slope of a curve changes as you move along it.**

✓ **To find the slope at a particular point on a curve, draw a line tangent to it and calculate the slope of that tangent.**

✓ **The slope at a point on a curve represents the instantaneous rate of change at that point.**

⚙ Instantaneous rate of change

The slope of a graph represents the rate of change of y with respect to x. For a curve, the slope is different at different parts of the graph. The curve has no constant rate of change, so the slope at any point is called the instantaneous rate of change at that point.

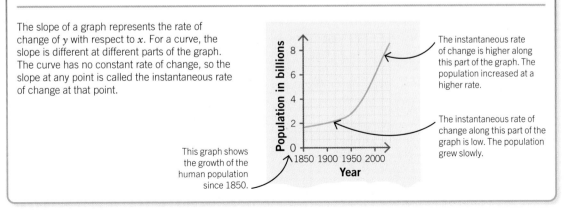

This graph shows the growth of the human population since 1850.

The instantaneous rate of change is higher along this part of the graph. The population increased at a higher rate.

The instantaneous rate of change along this part of the graph is low. The population grew slowly.

Linear real-life graphs

Real-life variables, such as length, can be plotted against each other on a graph. If one variable changes at a constant rate relative to the other, the slope of its line will be constant and the graph will be linear (straight).

Converting measurements

A linear graph can plot the relative values of two quantities, such as units of length, and be used to convert between them. This graph, called a conversion graph, shows how inches and centimeters relate to each other.

Draw a line from the measurement you need to convert until it hits the conversion rate line, then draw a line to the other axis to read its conversion.

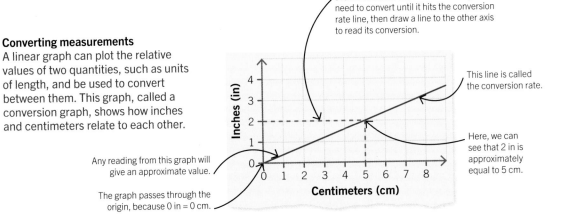

This line is called the conversion rate.

Here, we can see that 2 in is approximately equal to 5 cm.

Any reading from this graph will give an approximate value.

The graph passes through the origin, because 0 in = 0 cm.

Calculating a phone bill

If the relationship between two variables changes at a certain point, the graph will have sections with different slopes. A graph with this type of relationship between variables is called a piecewise linear graph, because the graph is made of different straight pieces. This graph shows the cost in cents per megabyte (¢/MB) of data used on a mobile phone plan.

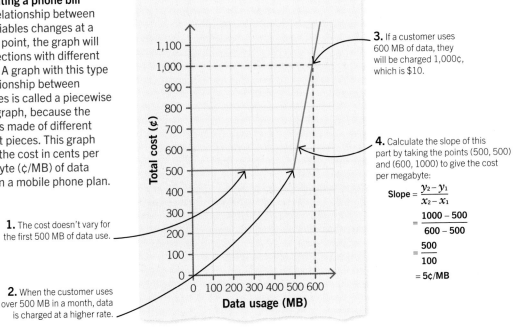

3. If a customer uses 600 MB of data, they will be charged 1,000¢, which is $10.

4. Calculate the slope of this part by taking the points (500, 500) and (600, 1000) to give the cost per megabyte:

$$\text{Slope} = \frac{y_2 - y_1}{x_2 - x_1}$$

$$= \frac{1000 - 500}{600 - 500}$$

$$= \frac{500}{100}$$

$$= 5¢/\text{MB}$$

1. The cost doesn't vary for the first 500 MB of data use.

2. When the customer uses over 500 MB in a month, data is charged at a higher rate.

Nonlinear real-life graphs

Not all real-life scenarios involve a linear relationship—for example, the filling of a container with sloped or curved sides. When a graph shows a nonlinear relationship between two variables, it will be a curve.

Filling containers with liquid
Imagine filling a container with liquid from a tap with a constant rate of flow. The height of the liquid in the container will increase over time. However, the rate of this change will depend on the shape of the container.

The graph is a line, because the fill rate is constant.

This container has straight sides, so the rate at which it fills up is constant.

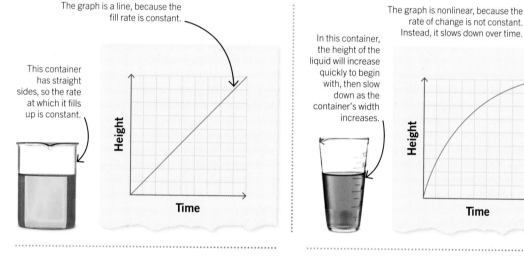

In this container, the height of the liquid will increase quickly to begin with, then slow down as the container's width increases.

The graph is nonlinear, because the rate of change is not constant. Instead, it slows down over time.

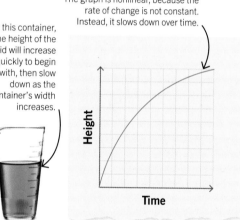

As this container fills, the height of the liquid will increase more and more quickly as the container's sides narrow.

The graph shows that the rate increases steadily as the container narrows, then becomes linear when its sides become straight.

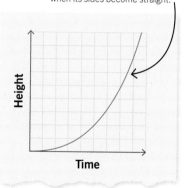

This spherical container will fill fastest at the beginning and end, where it is narrow.

The graph shows that the rate is lowest in the middle, where the container is widest, then becomes linear when the sides are straight.

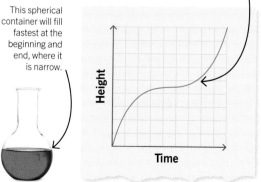

Domain and range of a function

A function is like a machine that takes an input (such as a number) and applies a rule to the input to give an output. The sets of possible values for the inputs and outputs of a function are called the domain and range.

Mapping inputs to outputs

Because a function is a rule for taking an input and giving an output, we can say it "maps" a set of inputs to a set of outputs. The possible set of inputs is called the domain of the function, and the possible set of outputs is the range.

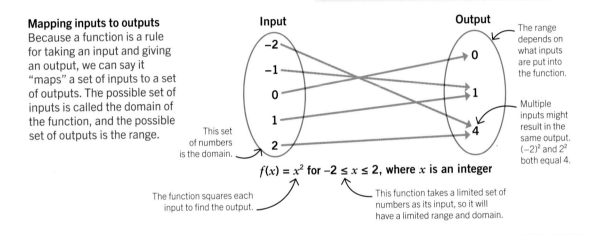

This set of numbers is the domain.

The range depends on what inputs are put into the function.

Multiple inputs might result in the same output. $(-2)^2$ and 2^2 both equal 4.

$f(x) = x^2$ for $-2 \leq x \leq 2$, where x is an integer

The function squares each input to find the output.

This function takes a limited set of numbers as its input, so it will have a limited range and domain.

Domain and range on a graph

While many functions can have any input and any output, some have a limited domain, a limited range, or both, like in the example above. A quadratic function will always have a limited range, even when its domain includes all real numbers, because the square of a real number cannot be negative. We can read the domain and range from a function's graph.

Any value of x can be used as the input for this quadratic function, but the output, y, will always be greater than or equal to 0.

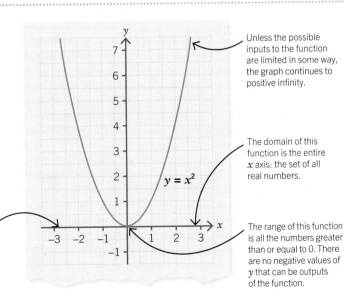

$y = x^2$

Unless the possible inputs to the function are limited in some way, the graph continues to positive infinity.

The domain of this function is the entire x axis: the set of all real numbers.

The range of this function is all the numbers greater than or equal to 0. There are no negative values of y that can be outputs of the function.

Interval notation

Because the range and domain of a function are sets of values, we can describe them using something called interval notation. We write the lowest value and the highest value separated by a comma within a combination of brackets and parentheses. Square brackets indicate a "closed" interval, while curved parentheses show "open" intervals.

A closed circle means −3 is a possible value of x.

This number line shows a domain for x.

An open circle means that 4 is not included in the possible values for x.

$$-4 \quad -3 \quad -2 \quad -1 \quad 0 \quad 1 \quad 2 \quad 3 \quad 4 \quad 5$$

We can write the possible values of x as an inequality (see page 154).

$-3 \leq x < 4$
Inequality notation

$[-3, 4)$
Interval notation

A curved parenthesis shows that the upper bound, 4, is not included in the set.

A square bracket shows that the lower bound, −3, is included in the set.

We can also express the set of possible x values in interval notation.

Limited functions

This is a graph of two limited functions: $f(x) = x + 1$ for $-1 < x \leq 2$ and $f(x) = 5 - x$ for $2 < x < 5$. It is called a piecewise function, because it is described by more than one equation. We can work out the interval notation for the domain (the possible x values) and range (the possible y values) by looking at the graph.

The range of this graph is $0 < y \leq 3$ or $(0, 3]$, because 0 is not included and 3 is included in the possible set of values for y.

A closed circle means these coordinates are included in the set of possible values.

An open circle means these coordinates are not included in the set of possible values.

$f(x) = x + 1$

$f(x) = 5 - x$

The domain of this graph is $-1 < x < 5$ or $(-1, 5)$, because −1 and 5 are not included in the set of possible values for x.

Unlimited functions

Sometimes a function will not be limited, so it will have an infinite set of values for its input and output. We can use the symbol ∞ to represent "infinity." This is the graph of the function $f(x) = x + 2$.

Any value of x can be the input, so the domain of the function includes all real numbers. We can use the infinity symbol to express the domain: $(-\infty, \infty)$.

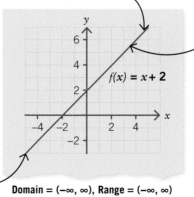

The graph will pass through every value of y, so the range is also the set of all real numbers. The range is $(-\infty, \infty)$.

$f(x) = x + 2$

The graph of this linear function could continue forever in both directions, because the function is not limited.

Domain = $(-\infty, \infty)$, Range = $(-\infty, \infty)$

Cubic graphs

While linear functions contain an x term and quadratic functions contain an x^2 term as their highest powers of x, cubic functions contain an x^3 term as the highest power of x. Graphs of cubic functions flatten or change direction twice and have a distinctive shape.

Key facts

✓ Cubic functions contain an x^3 term as their highest power.

✓ The graph of a cubic function will flatten or change direction in the middle.

✓ Positive cubic graphs move upward from left to right, while negative ones go downward.

Drawing a cubic graph

1. This is a cubic equation, because it contains an x^3 term as its highest power.

$$y = x^3 - 3x^2 - x + 3$$

2. To draw a cubic graph, make a table of x and y values to find the coordinates that can be plotted on the graph. Values of y are found by substituting a range of values for x into the function.

Input (x)	Output (y)	Coordinates of point
−2	$(-2)^3 - 3(-2)^2 - (-2) + 3 = -15$	(−2, −15)
−1	0	(−1, 0)
0	3	(0, 3)
1	0	(1, 0)
2	−3	(2, −3)
3	0	(3, 0)
4	15	(4, 15)

More points are needed to plot a cubic graph than a quadratic, because the shape is more complicated.

3. Plot the coordinates on the graph and join them with a smooth curve.

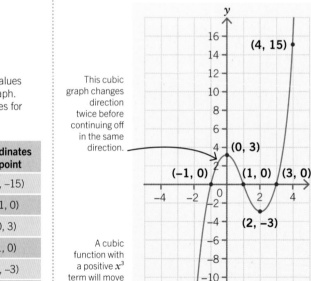

This cubic graph changes direction twice before continuing off in the same direction.

A cubic function with a positive x^3 term will move upward from left to right.

📑 How many roots?

Roots are the possible solutions to a function that equals zero. On a graph, they are the points where the graph crosses the x axis. Cubic functions can have a maximum of three roots, but some have only one or two.

This cubic graph has one root.

This cubic function has two roots.

Reciprocal graphs

The reciprocal of a number is 1 divided by that number. The reciprocal of x, for example, is $\frac{1}{x}$. Reciprocal functions can be graphed on the coordinate grid and always have the same characteristic shape.

A reciprocal function
This is a reciprocal function of x, because x appears as the denominator of the fraction.

$$f(x) = \frac{1}{x}$$

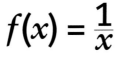

> 📌 **Key facts**
>
> ✓ The reciprocal of a number is 1 divided by that number.
>
> ✓ A reciprocal graph consists of two disconnected curved parts that don't touch and is symmetrical along both diagonals.

A table for the reciprocal function
As with any function, to work out coordinates to graph the function $f(x) = \frac{1}{x}$, we create a table of x and y values. Here is a table of values for $y = \frac{1}{x}$.

Input (x)	Output (y)	Coordinates
−3	$-\frac{1}{3}$	$(-3, -\frac{1}{3})$
−2	$-\frac{1}{2}$	$(-2, -\frac{1}{2})$
−1	−1	$(-1, -1)$
0	$\frac{1}{0}$	No value
1	1	$(1, 1)$
2	$\frac{1}{2}$	$(2, \frac{1}{2})$
3	$\frac{1}{3}$	$(3, \frac{1}{3})$

The function does not exist for $x = 0$. We say it is undefined for $x = 0$.

The graph of the reciprocal function
Plotting the coordinates reveals the characteristic shape of a reciprocal graph. The graph splits into two disconnected curved parts and has two diagonal lines of symmetry. Here is the graph of $y = \frac{1}{x}$.

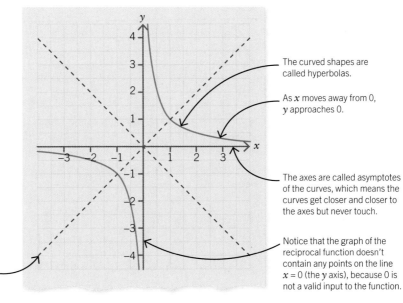

The curved shapes are called hyperbolas.

As x moves away from 0, y approaches 0.

The axes are called asymptotes of the curves, which means the curves get closer and closer to the axes but never touch.

The graph is symmetrical over both diagonals. The diagonals are the lines $y = x$ and $y = -x$.

Notice that the graph of the reciprocal function doesn't contain any points on the line $x = 0$ (the y axis), because 0 is not a valid input to the function.

Exponential graphs

An exponential graph is a graph in the form $y = k^x$, where x appears as the power of a constant. The graph's curve represents accelerating growth or decay, depending on its direction.

Exponential functions

This is an exponential function in the form $f(x) = k^x$. When k, called the base of the exponent, is greater than 1, the output of an exponential function will show exponential growth (see page 61).

$$f(x) = 2^x$$

In this example, the base is 2, so the output will double if the input increases by 1.

The number is raised to the power of x.

Table for $y = 2^x$

We identify coordinates for the graph of the exponential function $f(x) = 2^x$ by swapping $f(x)$ for y to turn the function into an equation. Substituting different values for x into the equation reveals the y values, and therefore the coordinates to plot.

Raising 2 to negative values of x gives values of y less than 1 but greater than 0.

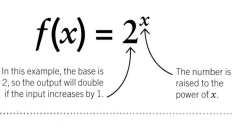

Input (x)	−2	−1	0	1	2
Output (y)	$\frac{1}{4}$	$\frac{1}{2}$	1	2	4

As 2 is raised to greater values of x, each value of y is further from the last.

Graph of $y = 2^x$

This is the graph of the exponential function $f(x) = 2^x$. It shows exponential growth. The graph is almost flat at one end, then as x increases, the curve climbs steeper and steeper upward.

For exponential growth, the higher the value of x, the faster the growth.

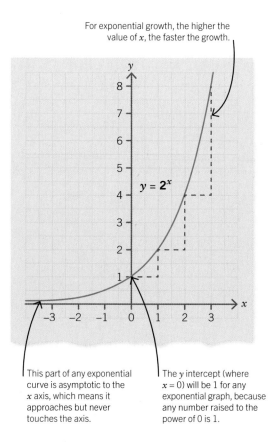

$y = 2^x$

This part of any exponential curve is asymptotic to the x axis, which means it approaches but never touches the axis.

The y intercept (where $x = 0$) will be 1 for any exponential graph, because any number raised to the power of 0 is 1.

Determining an exponential function

Some exponential functions have a second number in front of the base number, for example, $f(x) = 4 \times 2^x$. If you know some of the corresponding values of x and y, then you can work out what a and b are in an equation in the form $y = ab^x$.

1. Points $(0, 2)$ and $(1, 6)$ lie on an exponential curve with an equation in the form $y = ab^x$. Find the values of a and b to work out the equation of the exponential function.

2. Sketching the graph of the exponential equation will help us visualize and understand the problem. The first coordinate $(0, 2)$ gives us the y intercept, because it's where x is 0.

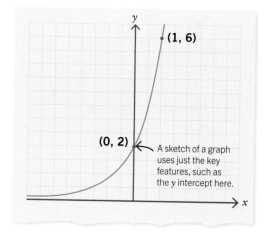

(1, 6)

(0, 2) ← A sketch of a graph uses just the key features, such as the y intercept here.

3. To begin to determine the equation, we substitute the coordinates of one of the points on the graph into the equation. First, substitute the coordinates of the y intercept.

$$y = ab^x$$
$$2 = ab^0 \quad \text{← Any number to the power of 0 is 1.}$$
$$2 = a \times 1$$
$$2 = a$$

4. Next, we substitute the coordinates of the second point into the equation.

$$y = ab^x$$
$$6 = ab^1$$

5. We know from step 3 that a is 2, so we can substitute that into this equation, too, then solve it to find b.

$$6 = ab^1$$
$$6 = 2b^1$$
$$3 = b^1 \quad \text{← Any number raised to the power of 1 is itself.}$$
$$3 = b$$

6. Now that we know that a is 2 and b is 3, we have the equation for the exponential function.

$$y = ab^x$$
$$y = 2 \times 3^x$$

🔎 Exponential decay

On a graph of an exponential function in the form $y = k^x$ where k is between 0 and 1, y will decrease as x increases. We call this exponential decay. This exponential graph approximately represents the radioactive decay of a form of uranium. It decays relatively rapidly at first but decays more slowly as time goes on.

For exponential decay, the higher the value of x, the slower the decay.

$f(x) = 0.5999^x$

k is between 0 and 1.

Mass (g)

Time (billion years)

Trigonometric graphs

Trigonometry is the area of math that explores triangles (see page 197). It uses ratios called sine, cosine, and tangent to explore the relationships between the angles and sides of triangles. Functions involving these ratios can be plotted on the coordinate grid to produce distinctive graphs.

Graphs of the sine and cosine functions
The graphs of sine (sin) and cosine (cos) are both wave-shaped curves that repeat every 360°. To draw the graphs of $y = \sin x$ and $y = \cos x$, use a calculator to work out $\sin x$ and $\cos x$ for various values of x.

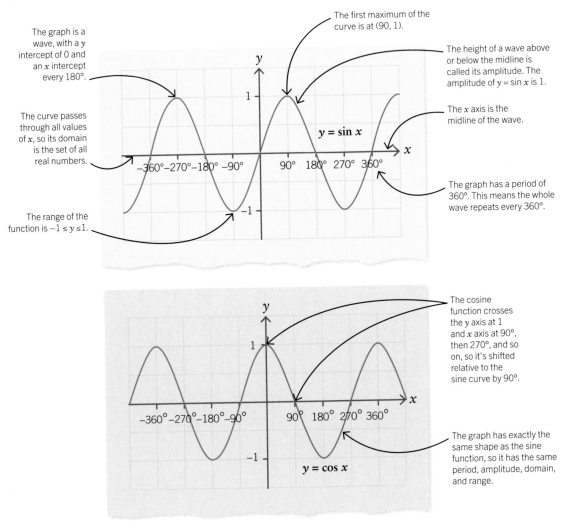

The graph is a wave, with a y intercept of 0 and an x intercept every 180°.

The curve passes through all values of x, so its domain is the set of all real numbers.

The range of the function is $-1 \le y \le 1$.

The first maximum of the curve is at (90, 1).

The height of a wave above or below the midline is called its amplitude. The amplitude of $y = \sin x$ is 1.

The x axis is the midline of the wave.

$y = \sin x$

The graph has a period of 360°. This means the whole wave repeats every 360°.

The cosine function crosses the y axis at 1 and x axis at 90°, then 270°, and so on, so it's shifted relative to the sine curve by 90°.

$y = \cos x$

The graph has exactly the same shape as the sine function, so it has the same period, amplitude, domain, and range.

Graph of the tangent function

The tangent (tan) function is a very different shape from the sine and cosine and has a repeating gap where the function is undefined. As for other functions, inputting values for x into the equation $y = \tan x$ will identify points to plot its graph.

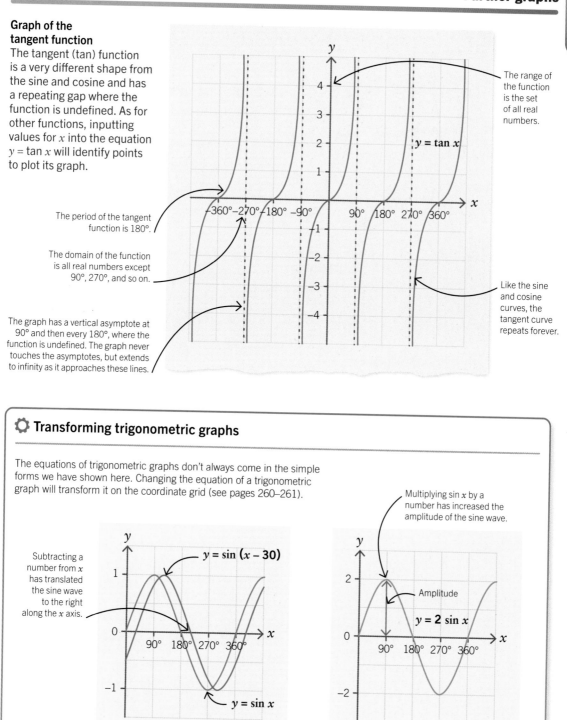

The range of the function is the set of all real numbers.

$y = \tan x$

The period of the tangent function is 180°.

The domain of the function is all real numbers except 90°, 270°, and so on.

Like the sine and cosine curves, the tangent curve repeats forever.

The graph has a vertical asymptote at 90° and then every 180°, where the function is undefined. The graph never touches the asymptotes, but extends to infinity as it approaches these lines.

⚙ Transforming trigonometric graphs

The equations of trigonometric graphs don't always come in the simple forms we have shown here. Changing the equation of a trigonometric graph will transform it on the coordinate grid (see pages 260–261).

Subtracting a number from x has translated the sine wave to the right along the x axis.

$y = \sin (x - 30)$

$y = \sin x$

Multiplying $\sin x$ by a number has increased the amplitude of the sine wave.

Amplitude

$y = 2 \sin x$

Transformations of graphs

Just as shapes and points can be transformed on the coordinate grid (see pages 174–175), graphs can be transformed, too. Changing a function will transform its graph.

Translations
By thinking of the equation of a graph as $y = f(x)$, we can describe how to translate it on the coordinate grid. Translating a function means moving it parallel to the x axis, the y axis, or both.

$y = f(x - a)$
Adding or subtracting a number to or from the x terms in an equation translates its graph in a negative or positive direction along the x axis. The translation is represented by the equation $y = f(x - a)$, where a is the number subtracted from x. Here, the graph of $y = x^2$ is transformed to $y = (x - 2)^2$ and $y = (x + 2)^2$.

Subtracting from the x term translates the graph in the positive direction.

Adding to the x term translates the graph in the negative direction.

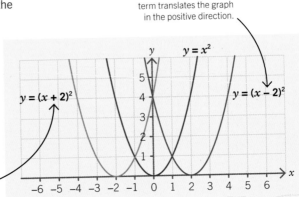

$y = f(x) + a$
Adding or subtracting a number to or from the whole of an equation translates its graph in a positive or negative direction along the y axis. The translation is represented by the equation $y = f(x) + a$, where a is the number added to the equation. Here, the graph of $y = x^2$ is transformed to $y = x^2 + 3$ and $y = x^2 - 3$.

Adding to the whole equation translates the graph in the positive direction.

Subtracting from the whole equation translates the graph in the negative direction.

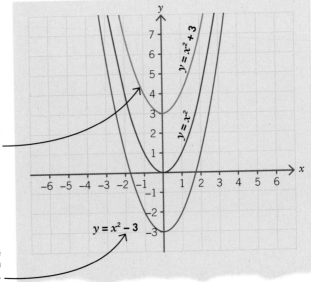

🔍 Combinations of transformations

Sometimes several transformations may be applied to a function. This graph shows what happens when the function $y = x^2$ is transformed to $y = (x - 5)^2 - 4$.

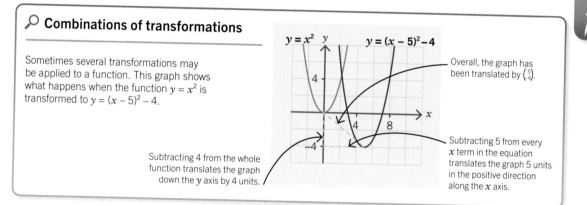

$y = x^2$ $y = (x - 5)^2 - 4$

Overall, the graph has been translated by $\binom{5}{4}$.

Subtracting 5 from every x term in the equation translates the graph 5 units in the positive direction along the x axis.

Subtracting 4 from the whole function translates the graph down the y axis by 4 units.

Reflections

By thinking of the equation of a graph as $y = f(x)$, we can describe how to reflect it on the coordinate grid. Reflecting a function means reflecting it in a mirror line, which is often the x axis or y axis.

$y = f(-x)$

Multiplying each x term by -1 will reflect it in the y axis. It is represented by the equation $y = f(-x)$. Here, the graph of $y = x^3 - 8x^2 + 19x - 10$ is transformed to $y = -x^3 - 8x^2 - 19x - 10$.

Multiplying each x in the equation by -1 reflects the graph in the y axis.

$y = -x^3 - 8x^2 - 19x - 10$ $y = x^3 - 8x^2 + 19x - 10$

$y = -f(x)$

Changing the sign of y in the equation of a graph by multiplying the whole equation by -1 will reflect the graph in the x axis. Here, the graph of $y = x^3 - 8x^2 + 19x - 10$ is transformed to $y = -x^3 + 8x^2 - 19x + 10$.

$y = x^3 - 8x^2 + 19x - 10$

$y = -x^3 + 8x^2 - 19x + 10$

Multiplying the entire function by -1 produces a reflection in the x axis.

Equation of a circle

Some functions will produce a circle when graphed on the coordinate grid. If we know the coordinates of the center of a circle and the length of its radius, we can find an equation for the circle.

When the center is the origin

A circle on the coordinate grid that has its center at (0, 0) has a very simple equation based on the Pythagorean theorem (see page 196). We can better understand how this equation works by imagining a right triangle between the circle's center and circumference.

A right triangle whose hypotenuse is the radius can be constructed at any point on the circle.

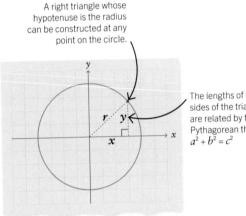

All the points on the circle will represent solutions to the equation $x^2 + y^2 = r^2$.

r is the radius of the circle.

The lengths of the sides of the triangle are related by the Pythagorean theorem: $a^2 + b^2 = c^2$

$$x^2 + y^2 = r^2$$

x and y are coordinates of any point on the circle when the center is at (0, 0).

Equation of any circle

A circle's center will not always be at (0, 0) on the coordinate grid. When this is the case, we use a different formula to find its radius, also based on the Pythagorean theorem. This formula is called the standard form and can be used for any circle on the coordinate grid, wherever its center lies.

The center of the circle is the point (a, b).

The point (x, y) is a radius away from the center.

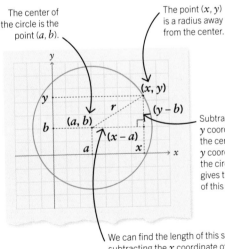

Subtracting the y coordinate of the center from the y coordinate of the circumference gives the length of this side.

$$(x - a)^2 + (y - b)^2 = r^2$$

We can calculate the length of the radius (r) by substituting the coordinates into this formula.

We can find the length of this side by subtracting the x coordinate of the center from the x coordinate of the circumference.

Standard and general form

This circle has its center at (3, 2) and a radius of 5. Its equation can be expressed in two different forms: the standard form and the general form.

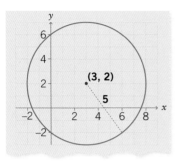

1. Substitute the center and radius into the standard form to get the equation of the circle.

$$(x - 3)^2 + (y - 2)^2 = 5^2$$

2. The equation of a circle may sometimes be written with the parentheses expanded out. This is called the general form.

$$x^2 + y^2 - 6x - 4y - 12 = 0$$

3. The general form for the equation of any circle is:

$$x^2 + y^2 + gx + fy + c = 0$$

In the example above, g was −6 and f was −4.

In the example above, the constant (c) was −12.

Converting between forms

To find the center and radius of a circle whose equation appears in the general form, it is best to convert the equation back to the standard form.

1. This equation is in the general form. We can convert it to the standard form by completing the square twice (see page 140)—once for the x terms and once for the y terms.

$$x^2 + y^2 - 6x - 4y - 12 = 0$$

2. First, add the constant to both sides, then group the x and y terms so they can be treated as separate quadratics.

$$x^2 + y^2 - 6x - 4y = 12$$
$$x^2 - 6x + y^2 - 4y = 12$$

3. Complete the square for the x terms and the y terms in turn.

$$(x - 3)^2 - 9 + (y - 2)^2 - 4 = 12$$

4. Gather the constant terms on the right-hand side of the equations. The equation is now in the standard form:

$$(x - 3)^2 + (y - 2)^2 = 25$$
$$(x - 3)^2 + (y - 2)^2 = 5^2$$

Equation of a tangent

A tangent to a circle meets a radius at 90° (see page 194) and is always a straight line, so its equation will be in the form $y = mx + b$ (see page 146). Find the equation for the tangent in the diagram.

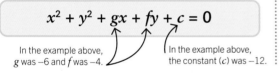

1. This tangent meets the circle $x^2 + y^2 = 169$ at the point (5, 12).

2. The tangent is perpendicular to the radius, so its slope (m) is the negative reciprocal of the slope of the radius (see page 147).

Slope of radius $= \dfrac{12}{5}$

Slope of tangent $= -1 \div \dfrac{12}{5} = -\dfrac{5}{12}$

3. Find b by substituting the coordinates of where the tangent meets the circle into the equation.

$$y = -\frac{5}{12}x + b$$
$$12 = -\frac{5}{12} \times 5 + b$$
$$12 = -\frac{25}{12} + b$$
$$b = \frac{169}{12}$$

4. The equation of the tangent is:

$$y = -\frac{5}{12}x + \frac{169}{12}$$

Sequences

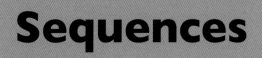

Number sequences

A number sequence is a list of numbers that follows a pattern or rule. Each number in a sequence is called a term.

Arithmetic sequences
In an arithmetic sequence, you can get from one term to the next by adding the same number each time.

Geometric sequences
In a geometric sequence, you can get from one term to the next by multiplying by the same number each time.

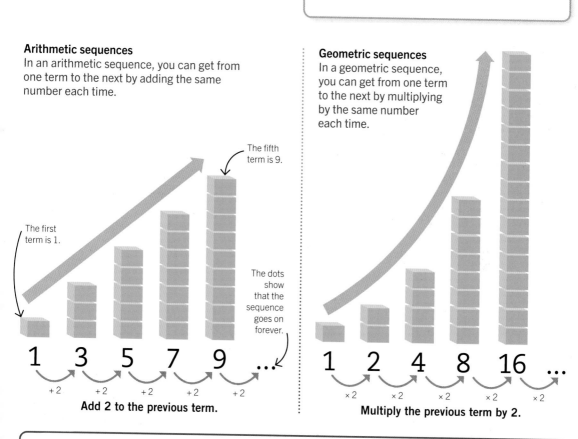

The fifth term is 9.

The first term is 1.

The dots show that the sequence goes on forever.

1 → 3 → 5 → 7 → 9 ...
+2 +2 +2 +2 +2

Add 2 to the previous term.

1 → 2 → 4 → 8 → 16 ...
×2 ×2 ×2 ×2 ×2

Multiply the previous term by 2.

📝 Finding the missing terms

Work out the missing term in each sequence by identifying the rule:

a) **−20, 10, 40, ..., 100**

b) **4, 16, ..., 256**

a) To get from one term to the next, the rule is to add 30.

−20, 10, 40, ..., 100
+30 +30 +30 +30

So the missing term is: 40 + 30 = 70.

b) The rule is to multiply by 4 to get to the next term.

4, 16, ..., 256
×4 ×4 ×4

So the missing term is: 16 × 4 = 64.

Term-to-term rule

In an arithmetic sequence, the term-to-term rule tells you how to work out the next term from the previous one. The difference between each term in the sequence is called the common difference.

Working out the term-to-term rule
To describe the term-to-term rule of an arithmetic sequence, start by giving the first term of the sequence, then describe how to get from one term to the next by giving the common difference. This rule allows you to find any term in a sequence by counting.

Key facts

✓ The term-to-term rule of an arithmetic sequence tells you how to go from one term to the next.

✓ To describe the term-to-term rule, start by giving the first term of the sequence, then describe the pattern.

✓ The common difference is the amount by which the number changes from one term to the next.

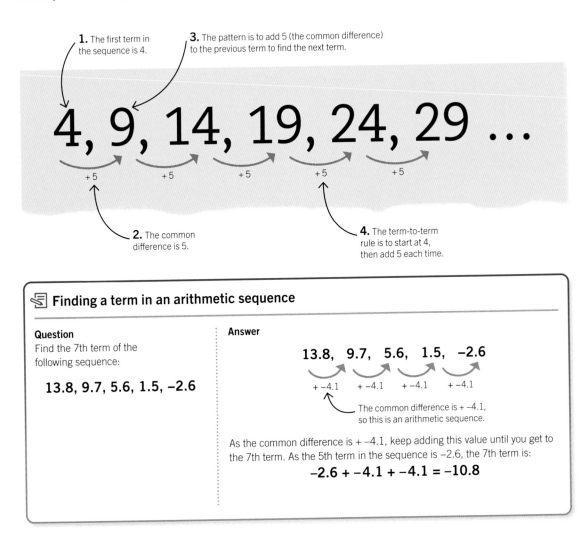

1. The first term in the sequence is 4.

3. The pattern is to add 5 (the common difference) to the previous term to find the next term.

4, 9, 14, 19, 24, 29 ...

+5   +5   +5   +5   +5

2. The common difference is 5.

4. The term-to-term rule is to start at 4, then add 5 each time.

Finding a term in an arithmetic sequence

Question
Find the 7th term of the following sequence:

13.8, 9.7, 5.6, 1.5, −2.6

Answer

13.8, 9.7, 5.6, 1.5, −2.6

+ −4.1   + −4.1   + −4.1   + −4.1

The common difference is + −4.1, so this is an arithmetic sequence.

As the common difference is + −4.1, keep adding this value until you get to the 7th term. As the 5th term in the sequence is −2.6, the 7th term is:

$$−2.6 + −4.1 + −4.1 = −10.8$$

Position-to-term rule

The term-to-term rule (see opposite) is useful for finding the next term in an arithmetic sequence but very time-consuming if you want to find out, say, the 50th term. The position-to-term rule describes the relationship between each term and its position in the sequence. You can use it to find the value of any term in an arithmetic sequence.

Key facts

✓ Each term in a sequence has its own unique position.

✓ The position-to-term rule allows you to find the value of any term in an arithmetic sequence without having to count from one term to the next.

Finding the position-to-term rule
Find the position-to-term rule for the sequence
4, 7, 10, 13, 16 ....

1. Write the position of each term in the sequence and work out the common difference between terms.

2. A common difference of + 3 implies that the sequence is linked to the three times table. We multiply the position by 3, so × 3 is the first operation of this rule.

3. Next, we need to work out what operation to apply to the three times table so that these numbers match the original sequence. We need to add 1 to each number, so + 1 is the second operation of the rule.

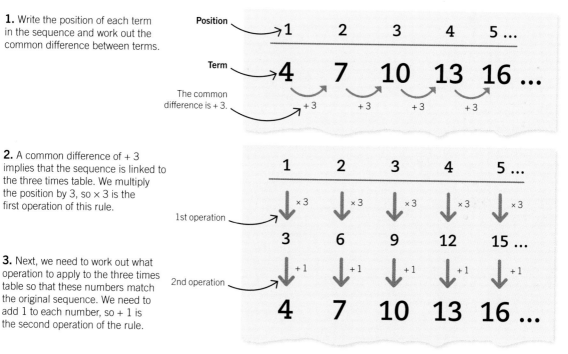

The position-to-term rule is:
multiply the position by 3, then add 1.

📑 Find the 10th term

Question
What is the 10th term in the sequence above?

Answer
As the position-to-term rule is multiply the position by 3 and add 1, apply this to the position of the term you want to find. You want to find the 10th term.

$$10 × 3 + 1 = 31$$

The 10th term in the sequence is 31.

Finding the nth term

We can describe the position-to-term rule of an arithmetic sequence using an algebraic expression. This expression can be used to find the value of any term in the sequence, and we form it by substituting the position number with n. We call the term we want to find the position for the "nth term."

Finding an expression for the nth term
Write the position-to-term rule for the sequence 3, 8, 13, 18, 23 ... as an expression.

1. The first step is to look for a common difference between the terms in the sequence. The common difference is + 5, meaning this is an arithmetic sequence.

2. To write the position-to-term rule as an algebraic expression, we represent the position number with the letter n. A common difference of + 5 suggests we should multiply n by 5, so the algebraic expression for the sequence will begin with $5n$.

3. We need to subtract 2 from each of these numbers to make them match the original sequence, so the expression also includes the operation − 2.

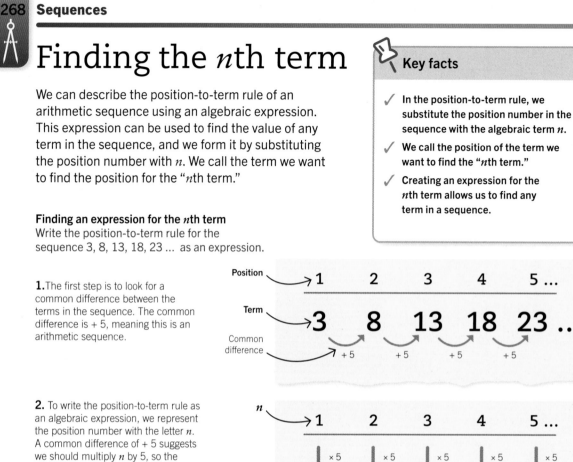

4. Putting these parts together gives us the expression for the nth term of the sequence. This expression can be used to find any term in the sequence.

This means "term." $\searrow a_n = 5n - 2$

n represents the position of any term in the sequence.

🖥 **Finding the 10th term**

Question
Use the position-to-term rule in the sequence above to find the value of the 10th term.

Answer
Substitute the position of the term you want to find into the expression.

$$a_{10} = 5(10) - 2 = 48$$

The nth term formula

In an arithmetic sequence, we can use a formula to find the nth term. The formula allows you to find any term in the sequence, if you know its position, n.

Finding a formula for the nth term

We can use algebraic terms to represent the first term and the common difference in an arithmetic sequence. Using these, we can create a formula that can be used to find the nth term of any arithmetic sequence.

1. Find the nth term formula for the arithmetic sequence 3, 5, 7, 9, 11.

2. The sequence works by adding successive amounts of the common difference to the first term. So to get from the first term to the second, you add $1 \times$ the common difference. To get to the third term, you add $2 \times$ the common difference, and so on.

3. This can be represented much more simply using algebra, from which we can create a formula for finding the nth term.

a_1 represents the first term.

Add $1 \times d$ (the common difference) to a_1 to get to the second term.

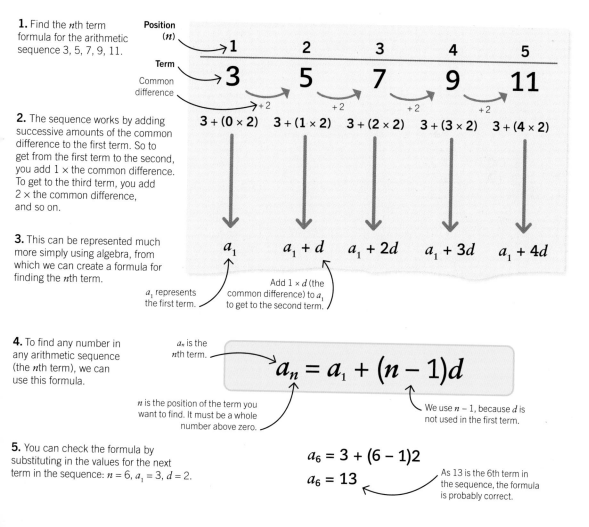

Position (n)

| 1 | 2 | 3 | 4 | 5 |

Term

Common difference

| 3 | 5 | 7 | 9 | 11 |

$+2$ $+2$ $+2$ $+2$

$3 + (0 \times 2)$ $3 + (1 \times 2)$ $3 + (2 \times 2)$ $3 + (3 \times 2)$ $3 + (4 \times 2)$

a_1 $a_1 + d$ $a_1 + 2d$ $a_1 + 3d$ $a_1 + 4d$

4. To find any number in any arithmetic sequence (the nth term), we can use this formula.

a_n is the nth term.

$$a_n = a_1 + (n - 1)d$$

n is the position of the term you want to find. It must be a whole number above zero.

We use $n - 1$, because d is not used in the first term.

5. You can check the formula by substituting in the values for the next term in the sequence: $n = 6$, $a_1 = 3$, $d = 2$.

$$a_6 = 3 + (6 - 1)2$$
$$a_6 = 13$$

As 13 is the 6th term in the sequence, the formula is probably correct.

Arithmetic pattern sequences

Number sequences can be made up of shapes or objects. If the pattern forms an arithmetic sequence, we can use the nth term formula for an arithmetic sequence to find the number of shapes or objects in any position in the sequence.

📌 **Key facts**

✓ You can form number sequences out of patterns.

✓ You can describe terms in an arithmetic pattern sequence using the nth term formula for an arithmetic sequence.

✓ You can use the nth term formula to find the number of objects for any pattern number.

Sequence of tiles
The patterns below are made up of blue and orange tiles. Find an expression for the number of blue tiles in the nth pattern using the nth term formula: $a_n = a_1 + (n − 1)d$.

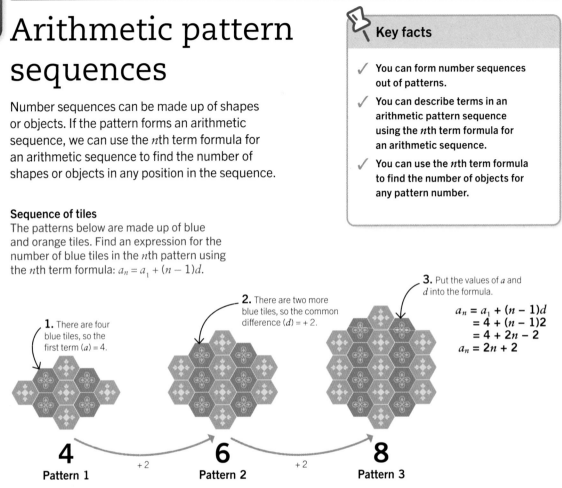

3. Put the values of a and d into the formula.

$$a_n = a_1 + (n − 1)d$$
$$= 4 + (n − 1)2$$
$$= 4 + 2n − 2$$
$$a_n = 2n + 2$$

2. There are two more blue tiles, so the common difference $(d) = + 2$.

1. There are four blue tiles, so the first term $(a) = 4$.

4
Pattern 1
$+ 2$
6
Pattern 2
$+ 2$
8
Pattern 3

📇 **Finding the nth term**

Question
In the arithmetic pattern sequence below, straws are added each time to make a new square with a triangle on top. How many straws will the 30th pattern have?

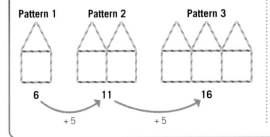

Pattern 1   Pattern 2   Pattern 3

6   11   16
$+5$ $+5$

Answer
1. Count the number of straws in each pattern to find the nth term expression. It is an arithmetic sequence 6, 11, 16 …, with a common difference of $+ 5$.

2. Substitute the values of a (6) and d (5) into the formula for the nth term of an arithmetic sequence.

$$a_n = a_1 + (n − 1)d$$
$$= 6 + (n − 1)5$$
$$= 6 + 5n − 5$$
$$a_n = 5n + 1$$

3. Then put $n = 30$ into this expression.

$$a_{30} = 5(30) + 1$$
$$= 150 + 1$$
$$= 151$$

The number of straws in the 30th pattern is 151.

Arithmetic series

An arithmetic series is the sum of terms in an arithmetic sequence. So for the arithmetic sequence 2, 4, 6, 8, 10, the arithmetic series is $2 + 4 + 6 + 8 + 10 = 30$. You can use sigma notation to represent an arithmetic series.

Sigma notation

The Greek letter sigma (Σ) means "take the sum of." Using sigma notation is a quick way to write out a long sum. The arithmetic series of the first five whole numbers ($1 + 2 + 3 + 4 + 5$) can be written out in the following way.

Key facts

✓ An arithmetic series is the sum of terms in an arithmetic sequence.

✓ Σ is the Greek letter sigma, and means "take the sum of."

✓ Sigma notation is a quick and neat way to write out a long sum.

✓ If you spot patterns in a series, you can calculate the sum of a long series.

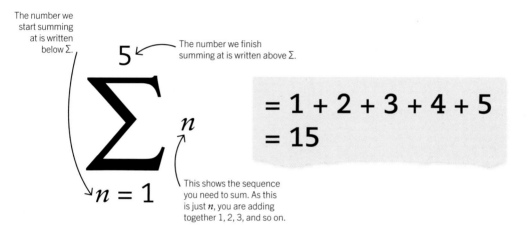

The number we start summing at is written below Σ.

The number we finish summing at is written above Σ.

$$\sum_{n=1}^{5} n = 1 + 2 + 3 + 4 + 5 = 15$$

This shows the sequence you need to sum. As this is just n, you are adding together 1, 2, 3, and so on.

Gauss's story

In the 1780s, a German schoolteacher asked his 9-year-old students, "What's the sum of all the numbers from 1 to 100?" So the students started counting and very swiftly one young boy shouted, "It's 5,050!" His teacher and fellow students couldn't believe it. The answer 5,050 was right. So how did he do it?

1. The boy paired each number in the series, joining 1 with 100, 2 with 99, and so on. Each pair now added up to 101.

1	2	3	...	98	99	100
+ 100	+ 99	+ 98	...	+ 3	+ 2	+ 1
101	101	101	...	101	101	101

2. Because the series ran from 1 to 100, he took the sum of these numbers by multiplying 101 by 100.

$$2\Sigma n = 100 \times 101 = 10\,100$$

3. In order to pair the numbers he'd counted each term twice, so he halved the total to make 50 pairs of numbers.

$$2\Sigma n = 10\,100$$
$$\text{So } \Sigma n = 5\,050$$

The boy's name was Carl Friedrich Gauss, and he would go on to become one of the world's most famous mathematicians.

Square and cube number sequences

Square and cube numbers (see page 22) are closely related to the properties of their shapes. They each form special sequences, because they each have a unique pattern. These sequences can be described using an nth term rule, from which you can find the value of any term in either sequence.

Key facts

✓ Square and cube numbers form special sequences.

✓ The nth term rule for square numbers is n^2.

✓ The nth term rule for cube numbers is n^3.

Square numbers
A square number is a whole number multiplied by itself. You can visualize square numbers by arranging objects into perfect squares, where you multiply the length of each side by itself to form the square number.

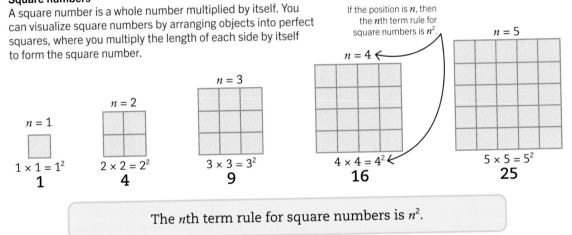

If the position is n, then the nth term rule for square numbers is n^2.

$n = 1$
$1 \times 1 = 1^2$
1

$n = 2$
$2 \times 2 = 2^2$
4

$n = 3$
$3 \times 3 = 3^2$
9

$n = 4$
$4 \times 4 = 4^2$
16

$n = 5$
$5 \times 5 = 5^2$
25

The nth term rule for square numbers is n^2.

Cube numbers
A cube number is a whole number multiplied by itself, then multiplied by itself again. Cube numbers can be visualized by arranging objects into perfect cubes, where you multiply the length by the width by the height to form the cube number.

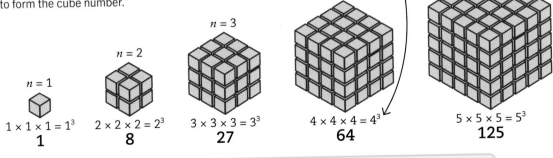

If the position is n, then the nth term rule for cube numbers is n^3.

$n = 1$
$1 \times 1 \times 1 = 1^3$
1

$n = 2$
$2 \times 2 \times 2 = 2^3$
8

$n = 3$
$3 \times 3 \times 3 = 3^3$
27

$n = 4$
$4 \times 4 \times 4 = 4^3$
64

$n = 5$
$5 \times 5 \times 5 = 5^3$
125

The nth term rule for cube numbers is n^3.

The triangular number sequence

Triangular numbers form a special sequence of numbers. You can express a sequence of triangular numbers using the term-to-term rule.

The term-to-term rule
Triangular numbers represent the number of identical objects that can be arranged to form an equilateral triangular pattern. You can represent the sequence of triangular numbers with a sequence of perfect triangular patterns.

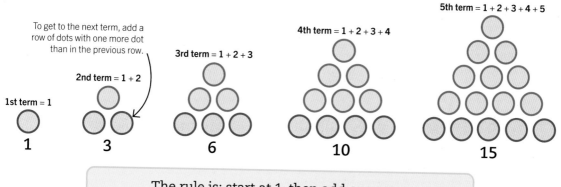

To get to the next term, add a row of dots with one more dot than in the previous row.

1st term = 1 : **1**

2nd term = 1 + 2 : **3**

3rd term = 1 + 2 + 3 : **6**

4th term = 1 + 2 + 3 + 4 : **10**

5th term = 1 + 2 + 3 + 4 + 5 : **15**

> The rule is: start at 1, then add one more than the value added to the previous term.

Finding the nth term
There's a neat trick you can use to find the nth term for triangular numbers: just add up all the numbers in the sequence from 1 to n. Each triangular number therefore represents the sum of an arithmetic series (see page 271), starting at 1. The formula is expressed using sigma notation.

Gauss's trick

You can use Gauss's trick of pairing numbers (see page 271) and then dividing by 2 to find the nth term. So the 50th term in the triangular sequence is:

$$a_n = (n + 1) \times \frac{n}{2}$$

$$a_{50} = 51 \times \frac{50}{2}$$

$$= 51 \times 25$$

$$= 1275$$

7th term = 1 + 2 + 3 + 4 + 5 + 6 + 7 = 28

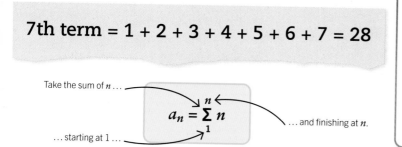

Take the sum of n ...

$$a_n = \sum_1^n n$$

... and finishing at n.

... starting at 1 ...

Quadratic sequences

Not all sequences behave like arithmetic sequences, with a common difference between terms (see page 266). In a quadratic sequence, the difference between terms varies. Quadratic sequences are linked to quadratic expressions (see page 100).

The nth term in a quadratic sequence

The difference between terms always changes in a quadratic sequence as it progresses. However, the difference between the differences remains constant each time. Quadratic sequences are connected to the sequences for square numbers (see page 272), so the expression for the nth term always contains n^2.

Sequence with the formula $n^2 - 1$

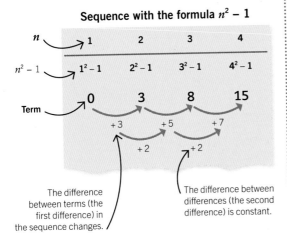

The difference between terms (the first difference) in the sequence changes.

The difference between differences (the second difference) is constant.

Sequence with the formula $4n^2 + 1$

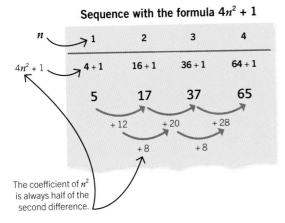

The coefficient of n^2 is always half of the second difference.

Finding the nth term: a simpler case

You need to follow several steps to find the nth term of a quadratic sequence.

1. Work out the differences between each term. As the second difference is constant, this is a quadratic sequence and the nth term will contain n^2.

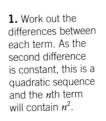

First difference

Second difference

2. To find the nth term, first find the coefficient of n^2. A second difference of 4 gives a coefficient for n^2 of 2, so the first part of the expression contains $2n^2$.

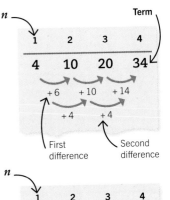

$2n^2$

3. Compare the $2n^2$ sequence with the original terms. You need to add 2 each time to get to the original terms of the sequence, so the formula contains $+2$.

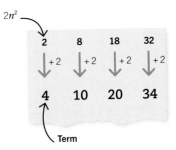

Term

4. Add $+2$ to $2n^2$ to form the nth term expression.

The nth term is $2n^2 + 2$.

Finding the nth term: a harder case

Sometimes, the nth term for a quadratic sequence contains a quadratic part and an arithmetic part (see page 268). You need to bolt them together to form one big expression.

(see page 268)

> **Key facts**
>
> ✓ In quadratic sequences, the difference between terms changes while the difference between the differences remains constant.
>
> ✓ The expression for the nth term of a quadratic sequence includes n^2.
>
> ✓ For some quadratic sequences, the expression for the nth term includes a quadratic part and an arithmetic part.

1. Work out the first and second differences between each term.

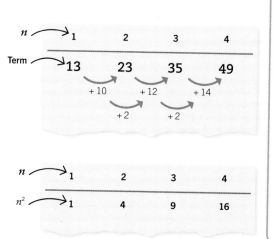

2. Divide the second difference by 2 to find the coefficient. Half of 2 is 1, so the quadratic part of the formula is n^2.

3. To find the arithmetic part of the expression, subtract the value of n^2 from each term in the original sequence. This gives you an arithmetic sequence with a common difference of $+7$.

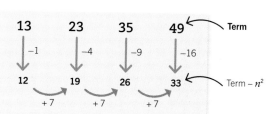

4. Work out the pattern of the arithmetic sequence using the common difference. A common difference of $+7$ means that you need to multiply n by 7. Then add 5 to get to the term. Therefore, the rule for the arithmetic part is $7n + 5$.

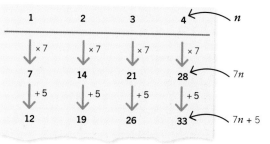

5. Combine the quadratic part (n^2; see step 2) with the arithmetic part (step 4) to find the nth term.

The nth term is $n^2 + 7n + 5$.

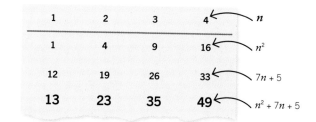

Geometric sequences

In a geometric sequence, you get from one term to the next term by multiplying by the same number each time. This number is known as the common ratio and can be used to find the nth term of any geometric sequence.

Bouncing a ball
You drop a tennis ball from a height. On the first bounce, the ball reaches a height of 80 cm, then loses half of its height on each bounce. These successive decreases in height form a geometric sequence.

Key facts

✓ In a geometric sequence, each term is found by multiplying the previous term by a constant amount called the common ratio (r).

✓ The nth term is given by the formula:
$$a_n = a_1 \times r^{n-1}$$

✓ r can be a positive or negative number, a decimal, a fraction, or an irrational square root.

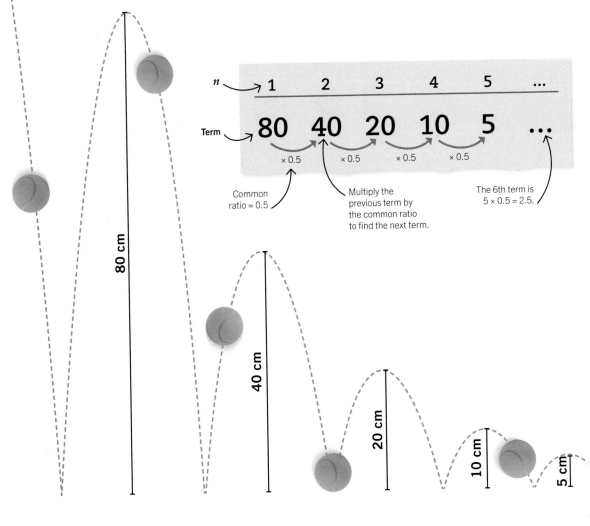

n	1	2	3	4	5	...
Term	80	40	20	10	5	...

×0.5 ×0.5 ×0.5 ×0.5

Common ratio = 0.5

Multiply the previous term by the common ratio to find the next term.

The 6th term is $5 \times 0.5 = 2.5$.

80 cm

40 cm

20 cm

10 cm

5 cm

Formula for a geometric sequence

You can find the value for any term (n) in a geometric sequence if you know the first term (a) and the common ratio (r).

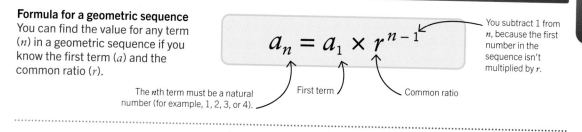

$$a_n = a_1 \times r^{n-1}$$

The nth term must be a natural number (for example, 1, 2, 3, or 4).

First term

Common ratio

You subtract 1 from n, because the first number in the sequence isn't multiplied by r.

More complex geometric sequences

You may come across more complicated geometric sequences involving negatives, fractions, or irrational square roots, but the same rules for finding the nth term always apply.

Alternating sequences

The common ratio in a geometric sequence can be negative. The result is an alternating sequence, where the terms switch between positive and negative. Remember to apply the correct rules when multiplying negative numbers (see page 14).

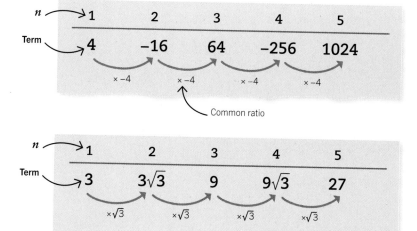

n	1	2	3	4	5
Term	4	−16	64	−256	1024

×−4   ×−4   ×−4   ×−4

Common ratio

Irrational square roots

Sometimes the common ratio can be an irrational square root (see page 122). You need to leave the term in square root form, as this is more accurate than writing it in decimals, which would require rounding.

n	1	2	3	4	5
Term	3	$3\sqrt{3}$	9	$9\sqrt{3}$	27

×$\sqrt{3}$ ×$\sqrt{3}$ ×$\sqrt{3}$ ×$\sqrt{3}$

🖩 Finding the nth term

Question

Find the 10th value in the sequence 100, 95, 90.25, 85.7375 …, rounded to four decimal places.

Answer

1. Find the common ratio.

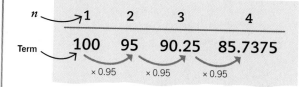

n	1	2	3	4
Term	100	95	90.25	85.7375

× 0.95   × 0.95   × 0.95

To get from the first term to the second term, you need to multiply by 0.95, so the common ratio is 0.95.

2. Put the values into the formula $a_n = a_1 \times r^{n-1}$.

$$a_1 = 100$$
$$r = 0.95$$

$$a_n = 100 \times 0.95^{n-1}$$

$$a_{10} = 100 \times 0.95^{10-1}$$
$$= 100 \times 0.95^9$$
$$= 63.0249$$

Rounded to four decimal places, the 10th term is 63.0249.

The Fibonacci sequence

Named after a 13th-century Italian mathematician, the Fibonacci sequence appears throughout nature. You'll see Fibonacci sequences in pine cones, flowers, and even galaxies in space.

Sunflower head
The number of spiraling patterns of seeds in the head of a sunflower follows the Fibonacci sequence. The seeds are formed in these spiraling patterns to make maximum use of space.

If you count the number of spirals, you'll always get a number from the Fibonacci sequence.

The spirals run in two different directions.

Any number in the Fibonacci sequence is called a Fibonacci number.

1   1   2   3   5   8   13   21 ...

1 + 1   1 + 2   2 + 3   3 + 5   5 + 8   8 + 13

The first two terms in the Fibonacci sequence are 1 and 1.

Each successive term is the sum of the two previous terms.

Fibonacci-type sequences

Fibonacci-type sequences follow the same rule as the Fibonacci sequence but don't start with the same numbers as the original sequence.

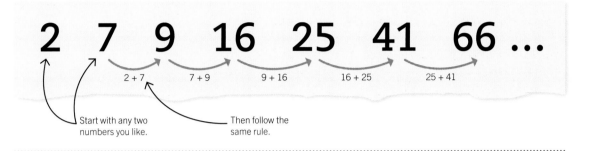

2   7   9   16   25   41   66 ...

2 + 7   7 + 9   9 + 16   16 + 25   25 + 41

Start with any two numbers you like.

Then follow the same rule.

Drawing a Fibonacci spiral

You can form a spiral using the numbers of the Fibonacci sequence by drawing adjacent squares with sides the length of each term in the sequence, then drawing a curve that passes through the opposite corners of each square.

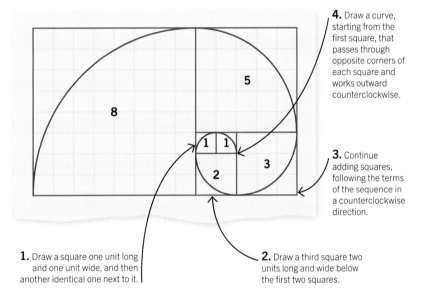

4. Draw a curve, starting from the first square, that passes through opposite corners of each square and works outward counterclockwise.

3. Continue adding squares, following the terms of the sequence in a counterclockwise direction.

1. Draw a square one unit long and one unit wide, and then another identical one next to it.

2. Draw a third square two units long and wide below the first two squares.

🔍 The Golden Ratio

The Fibonacci sequence is linked to the Golden Ratio, a proportion used frequently in art and architecture since the time of the ancient Greeks. A rectangle formed using the Golden Ratio—an "ideal" proportion of length to width—has long been considered to have the most visually appealing proportions.

Glossary

Acute angle An angle between 0° and 90°.

Addition Finding the sum or total of a set of values, represented by the symbol +.

Algebra The branch of math that uses letters or other symbols to stand for numbers that are unknown or might change.

Alternate angles Angles on different sides of a transversal line intersecting a pair of parallel lines. Alternate angles are equal.

Angle The amount of turn between two lines that meet at a point, measured in degrees (°).

Apex The top vertex of a shape.

Arc A curved line that forms part of the circumference of a circle.

Area The amount of space inside a 2D shape, measured in square units.

Arithmetic sequence A sequence in which each term after the first is found by adding the same amount each time.

Arithmetic series The sum of the terms in an arithmetic sequence.

Asymptote An asymptote of a curve is a line that the curve approaches but never meets as it approaches infinity.

Bar chart A diagram showing data as rectangular bars of different lengths.

Bearing An angle measured clockwise from north.

Bias A biased sample is one in which a group is over- or underrepresented owing to limitations in the sampling method.

Bisect To divide a line or angle into two equal parts.

Bounds of accuracy The lowest and highest possible values of a measurement.

Box plot A diagram used to represent the spread of statistical data.

Chord A line that connects two points on the circumference of a circle without passing through the center.

Circumference The distance around the edge of a circle.

Class In a grouped frequency table, continuous data is grouped into classes.

Coefficient The number by which a letter is multiplied in algebra. The coefficient of x in the term $5x$ is 5.

Common difference The difference between each term in an arithmetic sequence.

Common factor The factors shared by two or more numbers. The highest factor common to two or more numbers is called the greatest common factor (GCF).

Common multiple A whole number that is a shared multiple of two or more numbers. The lowest multiple shared by two or more numbers is called the least common multiple (LCM).

Common ratio The amount by which each term in a geometric sequence is multiplied in order to get to the next term.

Complementary angles Two angles that add up to 90°.

Compound interest Interest calculated based on the original amount plus any interest earned previously.

Compound shape A shape that can be broken down into simpler 2D or 3D shapes. Also called a composite shape.

Concave polygon A polygon with at least one reflex angle.

Conditional probability If the probability of one event is affected by another event, the two events are described as conditional.

Congruent Geometric shapes that have the same size and shape are congruent.

Constant A term, such as a number, that has a fixed value.

Continuous data Numerical data that can take any value in a range.

Convex polygon A polygon with no angles greater than 180°.

Coordinates Pairs of numbers that describe the position of a point, line, or shape on a grid or the position of something on a map.

Correlation There is a correlation between two variables if a change in one causes a change in the other.

Corresponding angles Two angles on the same side of a transversal line intersecting a pair of parallel lines. The angles are either both above or both below the parallel lines. Corresponding angles are equal.

Cosine In a right triangle, cosine is the ratio between the side adjacent to a given angle and the hypotenuse.

Cube number When you multiply a whole number by itself, then by itself again, the result is called a cube number.

Cube root A number's cube root is the number that, when multiplied by itself twice, equals the given number. It is indicated by the symbol $\sqrt[3]{}$.

Cumulative frequency A running total of the frequencies in a data set.

Cyclic quadrilateral A four-sided shape with vertices that each lie on the edge of a circle.

Data Information, such as numbers, facts, and statistics, gathered to test a hypothesis. A group of information collected about a subject or situation is called a data set.

Decay A pattern of repeated decrease.

Decimal A number that includes (or is entirely composed of) parts that are less than 1. These parts are separated from the parts more than 1 by a dot called a decimal point.

Denominator The number on the bottom of a fraction. The denominator of ⅔ is 3.

Density A measure of mass per unit of volume.

Diameter A line between two points on the edge of a circle or sphere that passes through the center.

Dilation The process of changing the size of a shape without changing the shape's angles or the ratios of its sides.

Direct proportion Two numbers are in direct proportion if their ratio to each other stays the same when they are changed by the same scale factor.

Discrete data Numerical data that can only have certain exact values.

Distribution In probability and statistics, the distribution gives the range of possible values and their probabilities.

Division The splitting of a number into equal parts, represented by the symbol ÷.

Domain The possible input values of a function.

Elevation A 2D representation of a 3D shape from the side or front.

Equation A statement in math that something is equal to something else, for example, $x + 2 = 4$.

Equilateral triangle A triangle with three equal sides and three equal angles.

Error interval The range of possible values of a measurement.

Estimation Finding an answer that's close to the correct answer, often by rounding one or more numbers up or down.

Experimental probability *See* relative frequency

Exponent *See* power

Exponential growth A pattern of repeated increase.

Expression A combination of numbers, symbols, and/or unknown variables that does not contain an equals sign.

Exterior angle An angle formed outside a polygon when a side is extended outward.

Factor The factors of a number are the whole numbers that it can be divided by exactly.

Factoring Rewriting a number or expression as the multiplication of its factors.

Fibonacci sequence The sequence starting with 1 and 1, with each subsequent term formed by adding the previous two together.

Formula A rule or statement that describes the fixed mathematical relationship between two or more variables.

Fraction A number that is not a whole number, represented as part of a whole, such as ¾.

Frequency In statistics, the number of occurrences of a value in a data set.

Frequency table A table showing the frequency of every value within a data set. A grouped frequency table organizes data into groups of values called classes.

Frequency tree A diagram used to display the frequencies of two or more combined events.

Function A mathematical expression that operates on an input to produce an output.

Geometric sequence A sequence in which each term after the first is found by multiplying the previous term by the same number each time (the common ratio).

Geometry The mathematics of shapes.

Histogram A type of bar chart in which the areas of bars represent frequency.

Hypotenuse The side opposite the right angle in a right triangle. It is the longest side of a right triangle.

Hypothesis An idea or theory tested by gathering and analyzing data.

Improper fraction A fraction in which the numerator is greater than the denominator.

Inequality An inequality shows the relationship between the sizes of two expressions or terms and will have a set of possible solutions.

Infinite Without a limit or end.

Integer A whole number, the negative of a whole number, or zero.

Interest An amount of money earned when money is invested, or charged when it is borrowed.

Interior angle An angle inside a polygon.

Interquartile range The difference between the lower and upper quartiles of a data set.

Intersect To meet or cross over.

Inverse operation An operation that reverses another operation.

Inverse proportion Two numbers are inversely proportional if an increase in one of the numbers results in a corresponding decrease in the other.

Irrational number A number that cannot be written as a whole number, as a fraction, or with a finite number of decimals.

Isosceles triangle A triangle with two equal sides and two equal angles.

Kite A quadrilateral with two pairs of adjacent sides of equal length.

Line graph A graph where data is plotted as points connected by straight lines.

Line of best fit A line on a scatter graph that shows the correlation between variables.

Linear equation An equation that forms a straight line when plotted on a coordinate grid. The variables in a linear equation have a highest power of 1.

Locus (plural: loci) A set of points that follow certain conditions or rules.

Mean A typical value found by adding up the values in a data set and dividing by the total number of values.

Median The middle value of a data set when ordered from lowest to highest.

Mixed number A fraction made up of a whole number and a proper fraction.

Mode The most frequent value in a data set.

Multiple The result of multiplying two numbers together.

Multiplication The process of repeated addition, represented by the symbol ×.

Multiplier A number by which another number is multiplied.

Mutually exclusive events Two events that cannot both be true at the same time.

Natural number All the counting numbers from 1 to infinity.

Negative number A number less than 0.

nth term An expression for any term in a sequence.

Numerator The number on the top of a fraction. The numerator of ⅔ is 2.

Obtuse angle An angle measuring between 90° and 180°.

Operation An action done to a number, such as adding or dividing.

Order of operations The conventional order in which to carry out operations in a calculation. The acronym PEMDAS is used to remember the order: parentheses, exponents, multiplication/division, addition/subtraction.

Parallel Two or more lines that are always the same distance apart and never meet.

Parallelogram A quadrilateral with opposite sides that are parallel and equal in length.

Percentage A number of parts out of 100. A percentage is shown by the symbol %.

Perimeter The distance around the edge of a shape.

Perpendicular A line is perpendicular to another line if the two lines are at right angles to each other.

Pi The circumference of any circle divided by its diameter always gives the same value, which is called pi. It is represented by the Greek symbol π.

Pictogram A type of chart that uses pictures to represent frequency.

Pie chart A chart in which frequencies are represented as sectors of a circle.

Piecewise graph A graph made of two or more different parts or functions.

Plan A 2D representation of a 3D shape from above.

Polygon A 2D closed shape with three or more straight sides.

Polyhedron A 3D object with flat faces and straight edges.

Population In statistics, a set of things about which data is collected.

Positive number A number greater than 0.

Power A number that indicates how many times a value is multiplied by itself.

Pressure A measure of a force applied to a particular surface area.

Prime number A number (excluding 1) that can only be divided exactly by 1 and itself.

Prism A 3D shape whose ends are two identical polygons. A prism is the same size and shape all along its length.

Probability The likelihood that something will happen.

Probability distribution A mathematical function sometimes shown in a graph, chart, or table that gives the probabilities of the possible outcomes of an experiment.

Product The result of multiplying two or more values together.

Proper fraction A fraction in which the numerator is less than the denominator.

Proportion A part of something considered in relation to another part or its whole.

The Pythagorean theorem A rule that states that the squared length of the hypotenuse of a right triangle equals the sum of the squares of the other two sides, as represented by the equation $a^2 + b^2 = c^2$.

Quadratic expression/equation An expression/equation that contains a term with a highest power of 2, for example, $x^2 + 5x + 6 = 0$.

Quadratic sequence A sequence in which the difference between terms is related to square numbers.

Quadrilateral A 2D shape that has four sides and four angles.

Qualitative data Data that is not in the form of numbers, but usually in the form of words.

Quantitative data Data in the form of numbers.

Quartiles In statistics, quartiles are points that split an ordered data set into four equal parts. The number that is a quarter of the way through is the lower quartile, halfway is the median, and three-quarters of the way through is the upper quartile.

Radius (plural: radii) Any line from the center of a circle to its circumference.

Range 1. The span between the smallest and largest values in a data set.
2. The possible output values of a function.

Rate of change A description of how one variable changes in relation to another.

Ratio The relationship between two quantities, expressed as a comparison of their sizes.

Reciprocal The reciprocal of a number is 1 divided by that number, so the reciprocal of 5 is ⅕. The reciprocal of a fraction is found by flipping the fraction's numerator and denominator, so the reciprocal of ⅔ is ³⁄₂.

Recurring decimal A recurring decimal never ends with a final digit. Instead, the number repeats a section of digits forever.

Reflection A type of transformation that produces a mirror image of the original object.

Reflex angle An angle measuring between 180° and 360°.

Relative frequency An estimate of probability found by experiment.

Remainder The number that is left over when one number cannot be divided by another exactly.

Rhombus A quadrilateral with two pairs of parallel sides and all four sides of the same length.

Right angle An angle measuring 90°.

Right triangle A triangle with one angle that is 90° (a right angle).

Root 1. A root of a number is a value that, when multiplied by itself a number of times, results in the original number. It is represented by the symbol $\sqrt{\ }$.
2. The roots of a function are the values of x when y is 0 (the x axis).

Rotation A type of transformation in which an object is turned around a point.

Rounding Approximating a number by writing it to the nearest whole number or to a given number of decimal places.

Sample A part of a population from which data is collected in a statistical inquiry.

Sample space diagram A diagram that displays the possible outcomes of a probability experiment.

Scalar A quantity with size but not direction.

Scale drawing A drawing with lengths in direct proportion to the object it represents.

Scale factor The ratio by which a number or object is made larger or smaller.

Scalene triangle A triangle where every side is a different length and every angle is a different size.

Scatter graph A graph in which plotted points are used to show the relationship between two variables.

Scientific notation A number, usually very large or small, written as a number between 1 and 10 multiplied by a power of 10.

Sector The region of a circle between two radii and an arc.

Segment 1. Part of a circle bounded by a chord and an arc.
2. A line with two endpoints.

Sequence A list of numbers or shapes that follow a rule.

Similar Shapes are similar if their corresponding lengths are in the same proportion.

Simple interest Interest calculated based on the original amount.

Simultaneous equations Two or more equations that contain the same variables and are solved together.

Sine In a right triangle, sine is the ratio between the side opposite a given angle and the hypotenuse of a right angle.

Slope The steepness of a line.

Spread A description of how a data set is distributed over a range.

Square number If you multiply a whole number by itself, the result is called a square number.

Square root The square root of a number is the number that, when multiplied by itself, gives the original number. It is represented by the symbol $\sqrt{}$.

Standard deviation A measure of spread that shows the amount of deviation from the mean. If the standard deviation is low, the data is close to the mean; if it is high, the data is widely spread.

Statistics The handling of data in order to better understand aspects of a population.

Subtraction Taking a value away from another value, represented by the symbol –.

Supplementary angles Two angles that add up to 180°.

Surface area The sum of the areas of the faces of a 3D shape.

Symmetry A measure of how unchanged a shape or object is after it has been rotated, reflected, or translated.

Tally marks Lines drawn to help record how many things you've counted.

Tangent 1. A straight line that touches a curve at a single point.
2. In a right triangle, tangent is the ratio between the side opposite a given angle and the side adjacent to the given angle.

Term 1. In algebra, a number, letter, or combination of both.
2. A number in a sequence or series.

Three-dimensional (3D) The term used to describe objects that have height, width, and depth.

Time series A series of measurements of a quantity over a period of time.

Transformation A change of position, size, or orientation. Reflections, rotations, dilations, and translations are all transformations.

Translation Movement of an object without changing its size, shape, or orientation.

Transversal A line that intersects two or more parallel lines.

Trapezoid A quadrilateral with one pair of parallel sides of unequal length.

Tree diagram A diagram used to find the combined probability of two or more events.

Trigonometry The study of triangles and the ratios of their sides and angles.

Two-dimensional (2D) The term used to describe flat shapes that have only width and length.

Unit 1. The standard amount in measuring, for example, meters, grams, or seconds.
2. A whole number between 0 and 9.

Variable A value that is unknown or might change. In algebra, a variable is usually represented by a letter.

Vector A quantity that has both size and direction, such as velocity.

Velocity The measure of speed in a particular direction.

Venn diagram A diagram consisting of two or more overlapping circles to represent sets of data.

Vertex The corner or point at which two or more surfaces or lines meet.

Vertically opposite angles Angles on the opposite sides of two intersecting lines. Vertically opposite angles are equal.

Volume The amount of space within a 3D object, measured in cubic units.

Whole number A positive number (including zero) that does not have a fractional part.

x **axis** The horizontal axis of a graph.

y **axis** The vertical axis of a graph.

y **intercept** The point at which a line crosses the y axis on a graph.

Index

Page numbers in **bold** refer to main entries.

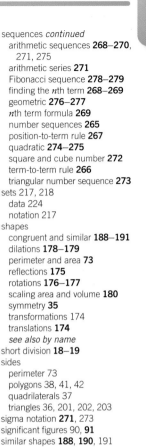

Acknowledgments

The publisher would like to thank the following people for their help with making the book: Tina Jindal, Mani Ramaswamy, and Amanda Wyatt for editorial assistance; Rabia Ahmad, Nobina Chakravorty, Meenal Goel, Arshti Narang, and Anjali Sachar for design assistance; Anita Yadav for technical assistance; Allen Ma and Amber Kuang for additional consulting; Priyanka Sharma and Saloni Singh for the jacket; Victoria Pyke for proofreading; and Helen Peters for the index.

Smithsonian Enterprises: Kealy Gordon, Product Development Manager; Jill Corcoran, Director, Licensed Publishing Sales; Janet Archer, DMM, Ecom and D-to-C; Carol LeBlanc, President.

The publisher would like to thank the following for their kind permission to reproduce their photographs:
(Key: a-above; b-below/bottom; c-center; f-far; l-left; r-right; t-top)

66 123RF.com: 29mokara (fbr). **Dorling Kindersley:** Mattel INC (cr). **Dreamstime.com:** Naruemon Mondee (br); Maxim Sergeenkov (cra). **71 Dreamstime.com:** Ken Cole. **73 Dreamstime.com:** Yuri Parmenov Yuri Parmenov. **82 Dreamstime.com:** Elena Tumanova (cr). **90 Dorling Kindersley:** Jerry Young (ca). **92 Getty Images / iStock:** DonNichols / E+ (cr). **126 Dreamstime.com:** Tomas Griger (ca). **150 Dreamstime.com:** Sergeyoch. **160 Dreamstime.com:**

Bakerjim (crb, clb). **Shutterstock.com:** New Africa (cra, cla). **251 Dreamstime. com:** Chernetskaya (cl); Serezniy (c); Hin255 (b). **278 Dreamstime.com:** Irochka. **279 Dreamstime.com:** Sergio Bertino / Serjedi.

All other images © Dorling Kindersley
For further information see:
www.dkimages.com